CRE▲TIVE
HOMEOWNER®

Southern
Inspired Home Designs

CREATIVE HOMEOWNER®, Upper Saddle River, New Jersey

VP/Business Development: Brian H. Toolan
VP/Editorial Director: Timothy O. Bakke
Production Manager: Rose Sullivan

Home Plans Publishing Consultant: James D. McNair III
Editorial Assistant: Nicole Porto

Design and Layout: Arrowhead Direct (David Kroha, Cindy DiPierdomenico, Judith Kroha)
Cover Design: 3r1

Current Printing (last digit)
10 9 8 7 6 5 4 3 2 1

Southern Inspired Home Designs
Library of Congress Control Number: 2004113796
ISBN: 1-58011-188-2

CREATIVE HOMEOWNER®
A Division of Federal Marketing Corp.
24 Park Way
Upper Saddle River, NJ 07458
www.creativehomeowner.com

Printed in China

Note: The homes as shown in the photographs and renderings in this book may differ from the actual blueprints. When studying the house of your choice, please check the floor plans carefully.

PHOTO CREDITS

Front cover: *top* plan 271081, page 101; *bottom row left to right* plan 161002, page 54; plan 211011, page 141; plan 131007, page 112 **back cover:** *top* plan 111003, page 203; *center* plan 121062, page 167; *bottom left* plan 131027, page 42; *bottom right* plan 111004, page 27 **page 1:** plan 311005, page 264 **page 3:** *top* plan 121072, page 177; *center* plan 111047, page 277; *bottom* plan 141031, page 15 **page 4:** plan 111003, page 203 **page 5:** plan 331005, page 228 **page 6:** *top* plan 141028, page 21; *bottom* plan 161002, page 54 **page 7:** plan 221022, page 168 **page 30:** courtesy of Kraftmaid Cabinetry **page 31:** *top* courtesy of Merillat Industries; *bottom* courtesy of Kraftmaid Cabinetry **pages 32–33:** *top right* courtesy of Kraftmaid Cabinetry; *bottom right* courtesy of American Olean; *center* courtesy of Kraftmaid Cabinetry **pages 34–35:** *center* courtesy of Kraftmaid Cabinetry; *bottom right* courtesy of Diamond Cabinets; *top left* courtesy of Wellborn **page 36:** *top* courtesy of Wellborn Cabinet; *bottom* courtesy of Diamond Cabinets **page 37:** *top left* courtesy of Iron-A-Way; *top right* courtesy of Rev-A-Shelf; *bottom right* courtesy of Merillat **page 38:** courtesy of Wellborn Cabinet **page 39:** *top* courtesy of Merillat Industries; *bottom* courtesy of Moen **page 40:** *top left* courtesy of Thibaut Wallcoverings; *top right* courtesy of Canac Cabinetry; *bottom right* courtesy of Wellborn Cabinet **page 41:** courtesy of American Olean **pages 71–85:** illustrator: Steve Buchanan/CH **page 114:** *top* courtesy of Thomasville; *both bottom* courtesy of Rubbermaid **page 115:** courtesy of IKEA **page 116:** courtesy of Closetmaid **page 117:** *top* courtesy of Closetmaid; *bottom* courtesy of Rubbermaid **pages 118–119:** *all* courtesy of Rubbermaid **page 120:** courtesy of Diamond Cabinets **page 121:** *top* courtesy of Diamond Cabinets **page 183:** *top* courtesy of Weber; *bottom right* courtesy of Frontgate; *bottom left* courtesy of Broilmaster **page 184:** courtesy of Sub-Zero **page 185:** *both* courtesy of Malibu Lighting/Intermatic, Inc. **pages 186–187:** *top right* Marvin Slobin/courtesy of California Redwood Association; *bottom center* courtesy of Southern Forest Products Association; *top left* courtesy of Malibu Lighting/Intermatic, Inc. **pages 204–205:** *all* courtesy of Sylvania **page 206:** courtesy of Kraftmaid Cabinetry **page 207:** *all* courtesy of Sylvania **page 234:** *both* courtesy of gidesigns.net **pages 235–236:** *both* courtesy of Trellis Structures **page 237:** *all* courtesy of Elyria Fence Co. **pages 238–239:** *left* David Freeman/Spectra Studios/CH; *right* courtesy of Elyria Fence Co. **pages 240–243:** *all* David Freeman/Spectra Studios/CH **page 244:** courtesy of California Redwood Association **page 245:** *both* courtesy of Intermatic, Inc. **page 280:** plan 271096, page 189

Photographers & Manufacturers: American Olean, Dallas, TX; 972-991-8904. California Redwood Association, Novato, CA; 888-225-7339. Diamond Cabinets, Jasper, IN; 812-482-2527. Elyria Fence Co., Elyria, OH; 800-779-7581. GI Designs, Denver, CO; 877-442-6773. Intermatic, Spring Grove, IL; 815-675-7000. Iron-A-Way, Morton, IL; 309-266-7232. Kraftmaid Cabinetry, Middlefield, OH; 440-632-5333. Merillat, Adrian, MI; 517-263-0771. Moen, North Olmstead, OH; 800-289-6636. Rev-A-Shelf, Louisville, KY; 800-626-1126. Rubbermaid, Wooster, OH; 888-895-2110. Thibaut, Newark, NJ; 973-643-3777. Thomasville Furniture, Thomasville, NC; 800-225-0265. Trellis Structures, Beverly, MA; 978-921-1235. Wellborn Cabinet, Ashland, AL; 800-336-8040.

Contents

Getting Started

Maybe you can't wait to bang the first nail. Or you may be just as happy leaving town until the windows are cleaned. The extent of your involvement with the construction phase is up to you. Your time, interests, and abilities can help you decide how to get the project from lines on paper to reality. But building a house requires more than putting pieces together. Whoever is in charge of the process must competently manage people as well as supplies, materials, and construction. He or she will have to

- Make a project schedule to plan the orderly progress of the work. This can be a bar chart that shows the time period of activity by each trade.
- Establish a budget for each category of work, such as foundation, framing, and finish carpentry.
- Arrange for a source of construction financing.
- Get a building permit and post it conspicuously at the construction site.
- Line up supply sources and order materials.
- Find subcontractors and negotiate their contracts.
- Coordinate the work so that it progresses smoothly with the fewest conflicts.
- Notify inspectors at the appropriate milestones.
- Make payments to suppliers and subcontractors.

You as the Builder

You'll have to take care of every logistical detail yourself if you decide to act as your own builder or general contractor. But along with the responsibilities of managing the project, you gain the flexibility to do as much of your own work as you want and subcontract out the rest. Before taking this path, however, be sure you have the time and capabilities. Do you also have the

time and ability to schedule the work, hire and coordinate subs, order materials, and keep ahead of the accounting required to manage the project successfully? If you do, you stand to save the amount that a general contractor would charge to take on these responsibilities, normally 15 to 30 percent of the construction cost. If you take this responsibility on but mismanage the project, the potential savings will erode and may even cost you more than if you had hired a builder in the first place. A subcontractor might charge extra for hav-

Acting as the builder, above, requires the ability to hire and manage subcontractors.

Building a home, opposite, includes the need to schedule building inspections at the appropriate milestones.

ing to return to the site to complete work that was originally scheduled for an earlier date. Or perhaps because you didn't order the windows at the beginning, you now have to pay for a recent cost increase. (If you had hired a builder in the first place he or she would absorb the increase.)

Hiring a Builder to Handle Construction

A builder or general contractor will manage every aspect of the construction process. Your role after signing the construction contract will be to make regular progress payments and ensure that the work for which you are paying has been completed. You will also consult with the builder and agree to any changes that may have to be made along the way.

Leads for finding builders might come from friends or neighbors who have had contractors build, remodel, or add to their homes. Real-estate agents and bankers may have some names handy but are more likely familiar with the builder's ability to complete projects on time and budget than the quality of the work itself.

The next step is to narrow your list of candidates to three or four who you think can do a quality job and work harmoniously with you. Phone each builder to see whether he or she is interested in being considered for your project. If so, invite the builder to an interview at your home. The meeting will serve two purposes. You'll be able to ask the candidate about his or her experience, and you'll be able to see whether or not your personalities are compatible. Go over the plans with the builder to make certain that he or she understands the scope of the project. Ask if they have constructed similar houses. Get references, and check the builder's standing with the Better Business Bureau. Develop a short list of builders, say three, and ask them to submit bids for the project.

Contracts

Lump-Sum Contracts

A lump-sum, or fixed-fee, contract lets you know from the beginning just what the project will cost, barring any changes made because of your requests or unforeseen conditions. This form works well for projects that promise few surprises and are well defined from the outset by a complete set of contract documents. You can enter into a fixed-price contract by negotiating with a single builder on your short list or by obtaining bids from three or four builders. If you go the latter route, give each bidder a set of documents and allow at least two weeks for them to submit their bids. When you get the bids, decide who you want and call the others to thank them for their efforts. You don't have to accept the lowest bid, but it probably makes sense to do so since you have already honed the list to builders you trust. Inform this builder of your intentions to finalize a contract.

Cost-Plus-Fee Contracts

Under a cost-plus-fee contract, you agree to pay the builder for the costs of labor and materials, as verified by receipts, plus a fee that represents the builder's overhead and profit. This arrangement is sometimes referred to as "time and materials." The fee can range between 15 and 30 percent of the incurred costs. Because you ultimately pick up the tab—whatever the costs—the contractor is never at risk, as he is with a lump-sum contract. You won't know the final total cost of a cost-plus-fee contract until the project is built and paid for. If you can live with that uncertainty, there are offsetting advantages. First, this form allows you to accommodate unknown conditions much more easily than does a lump-sum contract. And rather than being tied down by the project documents, you will be free to make changes at any point along the way. This can be a trap, though. Watching the project take shape will spark the desire to add something or do something differently. Each change costs more, and the accumulation can easily exceed your budget. Because of the uncertainty of the final tab and the built-in advantage to the contractor, you should think twice before entering into this form of contract.

Contract Content

The conditions of your agreement should be spelled out thoroughly in writing and signed by both parties, whatever contractual arrangement you make with your builder. Your contract should include provisions for the following:

- The names and addresses of the owner and builder.
- A description of the work to be included ("As described in the plans and specifications dated . . .").
- The date that the work will be completed if time is of the essence.
- The contract price for lump-sum contracts and the builder's allowed profit and overhead costs for changes.
- The builder's fee for cost-plus-fee contracts and the method of accounting and requesting payment.
- The criteria for progress payments (monthly, by project milestones) and the conditions of final payment.
- A list of each drawing and specification section that is to be included as part of the contract.
- Requirements for guarantees. (One year is the standard period for which contractors guarantee the entire project, but you may require specific guarantees on

When submitting bids, all of the builders should base their estimates on the same specifications. Once the work begins, communicate with your builder to keep the work proceeding smoothly.

Inspect your newly built home, if possible, before the builder closes it up and finishes it.

certain parts of the project, such as a 20-year guarantee on the roofing.)
- Provisions for insurance.
- A description of how changes in the work orders will be handled.

The builder may have a standard contract that you can tailor to the specifics of your project. These contain complete specific conditions with blanks that you can fill in to fit your project and a set of "general conditions" that cover a host of issues from insurance to termination provisions. It's always a good idea to have an attorney review the draft of your completed contract before signing it.

Working with Your Builder

The construction phase officially begins when you have a signed copy of the contract and copies of any insurance required from the builder. It's not unheard of for a builder to request an initial payment of 10 to 20 percent of the total cost to cover mobilization costs, those costs associated with obtaining permits and getting set up to begin the actual construction. If you agree to this, keep a careful eye on the progress of the work to ensure that the total paid out at any one time doesn't get too far out of sync with the actual work completed.

What about changes? From here on, it's up to you and your builder to proceed in good faith and to keep the channels of communication open. Even so, changes of one sort or another beset every project, and they usually add to its cost.

Light at the End of the Tunnel.

The builder's request for a final inspection marks the end of the construction phase—almost. At the final inspection meeting, you and the builder will inspect the work, noting any defects or incomplete items on a "punch list." When the builder tidies up the punch list items, you should reinspect. Sometimes, builders go on to another job and take forever to clean up the last few details, so only after all items on the list have been completed satisfactorily should you release the final payment, which often accounts for the builder's profit.

Some Final Words

Having a positive attitude is important when undertaking a project as large as building a home. A positive attitude can help you ride out the rigors and stress of the construction process.

Stay Flexible. Expect problems, because they certainly will occur. Weather can upset the schedule you have established for subcontractors. A supplier may get behind on deliveries, which also affects the schedule. An unexpected pipe may surprise you during excavation. Just as certain, every problem that comes along has a solution if you are open to it.

Be Patient. The extra days it may take to resolve a construction problem will be forgotten once the project is completed.

Express Yourself. If what you see isn't exactly what you thought you were getting, don't be afraid to look into changing it. Or you may spot an unforeseen opportunity for an improvement. Changes usually cost more money, though, so don't make frivolous decisions.

Finally, watching your home go up is exciting, so stay upbeat. Get away from your project from time to time. Dine out. Take time to relax. A positive attitude will make for smoother relations with your builder. An optimistic outlook will yield better-quality work if you are doing your own construction. And though the project might seem endless while it is under way, keep in mind that all the planning and construction will fade to a faint memory at some time in the future, and you will be getting a lifetime of pleasure from a home that is just right for you.

Plan #121084

Dimensions: 40' W x 42' D

Levels: 2

Square Footage: 1,728

Main Level Sq. Ft.: 845

Upper Level Sq. Ft.: 883

Bedrooms: 4

Bathrooms: 2½

Foundation: Basement

Materials List Available: Yes

Price Category: C

Images provided by designer/architect.

If you're looking for a home where the whole family will be comfortable, you'll love this design.

Features:

- **Great Room:** The heart of the home, this great room has a fireplace with a raised hearth, a sloped ceiling, and transom-topped windows.
- **Dining Room:** A cased opening lets you flow from the great room into this formal dining room. A built-in display hutch is the highlight here.
- **Kitchen:** What could be nicer than this wraparound kitchen with peninsula snack bar? The sunny, attached breakfast area has a pantry and built-in desk.
- **Master Suite:** A double vanity, whirlpool tub, shower, and walk-in closet exude luxury in this upper-floor master suite.

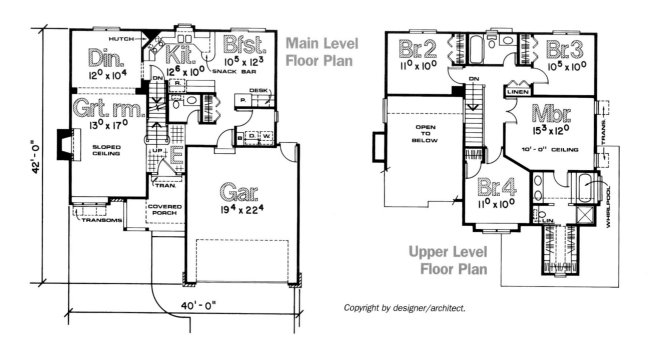

Copyright by designer/architect.

Plan #121014

Dimensions: 52' W x 47'4" D
Levels: 2
Square Footage: 1,869
Main Level Sq. Ft.: 1,421
Upper Level Sq. Ft.: 448
Bedrooms: 3
Bathrooms: 2½
Foundation: Basement
Materials List Available: Yes
Price Category: D

Images provided by designer/architect.

This compact home is packed with all the amenities you'll need for a gracious lifestyle.

Features:

• Ceiling Height: 8 ft. except as noted.

• Great Room: A soaring ceiling and six tall transom-topped windows make this a light and airy spot for entertaining.

• Formal Dining Room: This elegant room is ideal for entertaining dinner guests.

• Breakfast Area: This sunny area shares a see-through fireplace with the great room. It's the perfect place to start the day.

• Master Suite: Here are all the features you expect to find in large luxury homes. Wake up to tall, sloped ceilings, and enjoy the corner whirlpool, separate shower, and vanity. A large walk-in closet provides plenty of wardrobe storage.

• Attached Garage: The garage provides two bays of parking plus plenty of storage space.

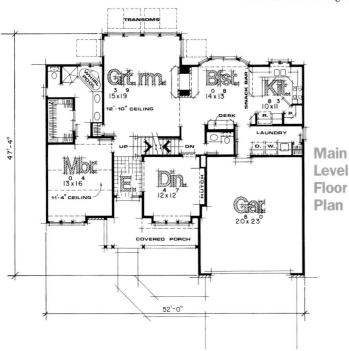

Main Level Floor Plan

Upper Level Floor Plan

Copyright by designer/architect.

Plan #151089

Dimensions: 84' W x 55'6" D
Levels: 1
Square Footage: 1,921
Bedrooms: 3
Bathrooms: 3
Foundation: Crawl space, slab, or basement
Materials List Available: Yes
Price Category: D

Images provided by designer/architect.

If your family loves to combine indoor and outdoor living, this home's fabulous porches and deck space make it perfect.

Features:

- **Porches:** A huge wraparound front porch, sizable rear porch, and deck that joins them give you space for entertaining or simply lounging.

- **Living Room:** A fireplace and built-in media center could be the focal points in this large room.

- **Hearth Room:** Open to both the living room and kitchen, this hearth room also features a fireplace.

- **Kitchen:** This step-saving kitchen includes ample storage and work space, as well as an angled bar it shares with the hearth room. Atrium doors lead to the rear porch.

- **Bonus Upper Level:** A large game room and a full bath make this area a favorite with the children.

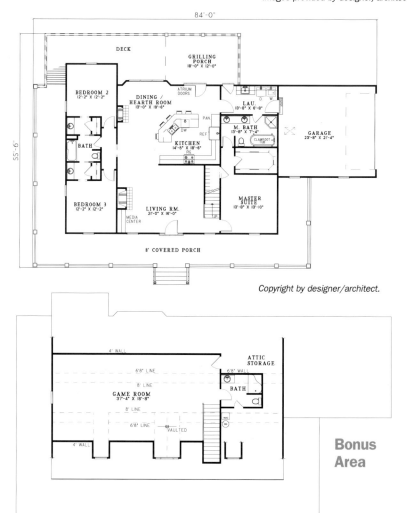

Copyright by designer/architect.

Bonus Area

Plan #361004

Dimensions: 77' W x 81' D

Levels: 1

Square Footage: 2,191

Bedrooms: 3

Bathrooms: 2

Foundation: Crawl space

Materials List Available: No

Price Category: D

Images provided by designer/architect.

If your family loves contemporary designs, this home with an open plan and unusually shaped rooms could be their dream house.

Features:

- **Great Room:** This area occupies the majority of the central hexagon.

- **Deck:** Doors from every living area, including the bedrooms, open to this wraparound deck, which surrounds the back of this home.

- **Living Room:** This area has a fireplace and sliding glass doors leading to the deck.

- **Dining Room:** Sliding glass doors and proximity to the kitchen define this dining area.

- **Kitchen:** The angled bar defines this room, where a walk-in pantry provides good storage space.

- **Master Suite:** This master wing includes a sitting room, door to the deck, window extension, walk-in closet, and luxury bath.

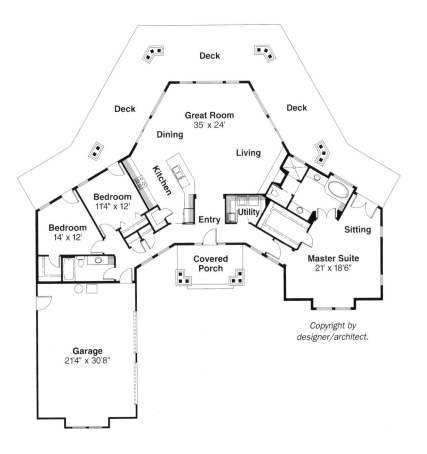

Copyright by designer/architect.

Plan #101017

Dimensions: 57' W x 51' D
Levels: 2
Square Footage: 2,253
Main Level Sq. Ft.: 1,719
Upper Level Sq. Ft.: 534
Opt. Upper Level Bonus Sq. Ft.: 247
Bedrooms: 4
Bathrooms: 3
Foundation: Basement
Materials List Available: No
Price Category: E

Images provided by designer/architect.

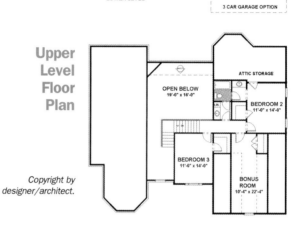

Main Level Floor Plan

Upper Level Floor Plan

Copyright by designer/architect.

Plan #141021

Dimensions: 70'10" W x 78'9" D
Levels: 1
Square Footage: 2,614
Bedrooms: 3
Bathrooms: 2½
Foundation: Basement
Materials List Available: Yes
Price Category: F

Images provided by designer/architect.

Living Room

Dining Room

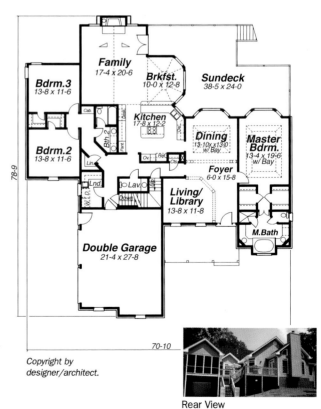

Copyright by designer/architect.

Rear View

Plan #241018

Dimensions: 83'7" W x 64'10" D

Levels: 1½

Square Footage: 2,519

Main Level Sq. Ft.: 2,096

Upper Level Sq. Ft.: 423

Bedrooms: 4

Bathrooms: 4

Foundation: Slab

Materials List Available: No

Price Category: E

Images provided by designer/architect.

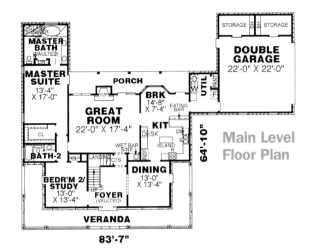

Main Level Floor Plan

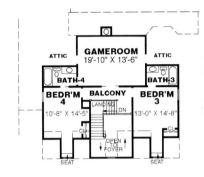

Upper Level Floor Plan

Copyright by designer/architect.

Plan #241019

Dimensions: 46'6" W x 34'2" D

Levels: 1

Square Footage: 1,397

Bedrooms: 3

Bathrooms: 2

Foundation: Slab

Materials List Available: No

Price Category: B

Images provided by designer/architect.

Copyright by designer/architect.

Plan #141029

Dimensions: 55' W x 42' D
Levels: 2
Square Footage: 2,289
Main Level Sq. Ft.: 1,382
Upper Level Sq. Ft.: 907
Bedrooms: 4
Bathrooms: 2½
Foundation: Basement
Materials List Available: Yes
Price Category: E

Images provided by designer/architect.

This well-appointed home combines elegance and style with a number of thoughtful interior amenities, allowing you to keep in step with current technological trends.

Features:

- Kitchen: Your family will naturally gravitate to this well-designed kitchen—and its innovative command center—through easy access both to and from the convenient garage entrance.

- Master Suite: Enjoy the style and comfort of this luxurious first-floor master suite, your own private haven from the cares and concerns that accompany a busy lifestyle.

- Additional Bedrooms: Your family will appreciate the convenience of the second-floor computer station, centrally located between two secondary bedrooms.

- Bonus Area: You can expand the optional space located on the second floor to meet future needs, or convert it to bedroom 5.

Main Level Floor Plan

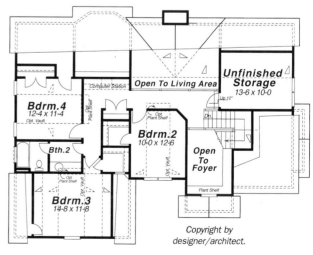

Upper Level Floor Plan

Copyright by designer/architect.

Plan #141031

Dimensions: 58'4" W x 30' D
Levels: 2
Square Footage: 2,367
Main Level Sq. Ft.: 1,025
Upper Level Sq. Ft.: 1,342
Bedrooms: 4
Bathrooms: 2½
Foundation: Basement
Materials List Available: No
Price Category: E

Images provided by designer/architect.

This inviting home combines traditional exterior lines, luxurious interior amenities, and innovative design to present a package that will appeal to all members of your family.

Features:

- Foyer: Formal living and dining rooms flank this impressive two-story foyer, which welcomes you to this delightful home with a staircase leading to a balcony.

- Command Center: You will enjoy the open flow of the main floor from the family room to this command center, beyond the kitchen, where you can plan your family activities.

- Master Suite: This master bedroom with optional window seat features a stepped tray ceiling. The master bath with cathedral ceiling offers an optional radius window.

- Additional Bedrooms: The secondary bedroom, next to the master, offers an over look to the foyer, well suited for a sitting room or study.

Main Level Floor Plan

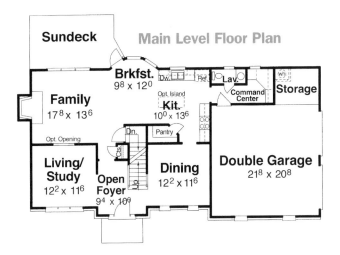

Upper Level Floor Plan

Copyright by designer/architect.

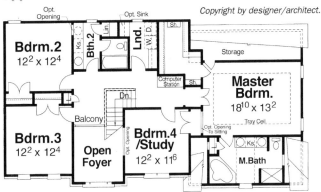

Plan #131005

Dimensions: 70' W x 37'4" D
Levels: 1
Square Footage: 1,595
Bedrooms: 3
Bathrooms: 2
Foundation: Basement, crawl space, or slab
Materials List Available: Yes
Price Category: D

With the finest features of an open design in the main living areas, this home gives privacy where you need it. Best of all, it's wheelchair accessible.

Features:

- Foyer: A high ceiling gives this area real presence and serves to blend it seamlessly with the great room and the dining room.

- Great Room: The open design allows you to use this room as an extension of the dining room or, if you wish, furnish it to create a private reading nook or visually separate media center.

- Breakfast Room: Both this room and the adjacent well-appointed kitchen flow into the rest of the living area. However, access to the rear porch, where you can sit out and enjoy the weather while you eat, distinguishes this room.

- Master Suite: Located in the same wing as the other bedrooms, this suite has a separate entrance and features a vaulted ceiling, three closets, and a compartmented bath.

SMARTtip

Create a Courtyard

Create a private walled-garden retreat with fences covered by climbing vines. Add height with trellises, and divide spaces with clipped boxwood hedges. Include an (almost) instant patio by digging away an area of sod and then covering it with a layer of sand and landscaping mesh to discourage weeds. Then cover it with pea gravel, and add a garden bench, statuary, and perhaps an antique or two. The result? European ambiance for even the most nondescript suburban yard.

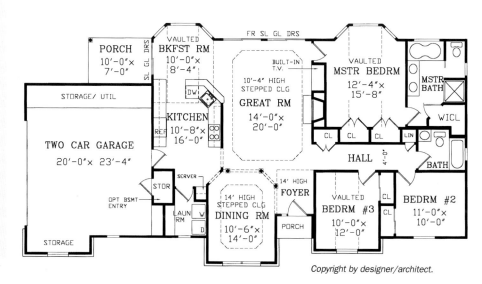

Copyright by designer/architect.

Foyer

Dining Room

Great Room

Living Room

SMARTtip

Natural Trellis

Create a natural rustic trellis that might even, if growing conditions are right, produce its own pretty blooms. Cut and place saplings in the ground as uprights. Then weave old grapevines with smaller saplings for the lattice.

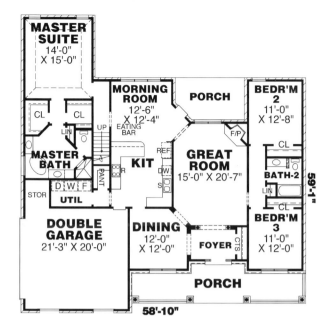

Plan #241016

Dimensions: 58'10" W x 59'1" D

Levels: 1

Square Footage: 2,011

Bedrooms: 3

Bathrooms: 2

Foundation: Slab

Materials List Available: No

Price Category: D

Images provided by designer/architect.

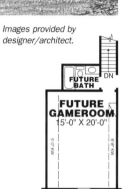

Bonus Area

Copyright by designer/architect.

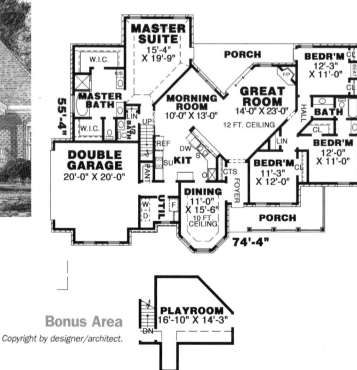

Plan #241017

Dimensions: 74'4" W x 55'4" D

Levels: 1

Square Footage: 2,431

Bedrooms: 4

Bathrooms: 2½

Foundation: Slab

Materials List Available: No

Price Category: E

Images provided by designer/architect.

Bonus Area

Copyright by designer/architect.

Main Level Floor Plan

Images provided by designer/architect.

Plan #151189

Dimensions: 50' W x 50' D
Levels: 1½
Square Footage: 2,196
Main Level Sq. Ft.: 1,672
Upper Level Sq. Ft.: 524
Opt. Bonus Sq. Ft.: 544
Bedrooms: 3
Bathrooms: 2½
Foundation: Crawl space, slab (basement or walk-out basement option for fee)
Materials List Available: Yes
Price Category: D

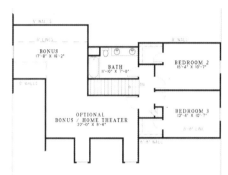

Upper Level Floor Plan

Copyright by designer/architect.

Images provided by designer/architect.

Plan #241015

Dimensions: 67'2" W x 46'10" D
Levels: 1
Square Footage: 1,609
Bedrooms: 3
Bathrooms: 2
Foundation: Slab
Materials List Available: No
Price Category: C

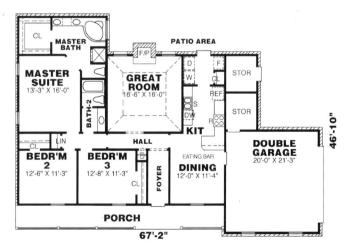

Copyright by designer/architect.

Plan #141032

Dimensions: 52' W x 44' D
Levels: 2
Square Footage: 2,476
Main Level Sq. Ft.: 1,160
Upper Level Sq. Ft.: 1,316
Bedrooms: 4
Bathrooms: 2½
Foundation: Basement
Materials List Available: Yes
Price Category: E

A refreshing design combines comfort, convenience, style, and modern innovations, inviting you to experience this family-oriented home.

Images provided by designer/architect.

Features:

- **Family Room:** Even as you enter the front door, you will be drawn to this impressive family room and its two-story fireplace wall.
- **Kitchen:** This well-designed kitchen with walk-in pantry makes meal preparation easy and enjoyable.
- **Command Center:** An innovative assist to managing a complex lifestyle, this command center, with its effective handling of additional work space and storage, will quickly become a family favorite.
- **Master Suite:** At the end of a busy day you can adjourn to the luxury and comfort of this master suite, which features a sitting room with a Palladian window.

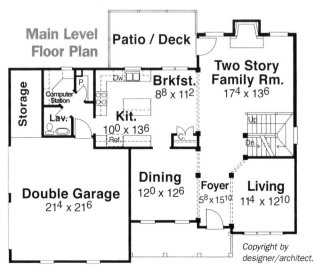

Copyright by designer/architect.

Plan #141028

Dimensions: 48' W x 36'4" D
Levels: 2
Square Footage: 2,215
Main Level Sq. Ft.: 1,075
Upper Level Sq. Ft.: 1,140
Bedrooms: 4
Bathrooms: 3
Foundation: Basement
Materials List Available: Yes
Price Category: E

Don't let appearances fool you. Designed to make efficient use of space without sacrificing style, this charming cottage offers more room than you might expect.

Images provided by designer/architect.

Features:

- Living Area: A delightful foyer with a U-shaped staircase that leads to the second floor welcomes you and introduces you to this comfortable living area, perfect for intimate gatherings of family or friends.

- Kitchen: Designed with convenience in mind, incorporating ample counter space and cabinets, this kitchen is a pleasure in which to work.

- Master Suite: This second-floor master suite, with windows overlooking the rear of the house, offers the option of a dramatic ceiling treatment. You will appreciate the closet behind the master bath, well-suited for clothing and low storage.

- Garage: An attached two-bay garage offers additional storage space.

Main Level Floor Plan

Patio / Sundeck

Bdrm.4
11^0 x 12^0

Two Story Living
16^4 x 14^6

Brkfst.
10^0 x 13^4

Kitchen
9^8 x 13^4

Dw.

Bath 3

Pantry   Ref.

Open Foyer
7^2 x 11^{10}

Dining
10^8 x 12^{10}

Double Garage
19^4 x 21^8

Up   Dn.

Upper Level Floor Plan

Bdrm.3
11^0 x 11^0

Opt. Plant Shelf Above

Open To Living Area

Laund.   W. D.

Sh.   Seat   Sh.
Stepped Tray

Master Bdrm.
13^6 x 17^6

Computer Station

Opt. Vault

Bath 2

Opt. Plant Shelf Above

Plant Shelf Above

Dn.

Open To Foyer

Bdrm.2
10^8 x 11^0

M.Bath
Tray

Opt. Vault

M.Clos.

Low Storage   Low Storage

Plan #361002

Dimensions: 62' W x 50' D
Levels: 1
Square Footage: 1,794
Bedrooms: 3
Bathrooms: 2
Foundation: Crawl space, basement
Materials List Available: No
Price Category: C

Images provided by designer/architect.

You'll love the contemporary open plan you'll find inside this home, with its wraparound front porch.

Features:

- **Family Room:** A vaulted ceiling adds to the spacious feeling in this room.

- **Deck:** Running the length of the house, this deck provides ample room for entertaining and dining.

- **Living Room:** This room has a fireplace and a deep bay perfectly suited for a sitting area.

- **Kitchen:** The angled island defines this space and makes a handy snack bar.

- **Eating Nook:** You'll love the vaulted ceiling and sliding glass doors to the rear deck.

- **Master Suite:** A walk-in closet and luxury bath complement this suite with doors to the deck.

- **Additional Bedrooms:** Both rooms have ample closet space and easy access to a nearby bath.

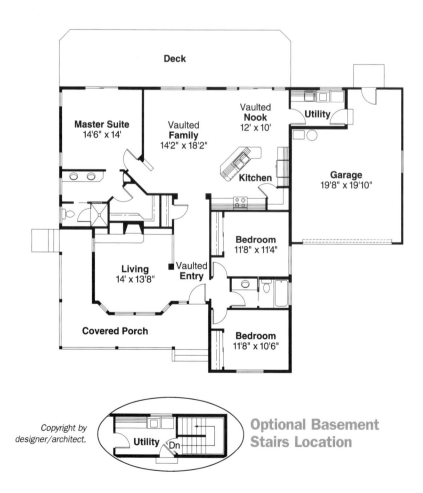

Copyright by designer/architect.

Optional Basement Stairs Location

Plan #321002

Dimensions: 72' W x 28' D
Levels: 1
Square Footage: 1,400
Bedrooms: 3
Bathrooms: 2
Foundation: Basement, crawl space
Materials List Available: Yes
Price Category: B

If you're looking for a well-designed compact home with contemporary amenities, this could be the home of your dreams.

Features:

- **Porch:** Just the right size for some rockers and a swing, this porch could become your outdoor living area when the weather is fine.

- **Living Room:** A vaulted ceiling adds to the spacious feeling in this room, where friends and family are sure to gather.

- **Kitchen:** This space-saving design, in combination with the ample counter and cabinet space, makes cooking a pleasure.

- **Utility Room:** This large room is fitted with cabinets for extra storage space. You'll find storage space in the large garage, too.

- **Master Bedroom:** This room is somewhat secluded for privacy, making it an ideal place for some quiet time at the end of the day.

Images provided by designer/architect.

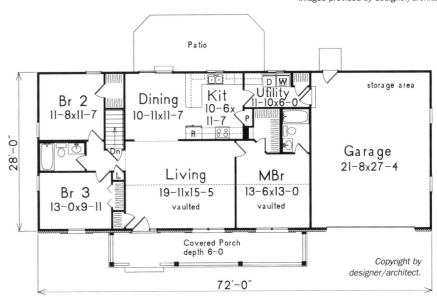

Copyright by designer/architect.

Plan #141027

Dimensions: 46' W x 38'4" D
Levels: 2
Square Footage: 2,088
Main Level Sq. Ft.: 1,048
Upper Level Sq. Ft.: 1,040
Bedrooms: 3
Bathrooms: 2½
Foundation: Basement
Materials List Available: Yes
Price Category: D

Specifically designed for narrow lots, this contemporary floor plan incorporates many features attractive to the discriminating buyer with a growing family.

Features:

• Living Area: You will enjoy the comfort and convenience of this casual living area, well-suited for family gatherings or entertaining friends.

• Kitchen: Designed for convenience and easy work patterns, this kitchen, with ample counter and cabinet space, is sure to become the hub of your family-oriented home.

• Master Bedroom: Enjoy the comfort and quiet of this relaxing room at the end of the day.

• Additional Bedrooms: One of the two secondary bedrooms features a Jack & Jill bath, perfect for a growing boy and girl. You will appreciate the gender-neutral features, abundant storage, and ample counter space that this room provides.

Main Level Floor Plan

Upper Level Floor Plan

Plan #161020

Dimensions: 60' W" x 50'4" D

Levels: 2

Square Footage: 2,082; 2,349 with bonus space

Main Level Sq. Ft.: 1,524

Upper Level Sq. Ft.: 558

Bedrooms: 3

Bathrooms: 2½

Foundation: Basement

Materials List Available: Yes

Price Category: D

Images provided by designer/architect.

You'll love the textured exterior finish and interesting roofline of this charming home.

Features:

- Great Room: Here you can enjoy the cozy fireplace, 12-ft. ceilings, and stylish French doors.

- Dining Room: A grand entry prepares you for the sloped ceiling that gives charm to this room.

- Kitchen: Natural light floods both the well-designed kitchen and adjacent breakfast room.

- Master Suite: Located on the first floor, this area boasts a whirlpool tub, a double-bowl vanity, and a large walk-in closet.

- Upper Level: Split stairs lead to a balcony over the foyer, a computer/study area, and two additional bedrooms.

- Bonus Room: Use this 267-sq.-ft. area over the garage for storage or a fourth bedroom.

Main Level Floor Plan

Upper Level Floor Plan

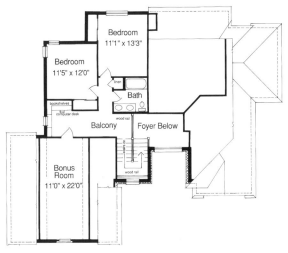

Copyright by designer/architect.

Living Room

Plan #111004

Dimensions: 76' W x 85' D

Levels: 1

Square Footage: 2,698

Bedrooms: 4

Full Bathrooms: 3½

Foundation: Slab

Materials List Available: No

Price Category: F

If you've been looking for a home that includes a special master suite, this one could be the answer to your dreams.

Features:

• **Living Room:** Make a sitting area around the fireplace here so that the whole family can enjoy the warmth on chilly days and winter evenings. A door from this room leads to the rear covered porch, making this room the heart of your home.

• **Kitchen:** An island with a cooktop makes cooking a pleasure in this well-designed kitchen, and the breakfast bar invites visitors at all times of day.

• **Utility Room:** A sink and a built-in ironing board make this room totally practical.

• **Master Suite:** A private fireplace in the corner sets a romantic tone for this bedroom, and the door to the covered porch allows you to sit outside on warm summer nights. The bath has two vanities, a divided walk-in closet, a standing shower, and a deluxe corner bathtub.

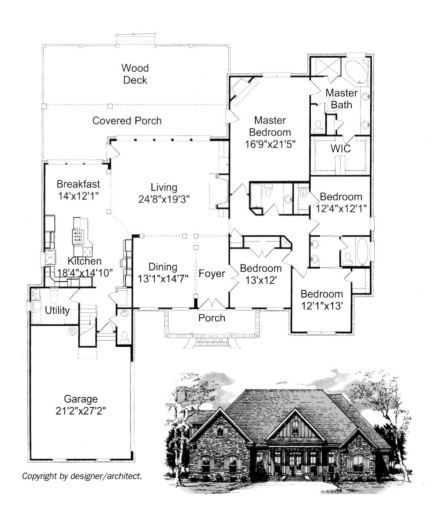

Copyright by designer/architect.

Kitchen

Dining Room

Master Bath

Master Bath

SMARTtip

How to Quit Smoking — Lighting Your Fireplace

Before attempting to light a wood fire, make certain that the damper is open all the way. This allows a good draft (flow of air up the chimney) to prevent smoke from blowing back into the room. To ensure a good draft—particularly if your home is well insulated—open a window a bit when lighting a fire.

The opposite of draft is downdraft, which occurs when cold air flows down the chimney and into the room. If the fireplace is properly designed and maintained, the smoke shelf will prevent backpuffing from downdraft most of the time by redirecting cold air currents back up the chimney. The open damper also helps prevent backpuffing.

Also, build a fire slowly to let the chimney liner heat up, which will create a good draft and minimize the chances of downdraft.

Don't wait until fall to inspect the chimney. Do this job, or call a chimney sweep, when the weather is mild. Because some repairs take a while to make, it's best to have them done when the fireplace is not normally in use. If you do the inspection yourself, wear old clothes, eye goggles, and a mask.

Plan #121027

Dimensions: 46' W x 48' D

Levels: 2

Square Footage: 1,660

Main Level Sq. Ft.: 1,265

Upper Level Sq. Ft.: 395

Bedrooms: 3

Bathrooms: 2½

Foundation: Basement

Materials List Available: Yes

Price Category: C

Images provided by designer/architect.

This elegant home is designed for architectural interest and gracious living.

Features:

• Ceiling Height: 8 ft. unless otherwise noted.

• Great Room: Family and guests will be drawn to this inviting, sun-filled room with its 13-ft. ceiling and raised-hearth fireplace.

• Formal Dining Room: An angled ceiling lends architectural interest to this elegant room. Alternately, this room can be used as a parlor.

• Master Bedroom: Corner windows are designed to ease window placement.

• Master Bath: The master bedroom is served by a private bath. The sunlit whirlpool bath invites you to take time to luxuriate and rejuvenate. There's a double vanity, separate shower, and a walk-in closet.

• Garage: This two bay garage offers plenty of space for storage in addition to parking.

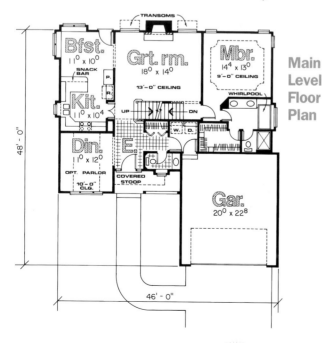

Main Level Floor Plan

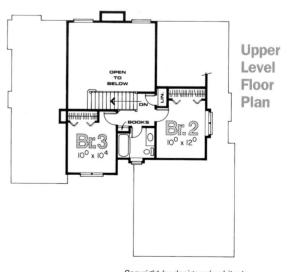

Upper Level Floor Plan

Copyright by designer/architect.

Plan #121083

Dimensions: 72' W x 45'4" D
Levels: 2
Square Footage: 2,695
Main Level Sq. Ft.: 1,881
Upper Level Sq. Ft.: 814
Bedrooms: 4
Bathrooms: 3½
Foundation: Basement
Materials List Available: Yes
Price Category: F

Images provided by designer/architect.

You'll love this home for its soaring entryway ceiling and well-designed layout.

Features:

• **Entry:** A balcony from the upper level looks down into this two-story entry, which features a decorative plant shelf.

• **Great Room:** Comfort is guaranteed in this large room, with its built-in bookcases framing a lovely fireplace and trio of transom-topped windows along one wall.

• **Living Room:** Save both this formal room and the formal dining room, both of which flank the entry, for guests and special occasions.

• **Kitchen:** This convenient work space includes a gazebo-shaped breakfast area where friends and family will gather at any time of day.

Main Level Floor Plan

Upper Level Floor Plan

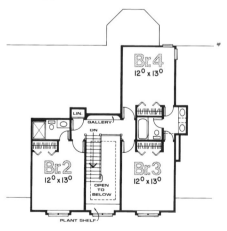

Copyright by designer/architect.

Kitchens and Baths

O f all the rooms in a house, kitchens present unique decorating challenges because so much tends to happen in these spaces. In addition to preparing meals, most families use kitchens as gathering and entertaining areas. Kitchens need to be functional, comfortable, and inviting.

Who can't relate to this scenario: you turn on the oven to preheat it, but wait, did you take out the large roasting pan first?

How about the lasagna dish, muffin tins, pizza stone, and cookie sheets that are in there, too? Now where can you put everything that was in the oven while the casserole is baking and the countertop is laden with the rest of tonight's dinner ingredients? Good cabinetry outfitted with an assortment of organizing options can help you there. It can make your kitchen more efficient and a whole lot neater while establishing a style, or "look," for the room.

Cabinet Construction

Basically, cabinets are constructed in one of two ways: framed or frameless. Framed cabinets have a traditional look, with a full frame across the face of the cabinet box that may show between closed doors. This secures adjacent cabinets and strengthens wider cabinet boxes with a center rail. Hinges on framed cabinets may or may not be visible around doors when they are closed. The door's face may be ornamented with raised or recessed panels, trimmed or framed panels, or a framed-glass panel with or without muntins (the narrow vertical and horizontal strips of wood that divide panes of glass).

Frameless Cabinets. Also known as European-style cabinets, although American manufacturers also make them, frameless cabinets are built without a face frame and sport a clean, contemporary look, often not befitting a Southern or Country style. There's no trim or molding with this simple design. Close-fitting doors cover the entire front of the box, no ornamentation appears on the face of the doors, and hinges are typically hidden inside the cabinet box.

Selecting Cabinets

Choosing one type over another is generally a matter of taste, although framed units offer slightly less interior space. But the quality of construction is a factor that should always be taken into consideration. How do you judge it? Solid wood is too expensive for most of today's budgets, but it might be used on just the doors and frames. More typical is plywood box construction, which offers good structural support and solid wood on the doors and frames. To save money, cabinetmakers sometimes use strong plywood for support elements, such as the box and frame, and medium-density fiberboard for other parts,

such as doors and drawer fronts. In yet another alternative, good-quality laminate cabinets can be made with high-quality, thick particleboard underneath the laminate finish.

Quality Points. There are other things to look for in cabinet construction. They include dovetail or mortise-and-tenon joinery and solidly mortised hinges. Also, make sure that the interior of every cabinet is well finished, with adjustable shelves that are a minimum ⅝ inch thick to prevent bowing.

Bead-board paneled doors, opposite, are at home in Southern-style kitchens.

Framed cabinets, above, offer a traditional look to an otherwise modern kitchen.

Country-style designs have many attributes of Cottage decor, right.

Unless you have the time and skill to build the cabinets yourself or can hire someone else to do it, you'll have to purchase them in one of four ways. **Knockdown cabinetry** (also known as RTA, ready to assemble) is shipped flat and, sometimes, unfinished because you put the pieces together. **Stock cabinetry** comes in standard sizes but limited styles and colors; it is often available on the spot or can be delivered quickly. Like stock, **semicustom cabinetry** comes in standard styles, but it is manufactured to fit a homeowner's specific size and finish needs. **Custom cabinetry** is not limited in terms of style or size because it is built to the designer's specifications.

The Decorative Role of Cabinets

The look you create in your kitchen will be largely influenced by the cabinetry you select. Finding a style that suits you and how you will use your new kitchen is similar to shopping for furniture. In fact, don't be surprised to see many furniture details dressing up the cabinets on view in showrooms and home centers today.

Details That Stand Out. Besides architectural elements such as fluted pilasters, corbels, moldings, and bull's-eye panels, look for details such as fretwork, rope motifs, gingerbread trim, balusters, composition ornamentation (it looks like carving), even footed cabinets that mimic separate furniture pieces. If your taste runs toward less fussy design, you'll also find handsome door and drawer styles that feature minimal decoration, if any. Woods and finishes are just as varied, and range from informal looks in birch, oak, ash, and maple to rich mahogany and cherry. Laminate finishes, though less popular than they were a decade ago, haven't completely disappeared from the marketplace, but an array of colors has replaced the once-ubiquitous almond and white finishes.

Color

Color is coming on strong on wood cabinetry, too. Accents in one, two, or more hues are pairing with natural wood tones. White-painted cabinets take on a warmer glow with tinted shades of this always pop-ular neutral. Special "vintage" finishes, such as translucent color glazes, continue to grow in popularity, as do distressed finishing techniques such as wire brushing and rubbed-through color that add both another dimension and the appeal of handcraftmanship, even on mass-produced items.

If you're shy about using color on such a high-ticket item as cabinetry, try it as an accent on molding, door trim, or island cabinetry. Just as matched furniture suites have become passé in other rooms of the house, the same is true for the kitchen, where mixing several looks can add sophistication and visual interest.

Cabinet Hardware

Another way to emphasize your kitchen's style is with hardware. From exquisite reproductions in brass, pewter, wrought iron, or ceramic to handsome bronze, chrome, nickel, glass, steel, plastic, rubber, wood, or stone creations, a smorgasbord of shapes and designs is available. Some pieces are highly polished; others are matte-finished, smooth, or hammered. Some are abstract or geometrical; others are simple,

elegant shapes. Whimsical designs take on the forms of animals or teapots, vegetables or flowers. Even just one or two great-looking door or drawer pulls can be showstoppers in a kitchen that may otherwise be devoid of much personality. Like mixing cabinet finishes, a combination of two hardware styles—perhaps picked up from other materials in the room—makes a big design statement. As the famed architect Mies Van der Rohe once stated, "God is in the details," and the most perfect detail in your new kitchen may be the artistic hardware that you select.

Cabinet style will set the tone for the design of the entire kitchen. The simple door styles keeps the room at left airy and casual.

The rustic look of the cabinets above is tailor-made for any Country style kitchen.

Color accents, such as the splash of color on the kitchen island shown right, can customize any simple cabinet design.

Cabinet hardware should complement the cabinet door and drawer designs, but it should also be easy for everyone in the household to grasp, above.

Kitchen storage comes in a variety of forms, including cabinets, drawers, pullout extensions, and the glass-front bins shown to the right.

Besides looks, consider the function of a pull or knob. You have to be able to grip it easily and comfortably. If your fingers or hands get stiff easily, or if you have arthritis, select C- or U-shaped pulls. If you like a knob, try it out in the showroom to make sure it isn't slippery or awkward when you grab it. Knobs and pulls can be inexpensive if you can stick to unfinished ones that you can paint in an accent color picked up from the tile or wallpaper. If you don't plan to buy new cabinets, changing the hardware on old ones can redefine their style. The right knob or pull can suggest any one of a number of vintage looks or decorative styles, from Colonial to Victorian, and reinforce your decor.

Types of Storage

Storage facilities can make or break a kitchen, so choose the places you'll put things with care. Here's a look at a few alternatives:

Pantries. How often you shop and how many groceries you typically bring home determine the amount of food storage space your family needs. If you like to stock up or take advantage of sales, add a pantry to your kitchen. To maximize a pantry's convenience, plan shallow, 6-inch-deep shelves so that cans and packages will never be stored more than two deep. This way, you'll easily be able to see what you've got on hand. Pantries range in size from floor-to-ceiling models to narrow units designed to fit between two standard-size cabinets.

Appliance Garages. Appliance garages make use of dead space in a corner, but they can be installed anywhere in the vertical space between wall-mounted cabinets and the countertop. A tambour (rolltop) door hides small appliances like a food processor or anything else you want within reach but hidden from view.

Lazy Susans and Carousel Shelves. Rotating shelves like lazy Susans and carousels maximize dead corner storage and put items like dishes or pots and pans within easy reach. A lazy Susan rotates 360 degrees, so just spin it to find what you're looking for. Carousel shelves, which attach to two right-angled doors, rotate 270 degrees; open the doors, and the shelves swing out allowing you to reach items easily.

Pivoting Shelves. Door-mounted shelves and in-cabinet swiveling shelf units offer easy access to kitchen supplies. Taller units serve as pantries that hold a great deal in minimal space.

Pullout Tables and Trays. In tight kitchens, pullout tables and trays are excellent ways to gain eating space or an extra work surface. Pullout cutting boards come in handy near cooktops, microwaves, and food prep areas. Pullout tea carts are also available.

Customized Organizers. If you decide to use value-priced cabinets or choose to forego the storage accessories offered by manufacturers, consider refitting their interiors with cabinet organizers you purchase yourself. These plastic, plastic-coated wire, or enameled-steel racks and hangers are widely available at department stores, hardware stores, and home centers.

Some of these units slide in and out of base cabinets, similar to the racks in a dishwasher. Others let you mount shallow drawers to the undersides of wall cabinets.

Still others consist of stackable plastic bins with plenty of room to hold kitchen sundries.

Beware of the temptation to overspecialize your kitchen storage facilities. Sizes and needs for certain items change, so be sure to allot at least 50 percent of your kitchen's storage to standard cabinets with one or more movable shelves. And don't forget to allow for storing recyclable items.

Today's cabinets can be customized with storage accessories, right.

Full-height pantries, above, provide a number of different types of storage near where you need the items. This pantry is next to the food-prep area.

Base cabinets can be outfitted with accessories for kitchen storage or for wet bar storage as shown in the cabinet below.

Storage Checklist

Here's a guide to help you get your storage needs in order.

■ **Do you like kitchen gadgets?**
Plan drawer space, countertop sorters, wall magnets, or hooks to keep these items handy near where you often use them.

■ **Do you own a food processor, blender, mixer, toaster oven, electric can opener, knife sharpener, juicer, coffee maker, or coffee mill?**
If you're particularly tidy, you may want small appliances like these tucked away in an appliance garage or cupboard to be taken out only when needed. If you pre-

fer to have frequently used machines sitting on the counter, ready to go, plan enough space, along with conveniently located electrical outlets.

■ **Do you plan to store large quantities of food?**
Be sure to allow plenty of freezer, bin, and shelf space for the kind of food shopping you do.

■ **Do you intend to do a lot of freezing or canning?**
Allow a work space and place to stow equipment. Also plan adequate storage for the fruits of your labor—an extra stand-alone freezer, a good-sized food safe in the kitchen, or a separate pantry or cellar.

■ **Do you bake often?**
Consider a baking center that can house your equipment and serve as a separate baking-ingredients pantry.

■ **Do you collect pottery, tinware, or anything else that might be displayed in the kitchen?**
Soffits provide an obvious place to hang small objects like collectible plates. Eliminating soffits provides a shelf on top of the wall cabinets for larger light-weight objects like baskets. Open shelving, glass-front cupboards, and display cabinets are other options.

■ **Do you collect cookbooks?**
If so, you'll need expandable shelf space and perhaps a bookstand.

Personal Profile of You and Your Family

■ **How tall are you and everyone else who will use your kitchen?**
Adjust your counter and wall-cabinet heights to suit. Multilevel work surfaces for special tasks are a necessity for good kitchen design.

■ **Do you or any of your family members use a walker, leg braces, or a wheelchair?**
Plan a good work height, knee space, grab bars, secure seating, slide-out work

Fold-down ironing boards, above left, are a true luxury. If you have the space, install one near the kitchen or laundry room.

Corner cabinets often contain storage space you can't reach. Make it accessible by installing swing-out shelves, above right, or a lazy Susan.

Glass doors put your kitchen items on display. The owners of the kitchen below chose distinctive pottery and glassware for their glass-door cabinets.

boards, and other convenience features to make your kitchen comfortable for all who will use it.

■ **Are you left- or right-handed?**
Think about your natural motion when you choose whether to open cupboards or refrigerator doors from the left or right side, whether to locate your dishwasher to the left or right of the sink, and so on.

■ **How high can you comfortably reach?**
If you're tall, hang your wall cabinets high. If you're petite, you may want to hang the cabinets lower and plan a spot to keep a step stool handy.

■ **Can you comfortably bend and reach for something in a base cabinet? Can you lift heavy objects easily and without strain or pain?**
If your range is limited in these areas, be sure to plan roll-out shelving on both upper and lower tiers of your base cabinets. Also, look into spring-up shelves designed to lift mixer bases or other heavy appliances to counter height.

■ **Do you frequently share cooking tasks with another family member?**
If so, you may each prefer to have your own work area.

ous plan demands this kind of attention. Even if you are designing a modest bath, you can greatly increase its performance and your ultimate comfort by thoughtfully planning out every square inch of floor and wall space. In fact, small spaces require more attention to details than larger spaces.

Types of bathrooms

The most-common-size American bathroom measures 60 x 84 inches or 60 x 96 inches. The most common complaint about it is the lack of space. The arrangement may have suited families 50 years ago, but times and habits have changed. If it's the only bathroom in the house, making it work better becomes even more important.

When planning the layout, try angling a sink or shower unit in a corner to free up some floor space. Unlike a traditional door, which swings into the room and takes up wall space when it is open, a pocket door slides into the wall. Another smart way to add function to a small bathroom is to remove the drywall and install shelves between the studs.

The Importance of Lighting. You can also make a small bathroom feel roomier by bringing in natural light with a skylight or roof window or by replacing one small standard window with several small casement units that can be installed high on the wall to maintain privacy while admitting light.

Bath Design

Many professionals believe that bathrooms may be the most difficult rooms in the house to design properly. The space is often small, yet it must be able to accommodate a variety of large fixtures. In addition, many homeowners tend to focus, at least initially, on the way the bathroom looks. They fall in love with the whirlpool tub that is really too large for the space or the exquisite hand-painted sink that, while beautiful, demands too much effort to keep it

looking that way. Design your bath to be functional as well as beautiful.

Architect Louis Sullivan said, "Form follows function." That does not mean that style has to be subservient to function, but there must be a balance between the two. So even if you have a clear picture about how you want the new bathroom to look, put that thought on hold—temporarily—and think about how it will work.

Thorough Planning. Don't mislead yourself into believing that only a luxuri-

The Master Bath

The concept of the master bath has come of age in the past decade. It is one of the most popular rooms for splurging on high-end items and gives one of the highest returns on investment upon resale. It's where you can create that sought-after getaway—the home version of a European spa.

Latest Trends. Some popular amenities to include in your plan are a sauna, greenhouse, exercise studio, fireplace, audio and video systems, faucets and sprayers with full massaging options, steam room,

Windows placed high on the wall let in light while maintaining privacy, opposite.

Master baths, above, often contain an attached dressing area.

Traditional designs do not prevent you from using the latest shower products, right.

Cottage baths tend to be bright and airy, such as the one shown to the left.

A simple floral design decorates the border of the medicine cabinet above.

Traditional bathroom cabinetry should be simple in design, below.

whirlpool tub, and dressing table. You are only limited by size and imagination.

Planning for Extras. Extras can be tempting but may require special planning. For example, you may need additional support in the floor, as well as supplemental heating and ventilation. You would not want to slip into a tub and have it fall two floors to the middle of the living room.

Some of the best floor plans for the modern adult bath also include a separate room for the toilet and bidet, a detached tub and shower, and dual sinks on opposite sides of the room with adjacent dressing rooms and walk-in closets. Modern couples

want to share a master bed and bath, but they also want to have privacy and the ease of getting ready in the morning without tripping over their mates. The only way to do this harmoniously is to mingle the parts of the room that invite sharing and separate those elements that are always private. Such items as a sauna, exercise area, and a whirlpool tub would be part of shared space. Dressing tables and clothes closets would be private spaces.

The Powder Room

The guest bath. The half bath. It has a lot of names, and it may be the most efficient room in the house, providing just what you

need often in tight quarters. A powder room normally includes nothing more than a lavatory and a toilet. You can find small-scale fixtures specifically designed for the powder room, from the tiniest lavs to unusually narrow toilets.

Keep a small powder room as light and open as possible. Plan to install good lighting because the powder room is often used for touching up makeup.

Focal Points. In the powder room, the vanity is often the focal point. The room offers the best opportunity to showcase a decorative piece, such as a hand-painted pedestal sink or a custom-made vanity.

Because the powder room is often for guests and is normally located on the ground floor near the living area, take extra care to ensure privacy. If possible, the best location is in a hallway, away from the living room, kitchen, and dining area. This room can also handle stronger wall colors—either dark or bright ones—as well as larger, bolder wallpaper patterns because it is a short-stay room.

The Family Bath

Compartmentalizing is the best way to start planning the family bath. But remember, when you separate the bathroom into smaller, distinct areas, you run the risk of making the room feel cramped. Try to alleviate this with extra natural light, good artificial lighting, and translucent partitions made of glass blocks or etched glass. Anything that divides with privacy while also allowing light to enter will help ease the closed-in feeling.

Separate Areas. If separating the fixtures is not possible because of the size of the room, include a sink in the dressing area within the master bedroom to provide a second place for applying makeup or shaving. It will help relieve bottlenecks when everyone is dressing in the morning.

Investigate building a back-to-back bath in lieu of one large shared room. Another popular option is to locate the bathing fixtures, both the tub and separate shower, in the center of the room; install the bidet, a toilet, and sink on either side in their own separate areas. To make the arrangement work, keep each side of the room accessible to the door.

There are other options you can use. It is important to remember that you don't need to do them all at once; you can do some remodeling once you've moved into your house.

Ceramic-tile counters for bathroom vanities are easy to clean and can stand up to abuse.

Plan #131027

Dimensions: 62'4" W x 53'6" D
Levels: 2
Square Footage: 2,567
Main Level Sq. Ft.: 2,017
Upper Level Sq. Ft.: 550
Bedrooms: 4
Bathrooms: 3
Foundation: Crawl space, slab, or basement
Materials List Available: Yes
Price Category: F

Images provided by designer/architect.

The features of this home are so good that you may have trouble imagining all of them at once.

Features:

- **Great Room:** Imagine a stepped ceiling, corner fireplace, built-media center, and wall of windows with a glass door to the backyard—in one room.
- **Dining Room:** A stepped ceiling and server with a sink add to the elegance of this formal room.
- **Breakfast Room:** Eat at the bar this room shares with the island kitchen, and admire the 12-ft. cathedral ceiling and bayed group of

8- and 9-ft. windows. Or go through the sliding glass door to the covered side porch.

- **Master Suite:** The bedroom has a tray ceiling and cozy sitting area, and a whirlpool tub, shower, and walk-in closet are in the skylighted bath.
- **Optional Study:** The private bath in bedroom 2 makes it ideal for a study or home office.
- **Bonus Room:** Enjoy the extra 300 sq. ft.

Breakfast Nook

Rear View

Great Room

Main Level Floor Plan

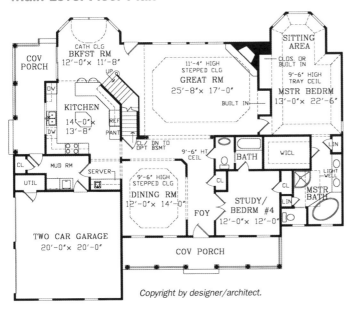

Copyright by designer/architect.

Upper Level Floor Plan

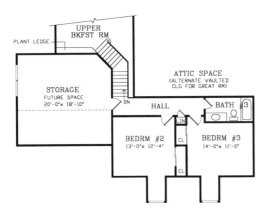

Painting Tips

As with any skill, there is a right and a wrong way to paint. There is a right way to hold a brush, a right way to maneuver a roller, a right way to spray a wall, etc. Follow these basic professional tips:

Brushing vs. Rolling. Some painters insist that only a brush-painted job looks right. However, most painters will "cut in" the edges with a brush, and then finish the main body of a wall or ceiling using a roller. Brushing alone can be time-consuming, and it is typically reserved for architectural woodwork.

Using the Right Brush. Use the largest brush with which you are comfortable. Professional painters seldom pick up anything smaller than a 4-inch brush. Most homeowners will achieve good results using a 4-inch brush for "cutting in" and for large surfaces, and an angled 2½- to 3-inch sash brush for trim around windows and doors. Be sure, also, to use brushes that are appropriate for the type of paint being applied. Oil-based paints require a natural bristle (also called "China bristles"), while water-based paints are applied with a synthetic bristle brush.

Handling a Brush. Many people grip a paintbrush as if they were shaking someone's hand. It is better to grip a brush more like a pencil, with the fingers and thumb wrapped around the metal ferrule. This grip provides the hand and wrist with a wider range of motion and therefore greater speed and precision. If your hand cramps, switch hands or switch temporarily to the handshake grip.

Wiping Rags. Before you begin painting, put a dust rag in your pocket. This is helpful for clearing away cobwebs and dust before painting. It is also handy for wiping off paint drips before they have a chance to dry.

Paint Hooks. When working on a ladder, use a good-quality paint hook to secure the paint bucket to your ladder. Avoid makeshift hooks made with wire or coat hangers. Paint hooks are inexpensive and available at virtually all paint and hardware stores.

Plan #151195

Dimensions: 52'6" W x 55'6" D

Levels: 1½

Square Footage: 1,710

Main Level Sq. Ft.: 1,710

Opt. Bonus Sq. Ft.: 557

Bedrooms: 3

Bathrooms: 2

Foundation: Crawl space, slab (basement or walk-out basement option for fee)

Materials List Available: Yes

Price Category: C

Images provided by designer/architect.

**Main Level
Floor Plan**

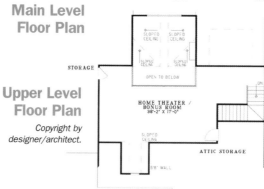

**Upper Level
Floor Plan**

Copyright by designer/architect.

Plan #151198

Dimensions: 54'10" W x 56'8" D

Levels: 1

Square Footage: 1,807

Bedrooms: 3

Bathrooms: 2

Foundation: Crawl space, slab (basement or walk-out basement option for fee)

Materials List Available: Yes

Price Category: D

Images provided by designer/architect.

Copyright by designer/architect.

Plan #151199

Dimensions: 52' W x 42'10" D

Levels: 1

Square Footage: 1,295

Bedrooms: 3

Bathrooms: 2

Foundation: Crawl space, slab (basement or walk-out basement option for fee)

Materials List Available: Yes

Price Category: B

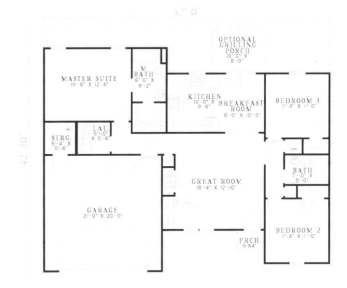

Images provided by designer/architect.

Copyright by designer/architect.

Plan #211144

Dimensions: 52' W x 74' D

Levels: 2

Square Footage: 2,542

Main Level Sq. Ft.: 1,510

Upper Level Sq. Ft.: 1,032

Bedrooms: 4

Bathrooms: 3½

Foundation: Basement, crawl space, or slab

Materials List Available: Yes

Price Category: E

Images provided by designer/architect.

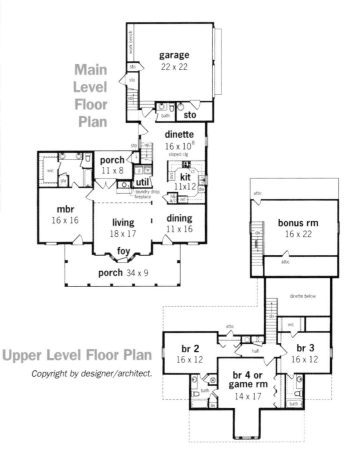

Copyright by designer/architect.

Plan #131003

Dimensions: 60' W x 39'10" D
Levels: 1
Square Footage: 1,466
Bedrooms: 3
Bathrooms: 2
Foundation: Basement, crawl space, or slab
Materials List Available: Yes
Price Category: B

Victorian styling adds elegance to this compact and easy-to-maintain ranch design.

Features:

- Ceiling Height: 8 ft.

- Foyer: Bridging between the front door and the great room, this foyer is a surprise feature.

- Great Room: A 10-ft. ceiling adds to the spacious feeling of this room, while the corner fireplace gives it an intimate feeling. Sliding glass doors at the rear of the room open to the backyard.

- Dining Room: This formal room adjoins the great room, allowing guests and family to flow between the rooms.

- Breakfast Room: Turrets add a Victorian feeling to this room that's just off the kitchen and overlooks the front porch.

- Master Suite: Privacy is assured in this suite, which is separated from the main part of the house. A compartmented bath and large walk-in closet add convenience to its beauty.

Images provided by designer/architect.

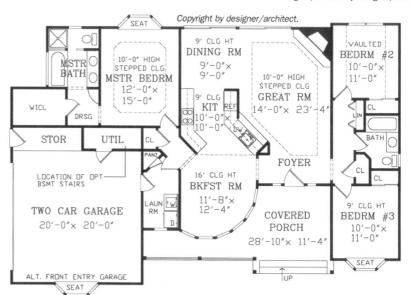

Copyright by designer/architect.

Breakfast Room

Plan #131002

Dimensions: 70'1" W x 60'7" D
Levels: 1
Square Footage: 1,709
Bedrooms: 3
Bathrooms: 2½
Foundation: Basement, crawl space, or slab
Materials List Available: Yes
Price Category: D

Images provided by designer/architect.

Rear View

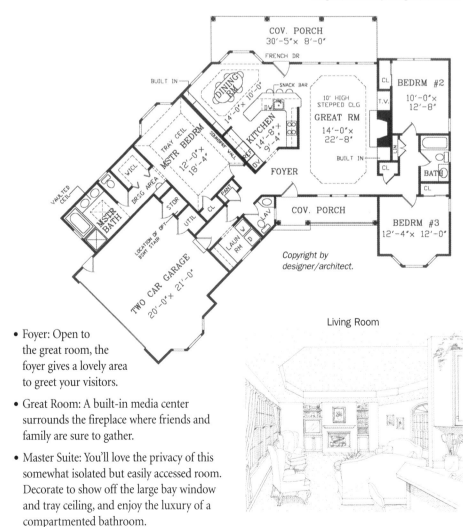

Living Room

You'll love the way this angled ranch brings out the best in a corner lot or on a slope.

Features:

Ceiling Height: 8 ft.

- Front Porch: Hang baskets of plants from the roof of this porch, which is just the right size for a couple of rockers and a side table.

- Dining Room: Well-placed windows flood this room with sunlight during the day and a built-in cabinet gives ample storage space for all your china, linens, and collectables.

- Foyer: Open to the great room, the foyer gives a lovely area to greet your visitors.

- Great Room: A built-in media center surrounds the fireplace where friends and family are sure to gather.

- Master Suite: You'll love the privacy of this somewhat isolated but easily accessed room. Decorate to show off the large bay window and tray ceiling, and enjoy the luxury of a compartmented bathroom.

Plan #101012

Dimensions: 69'4" W x 62'9" D

Levels: 1

Square Footage: 2,288

Bedrooms: 3

Bathrooms: 2½

Foundation: Slab, crawl space, or basement

Materials List Available: No

Price Category: E

Images provided by designer/architect.

This classic brick ranch boasts traditional styling and an exciting up-to-date floor plan.

Features:

- Ceiling Height: 9 ft. unless otherwise noted.

- Front Porch: Guests will be welcome by this inviting front porch, which features a 12-ft. ceiling.

- Family Room: This warm and inviting room measures 16 ft. x 19 ft. It features a 14-ft. ceiling and a rear wall of windows. French doors lead to an enormous deck.

- Kitchen: This unique angled kitchen is open to the hearth room and eating areas, all of which enjoy vaulted ceilings and are surrounded by windows. The hearth room has a TV niche.

- Master Suite: This 16-ft. x 15-ft. master suite is truly sumptuous, with its 12-ft. ceiling, sitting area, two walk-in closets, and full-featured bath.

- Bonus Room: Here is plenty of storage or room for future expansion. Just beyond the entry are stairs leading to a bonus room measuring approximately 12 ft. x 21 ft.

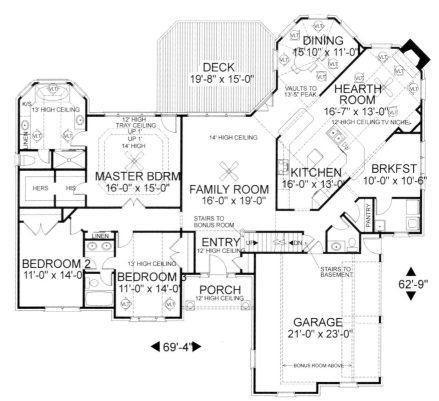

Copyright by designer/architect.

Plan #361006

Dimensions: 70' W x 62' D
Levels: 1
Square Footage: 2,274
Bedrooms: 3
Bathrooms: 2½
Foundation: Crawl space, basement
Materials List Available: No
Price Category: E

Images provided by designer/architect.

You'll love the features that make this home with an open plan as comfortable as it is beautiful.

Features:

- Great Room: The vaulted ceiling emphasizes the spacious feeling of this room.

- Living Room: A corner fireplace and extensive window areas are the focal points here.

- Dining Room: Double doors lead to the covered patio, making it easy to dine outside.

- Kitchen: The angled work spaces, snack bar, and walk-in pantry all add convenience to this room.

- Study: Use this room as a media center or a quiet place to get away from it all.

- Master Suite: This suite has double doors to the patio, two walk-in closets, and a luxury bath.

- Additional Bedrooms: Both have large closets and a shared bath, and one has a vaulted ceiling.

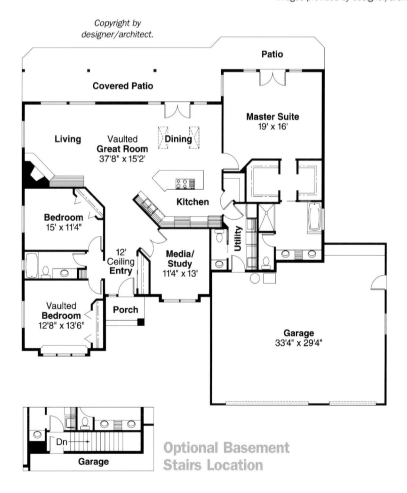

Copyright by designer/architect.

Plan #151201

Dimensions: 55' W x 52'10" D

Levels: 2

Square Footage: 2,642

Main Level Sq. Ft.: 1,747

Upper Level Sq. Ft.: 895

Opt. Bonus Sq. Ft.: 263

Bedrooms: 4

Bathrooms: 3½

Foundation: Crawl space, slab (basement or walk-out basement option for fee)

Materials List Available: Yes

Price Category: F

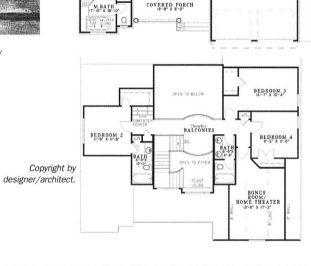

Images provided by designer/architect.

Main Level Floor Plan

Upper Level Floor Plan

Copyright by designer/architect.

Plan #151202

Dimensions: 55'10" W x 65'8" D

Levels: 2

Square Footage: 2,651

Main Level Sq. Ft.: 1,793

Upper Level Sq. Ft.: 858

Opt. Bonus Sq. Ft.: 418

Bedrooms: 4

Bathrooms: 2

Foundation: Crawl space, slab (basement or walk-out basement option for fee)

Materials List Available: Yes

Price Category: F

Images provided by designer/ architect.

Main Level Floor Plan

Upper Level Floor Plan

Copyright by designer/architect.

Plan #141007

Dimensions: 65' W x 56'5" D
Levels: 1
Square Footage: 1,854
Bedrooms: 3
Bathrooms: 2½
Foundation: Basement
Materials List Available: No
Price Category: D

Images provided by designer/architect.

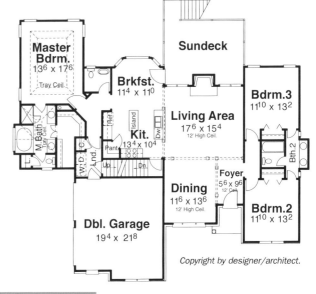

Copyright by designer/architect.

SMARTtip

Painting Walls

Paint won't hide imperfections. Rather, it will make them stand out. So shine a bright light at a low angle across the surface to spot problem areas before painting.

Plan #131035

Dimensions: 65'4" W x 45'10" D
Levels: 1
Square Footage: 1,892
Bedrooms: 3
Bathrooms: 2½
Foundation: Basement, crawl space, or slab
Materials List Available: Yes
Price Category: D

Images provided by designer/architect.

Rear Elevation

Bonus Area

Copyright by designer/architect.

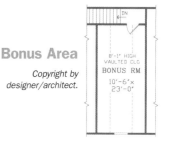

Plan #131004

Dimensions: 59'4" W x 35'8" D
Levels: 1
Square Footage: 1,097
Bedrooms: 3
Bathrooms: 2
Foundation: Basement, crawl space, or slab
Materials List Available: Yes
Price Category: B

Images provided by designer/architect.

You'll love the extra features you'll find in this charming but easy-to-build ranch home.

Features:

- **Porch:** This full-width porch is graced with impressive round columns, decorative railings, and ornamental moldings.

- **Living Room:** Just beyond the front door, the living room entrance has a railing that creates the illusion of a hallway. The 10-ft. tray ceiling makes this room feel spacious.

- **Dining Room:** Flowing from the living room, this room has a 9-ft.-high stepped ceiling and leads to sliding glass doors that open to the large rear patio.

- **Kitchen:** This kitchen is adjacent to the dining room for convenience and has a large island for efficient work patterns.

- **Master Suite:** Enjoy the privacy in this bedroom with its private bathroom.

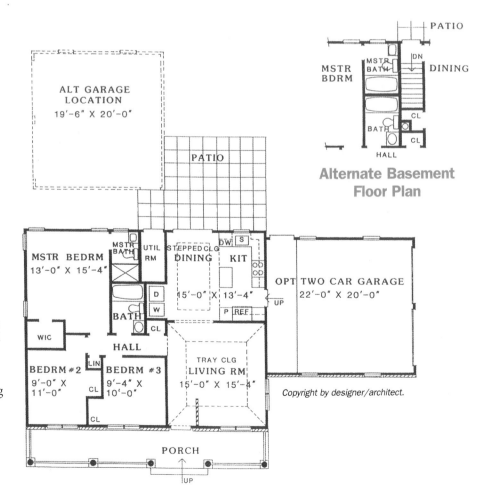

Alternate Basement Floor Plan

Copyright by designer/architect.

Plan #161015

Dimensions: 55'4" W x 40'4" D
Levels: 2
Square Footage: 1,768
Main Level Sq. Ft.: 960
Upper Level Sq. Ft.: 808
Bedrooms: 3
Bathrooms: 2½
Foundation: Basement
Materials List Available: No
Price Category: C

Images provided by designer/architect.

One look at this dramatic exterior—a 12-ft. high entry with a transom and sidelights, multiple gables, and an impressive box window—you'll fall in love with this home.

Features:

- Foyer: This 2-story area announces the grace of this home to everyone who enters it.

- Great Room: A natural gathering spot, this room is sunken to set it off from the rest of the house. The 12-ft. ceiling adds a spacious feeling, and the access to the rear porch makes it ideal for friends and family.

- Kitchen: The kids will enjoy the snack bar and you'll love the adjoining breakfast room with its access to the rear porch.

- Master Suite: A whirlpool in the master bath and walk-in closets in the bedroom spell luxury.

- Laundry Area: Two large closets are so handy that you'll wonder how you ever did without them.

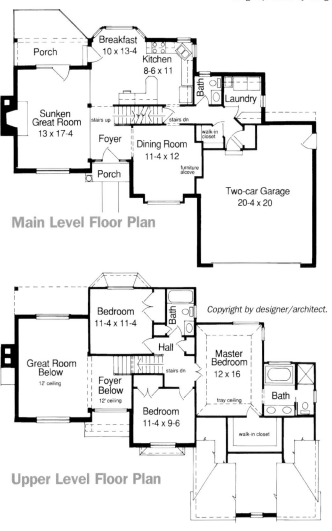

Main Level Floor Plan

Upper Level Floor Plan

Copyright by designer/architect.

Plan #161002

Dimensions: 64'2" W x 44'2" D

Levels: 1

Square Footage: 1,860

Bedrooms: 3

Bathrooms: 2

Foundation: Basement

Materials List Available: Yes

Price Category: D

Images provided by designer/architect.

The brick, stone, and cedar shake facade provides color and texture to the exterior, while the unique nooks and angles inside this delightful one-level home give it character.

Features:

- **Great Room/Dining Room:** This spacious great room is furnished with a wood-burning fireplace, a high ceiling, and French doors. Wide entrances to the breakfast room and dining room expand its space to comfortably hold large gatherings.

- **Kitchen:** The breakfast bar offers additional seating. The covered porch lets you enjoy a view of the landscape and is conveniently located for outdoor meals off this kitchen and breakfast area.

- **Master Bedroom:** The master bedroom is a private retreat. An alcove creates a comfortable sitting area, and an angled entry leads to the bath with whirlpool and a double-bowl vanity.

Left Side Elevation

Right Side Elevation

Rear Elevation

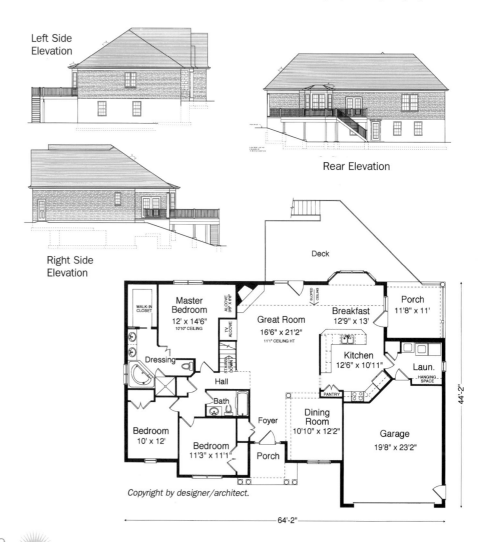

Copyright by designer/architect.

Dining Room

Living Room / Dining Room

Great Room/Breakfast Area

Great Room

Installing Rods and Poles

The way to install a rod or pole depends on the type it is, the brackets that will hold it, the weight of the window treatment, and the surface to which it is being fastened. Given below are some general guidelines, but for specific installation procedures, refer to the instructions that accompany the rod or pole.

- Use a stepladder to reach high places.

- Use the proper tools.

- Take accurate measurements.

- Work with a helper.

- If attaching a bracket to wood, first drill small pilot holes to avoid splitting the wood.

- Consider using wall anchors, particularly for the heavier window treatments.

- Use a level as needed to help you position the brackets for the pole or rod.

- Take care not to drill or hammer into any pipes or electrical wiring.

Because they're designed to stand out, decorative poles and their finials require more room for installation than conventional drapery rods. Finials add inches to the ends of a window treatment, so make sure you have enough wall room to display your hardware to its full advantage. And because decorative rods are often heavy, be certain your window frames and walls can support the weight.

Plan #131001

Dimensions: 72'4" W x 32'4" D
Levels: 1
Square Footage: 1,615
Bedrooms: 3
Bathrooms: 2
Foundation: Basement, crawl space, or slab
Materials List Available: Yes
Price Category: D

Images provided by designer/architect.

Cathedral ceilings and illuminating skylights add drama and beauty to this practical ranch house.

Features:

Ceiling Height: 8 ft.

- **Front Porch:** Watch the rain in comfort from the covered front porch.

- **Foyer:** The stone-tiled foyer flows into the living areas.

- **Living Room:** Oriented towards the front of the house, the living room opens to the dining room and shares a lovely three-sided fireplace with the family room.

- **Family Room:** Conveniently located to share the fireplace with the living room, this room is bright and cheery thanks to its skylights as well as the sliding glass doors that open onto the rear patio.

- **Kitchen:** An island makes this sunny room both efficient and attractive.

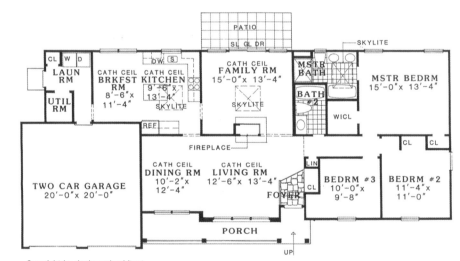

Copyright by designer/architect.

- **Breakfast Nook:** Located just off the kitchen, this area can serve double-duty as a spot for kitchen visitors to sit.

- **Dining Room:** The open design between the dining and living rooms adds to the spacious feeling that the cathedral ceiling creates in this area.

- **Laundry Room:** This area opens from the kitchen for convenience.

- **Master Suite:** A walk-in closet makes this room practical, but the master bathroom with a skylight, dual-sink vanity, soaking tub, and separate shower makes it luxurious.

- **Bedrooms:** The two additional bedrooms share a bathroom.

Plan #121064

Dimensions: 44' W x 40' D
Levels: 2
Square Footage: 1,846
Main Level Sq. Ft.: 919
Upper Level Sq. Ft.: 927
Bedrooms: 4
Bathrooms: 2½
Foundation: Basement
Materials List Available: Yes
Price Category: D

Images provided by designer/architect.

You'll love the features and design in this compact but amenity-filled home.

Features:

• **Entry:** A balcony overlooks this two-story entry, where a plant shelf tops the coat closet.

• **Great Room:** A trio of tall windows points up the large dimensions of this room, which is sure to be the hub of your home. Arrange the

furniture to create a cozy space around the fireplace, or leave it open to the room.

• **Kitchen:** You'll love to work in this well-designed kitchen area.

• **Master Suite:** On the second floor, this master suite features a tiered ceiling and two walk-in closets. In the bath, you'll find a double vanity, whirlpool tub, and separate shower.

Main Level Floor Plan

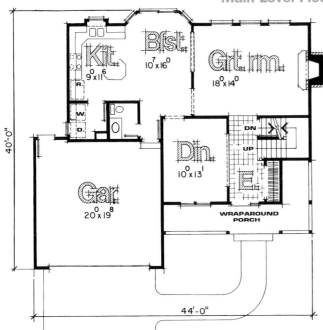

Upper Level Floor Plan

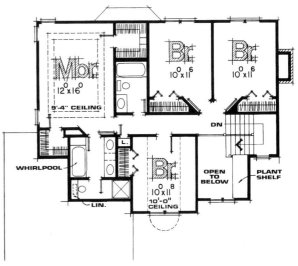

Copyright by designer/architect.

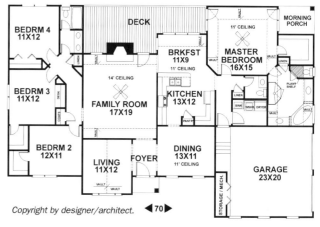

Copyright by designer/architect. ◄ 70 ►

Plan #101010

Dimensions: 70' W x 47' D
Levels: 1
Square Footage: 2,187
Bedrooms: 4
Bathrooms: 2½
Foundation: Slab, crawl space, or basement
Materials List Available: Yes
Price Category: D

Images provided by designer/architect.

Copyright by designer/architect.

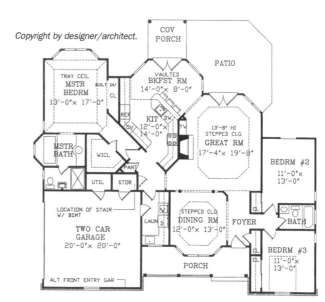

Plan #131015

Dimensions: 57'4" W x 56'10" D
Levels: 1
Square Footage: 1,860
Bedrooms: 3
Bathrooms: 2
Foundation: Basement, crawl space, or slab
Materials List Available: Yes
Price Category: D

Images provided by designer/architect.

Rear Elevation

Great Room

Plan #241022

Dimensions: 55'6" W x 51'1" D

Levels: 1

Square Footage: 1,779

Bedrooms: 3

Bathrooms: 2

Foundation: Slab

Materials List Available: No

Price Category: C

Images provided by designer/architect.

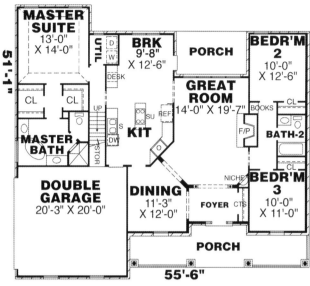

Copyright by designer/architect.

Plan #311021

Dimensions: 70' W x 46' D

Levels: 1

Square Footage: 1,670

Bedrooms: 3

Bathrooms: 2

Foundation: Basement, crawl space, or slab

Materials List Available: Yes

Price Category: C

Images provided by designer/architect.

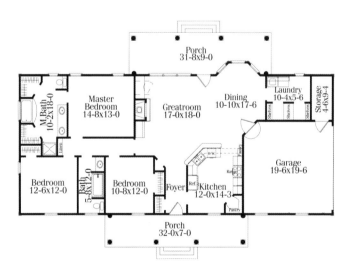

Stair Location for Basement Option

Copyright by designer/architect.

Plan #121051

Dimensions: 64' W x 44' D
Levels: 1
Square Footage: 1,808
Bedrooms: 3
Bathrooms: 2½
Foundation: Basement
Materials List Available: Yes
Price Category: D

Images provided by designer/architect.

You'll love the way that natural light pours into this home from the gorgeous windows you'll find in room after room.

Features:

- Great Room: You'll notice the bayed, transom-topped window in the great room as soon as you step into this lovely home. A wet-bar makes this great room a natural place for entertaining, and the see-through fireplace makes it cozy on chilly days and winter evenings.

- Kitchen: This well-designed kitchen will be a delight for everyone who cooks here, not only because of the ample counter and cabinet space but also because of its location in the home.

- Master Suite: Angled ceilings in both the bedroom and the bathroom of this suite make it feel luxurious, and the picturesque window in the bedroom gives it character. The bath includes a corner whirlpool tub where you'll love to relax at the end of the day.

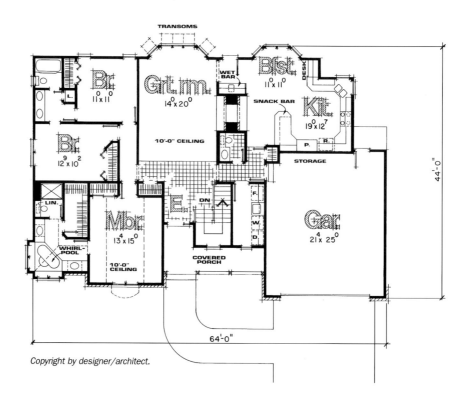

Copyright by designer/architect.

Plan #121052

Dimensions: 56' W x 70' D
Levels: 1
Square Footage: 2,093
Bedrooms: 4
Bathrooms: 2
Foundation: Basement
Materials List Available: Yes
Price Category: D

You'll love this one story home with all the amenities that usually go with a larger home with more levels.

Features:

- Entry: As you enter this home, you'll have a long view into the great room, letting you feel welcome right away.

- Great Room: Enjoy the fireplace in this large room during cool evenings, and during the day, bask in the sunlight streaming through the arched windows that flank the fireplace.

- Den: French doors from the great room open into this room that features a spider-beamed ceiling.

- Kitchen: An island, pantry, and built-in desk make this kitchen a versatile work space. It includes a lovely breakfast area, too, that opens into the backyard.

- Master Suite: This secluded suite features an angled ceiling in the private bathroom.

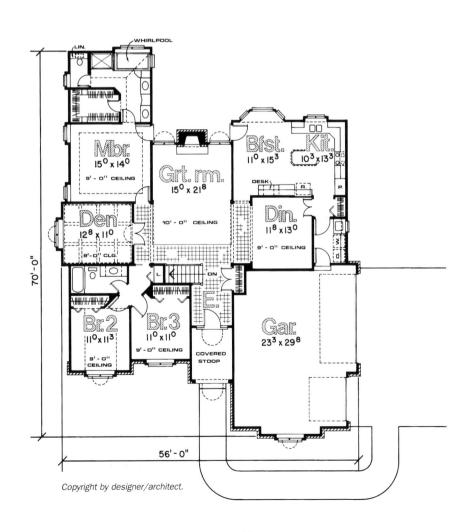

Plan #361005

Dimensions: 68' W x 71' D

Levels: 1

Square Footage: 2,759

Bedrooms: 4

Bathrooms: 2½

Foundation: Crawl space

Materials List Available: No

Price Category: F

This spacious home is ideal for a large family who spends time at home or entertains a crowd.

Features:

- **Great Room:** This vaulted great room has a fireplace and easy access to the kitchen, dining nook, and covered patio.

- **Dining Room:** Double doors from the vaulted entry and a pocket door to the hall make it easy to keep this room for formal dinner parties.

- **Nook:** Sliding glass doors lead to the rear patio, which is equally perfect for a relaxed breakfast or an informal dinner party.

- **Kitchen:** The angled work and snack bar creates a convenient design in this compact kitchen.

- **Master Suite:** The door to the patio, the walk-in closet, and the luxury bath are delightful.

- **Bedrooms:** In a wing of their own, each of the three bedrooms has a roomy closet.

Images provided by designer/architect.

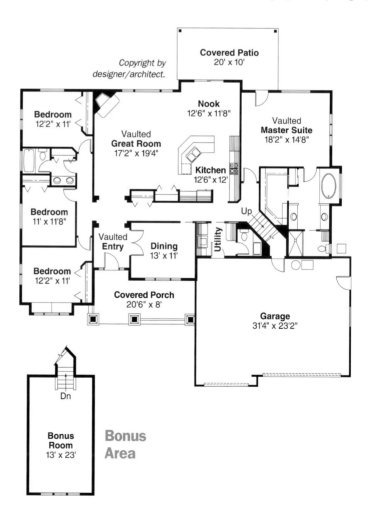

Plan #151171

Dimensions: 63'10" W x 72'2" D

Levels: 1

Square Footage: 2,131

Bedrooms: 3

Bathrooms: 2½

Foundation: Crawl space, slab (basement or daylight basement option for fee)

Materials List Available: Yes

Price Category: D

Images provided by designer/architect.

This home has everything an active family could possibly want—beauty, luxury, and plenty of space to relax and entertain, both inside and out.

Features:

• Great Room: Skylights in the vaulted ceiling, a fireplace, and the door to the rear screened porch make this a favorite place to spend time.

• Dining Area: Bay windows let light flood the area.

• Kitchen: The central island and snack bar, pantry, computer center, and ample counter and cabinet space make a great working area.

• Storm Shelter: You'll be happy to have this room, and even happier not to have to use it.

• Master Suite: The vaulted ceiling, door to the grilling patio, two walk-in closets, and luxury bath combine to create a suite you'll love.

• Additional Bedrooms: A window seat in one room is a child's dream, and you'll love the big closets.

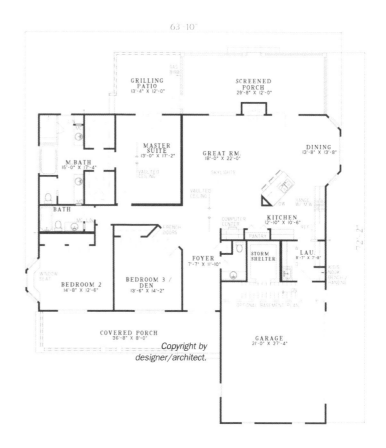

Copyright by designer/architect.

Plan #151065

Dimensions: 51' W x 71'4" D

Levels: 1

Square Footage: 1,881

Bedrooms: 3

Bathrooms: 2

Foundation: Crawl space, slab

Materials List Available: Yes

Price Category: D

Images provided by designer/architect.

Copyright by designer/architect.

Plan #151108

Dimensions: 84'6" W x 58'6" D

Levels: 1

Square Footage: 2,742

Bedrooms: 4

Bathrooms: 2½

Foundation: Crawl space, slab, or basement

Materials List Available: Yes

Price Category: F

Images provided by designer/architect.

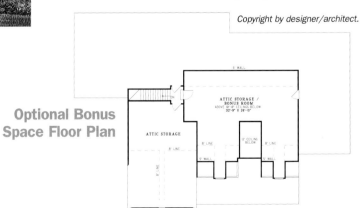

Copyright by designer/architect.

Optional Bonus Space Floor Plan

Plan #151037

Dimensions: 50' W x 56' D

Levels: 1

Square Footage: 1,538

Bedrooms: 3

Bathrooms: 2

Foundation: Crawl space, slab, or basement

Materials List Available: Yes

Price Category: C

Images provided by designer/architect.

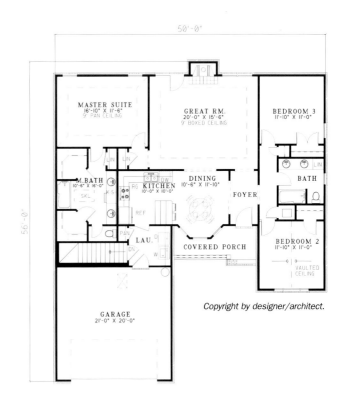

Copyright by designer/architect.

Plan #151050

Dimensions: 69'2" W x 74'10" D

Levels: 1

Square Footage: 2,096

Bedrooms: 3

Bathrooms: 2½

Foundation: Crawl space, slab, or basement

Materials List Available: Yes

Price Category: D

Images provided by designer/architect.

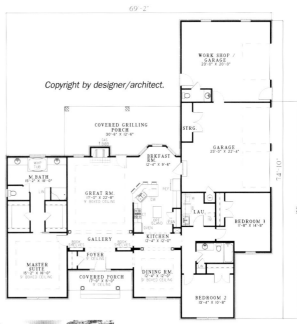

Copyright by designer/architect.

Plan #121077

Dimensions: 64' W x 46' D

Levels: 2

Square Footage: 2,480

Main Level Sq. Ft.: 1,369

Upper Level Sq. Ft.: 1,111

Bedrooms: 4

Bathrooms: 2½

Foundation: Basement

Materials List Available: Yes

Price Category: E

Images provided by designer/architect.

You'll love this design if you've been looking for a home that mixes formal and informal living spaces.

Features:

• Entry: An angled staircase is the focal point in this lovely two-story entry.

• Living Room: To the left of the entry, a boxed ceiling, transom-topped windows, and corner columns highlight this formal living room and the dining room.

• Den: On the right side of the entry, French doors open to this cozy den with its boxed window and built-in bookcase.

• Family Room: Sunken to set it off, the family room has a beamed ceiling and a fireplace flanked by windows.

Main Level Floor Plan

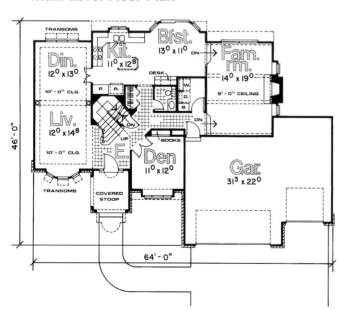

Upper Level Floor Plan

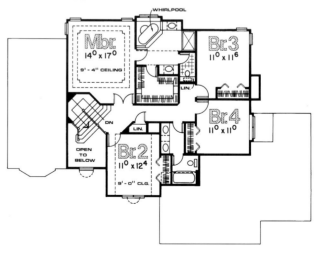

Copyright by designer/architect.

Plan #141025

Dimensions: 52' W x 36' D

Levels: 2

Square Footage: 1,721

Main Level Sq. Ft.: 902

Upper Level Sq. Ft.: 819

Bedrooms: 4

Bathrooms: 2½

Foundation: Basement

Materials List Available: Yes

Price Category: C

Features:

- **Living Room:** This formal living room, certain to become a gathering place for friends and family, is accessible through an open foyer, with U-shaped stairs leading to the second floor.

- **Dining Room:** This formal dining room is particularly well-suited for those special entertainment occasions.

- **Kitchen:** This kitchen, which is designed for convenience and easy work patterns, makes food preparation a pleasure.

- **Bedrooms:** In addition to the master bedroom, this delightful home offers two secondary bedrooms. Also, you can convert the bonus room above the garage into a fourth bedroom.

Living Room

This traditional two-story home, with its typical roof and multi-directional ridge lines, presents a grand appearance. While modest in size, this lovely home incorporates many amenities found in much larger offerings.

Main Level Floor Plan

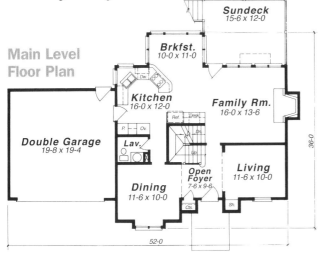

Upper Level Floor Plan

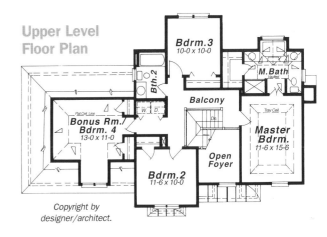

Copyright by designer/architect.

Plan #131032

Dimensions: 69'2" W x 46' D
Levels: 2
Square Footage: 2,455
Main Level Sq. Ft.: 1,499
Upper Level Sq. Ft.: 956
Bedrooms: 4
Bathrooms: 3
Foundation: Crawl space, slab, or basement
Materials List Available: Yes
Price Category: F

Images provided by designer/architect.

If you love Victorian styling, you'll be charmed by the ornate, rounded front porch and the two-story bay that distinguish this home.

Features:

• Living Room: You'll love the 13-ft. ceiling in this room, as well as the panoramic view it gives of the front porch and yard.

• Kitchen: Sunlight streams into this room, where an angled island with a cooktop eases both prepping and cooking.

• Breakfast Room: This room shares an eating bar with the kitchen, making it easy for the family to congregate while the family chef is cooking.

• Guest Room: Use this lovely room on the first level as a home office or study if you wish.

• Master Suite: The dramatic bayed sitting area with a high ceiling has an octagonal shape that you'll adore, and the amenities in the private bath will soothe you at the end of a busy day.

Rear View

Upper Level Floor Plan

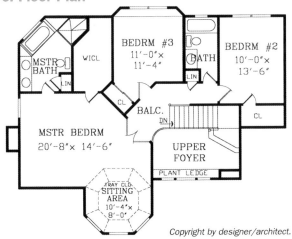

MSTR BATH

WICL

BEDRM #3
11'-0" ×
11'-4"

BATH

BEDRM #2
10'-0" ×
13'-6"

LIN

CL

BALC.
DN

CL

MSTR BEDRM
20'-8" × 14'-6"

UPPER
FOYER

PLANT LEDGE

TRAY CLG.
SITTING
AREA
10'-4" ×
8'-0"

Copyright by designer/architect.

Dining Room

Main Level Floor Plan

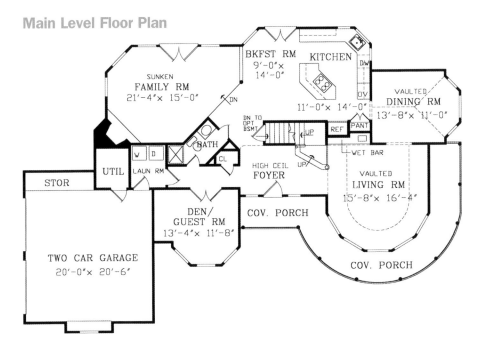

BKFST RM
9'-0" ×
14'-0"

KITCHEN

DW

SUNKEN
FAMILY RM
21'-4" × 15'-0"

DN

11'-0" × 14'-0"

OV

VAULTED
DINING RM
13'-8" × 11'-0"

DN TO
OPT
BSMT

UP

REF

PANT

BATH

WET BAR

W   D

UP

HIGH CEIL
FOYER

VAULTED
LIVING RM
15'-8" × 16'-4"

UTIL

LAUN RM

CL

STOR

DEN/
GUEST RM
13'-4" × 11'-8"

COV. PORCH

TWO CAR GARAGE
20'-0" × 20'-6"

COV. PORCH

Living Room

Kitchen

Breakfast

Foyer

Planning Your Landscape

Landscapes change over the years. As plants grow, the overall look evolves from sparse to lush. Trees cast cool shade where the sun used to shine. Shrubs and hedges grow tall and dense enough to provide privacy. Perennials and ground covers spread to form colorful patches of foliage and flowers. Meanwhile, paths, arbors, fences, and other structures gain the patina of age.

Constant change over the years—sometimes rapid and dramatic, sometimes slow and subtle—is one of the joys of landscaping. It is also one of the challenges. Anticipating how fast plants will grow and how big they will eventually get is difficult, even for professional designers, and was a major concern in formulating the designs for this book.

To illustrate the kinds of changes to expect in a planting, these pages show one of the designs at three different "ages." Even though a new planting may look sparse at first, it will soon fill in. And because of careful spacing, the planting will look as good in 10 to 15 years as it does after 3 to 5. It will, of course, look different, but that's part of the fun.

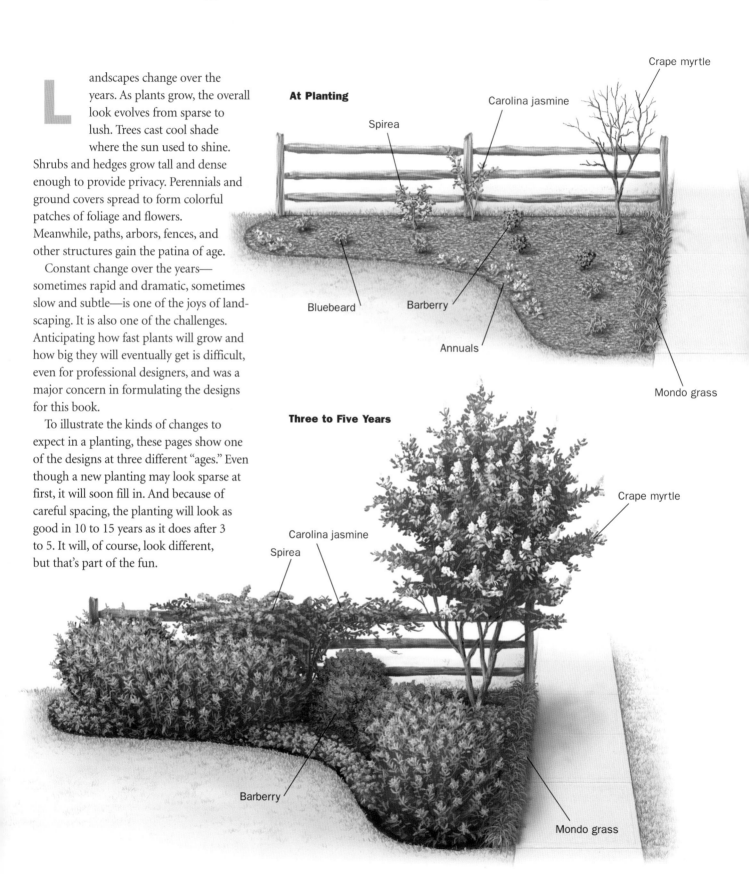

At Planting

Crape myrtle

Carolina jasmine

Spirea

Bluebeard

Barberry

Annuals

Mondo grass

Three to Five Years

Crape myrtle

Carolina jasmine

Spirea

Barberry

Mondo grass

At Planting—Here's how the corner planting (pp. 38–39) might appear in spring immediately after planting. The fence and mulch look conspicuously fresh, new, and unweathered. The crape myrtle is only 4 to 5 ft. tall, with trunks no thicker than broomsticks. It hasn't leafed out yet. The spirea and barberries are 12 to 18 in. tall and wide, and the Carolina jasmine just reaches the bottom rail of the fence. Evenly spaced tufts of mondo grass edge the sidewalk. The bluebeards are stubby now but will grow 2 to 3 ft. tall by late summer, when they bloom. Annuals such as vinca and ageratum start flowering right away and soon form solid patches of color. The first year after planting, be sure to water during dry spells and to pull or spray any weeds that pop through the mulch.

Three to Five Years—Shown in summer now, the planting has begun to mature. The mondo grass has spread to make a continuous, weed-proof patch. The Carolina jasmine reaches partway along the fence. The spirea and barberries have grown into bushy, rounded specimens. From now on, they'll get wider but not much taller. The crape myrtle will keep growing about 1 ft. taller every year, and its crown will broaden. As you continue replacing the annuals twice a year, keep adding compost or organic matter to the soil and spreading fresh mulch on top.

Ten to Fifteen Years—As shown here in late summer, the crape myrtle is now a fine specimen, about 15 ft. tall, with a handsome silhouette, beautiful flowers, and colorful bark on its trunks. The bluebeards recover from an annual spring pruning to form bushy mounds covered with blooms. The Carolina jasmine, spirea, and barberry have reached their mature size. Keep them neat and healthy by pruning out old, weak, or dead stems every spring. If you get tired of replanting annuals, substitute low-growing perennials or shrubs in those positions.

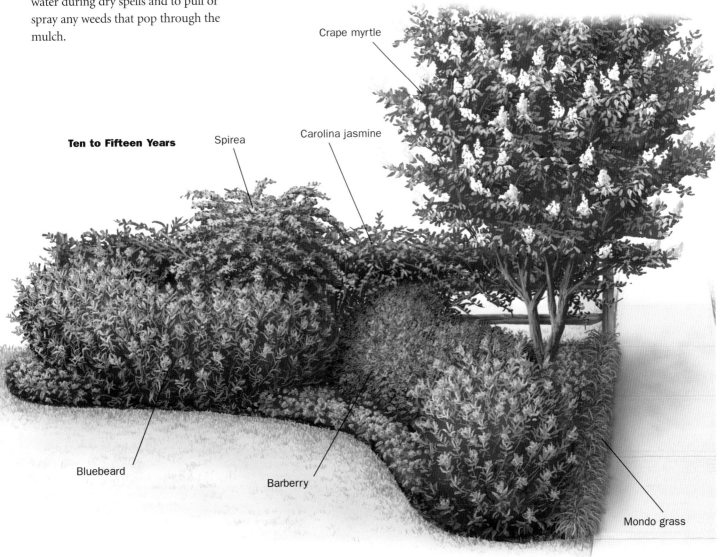

Ten to Fifteen Years

Crape myrtle

Spirea

Carolina jasmine

Bluebeard

Barberry

Mondo grass

Southern Hospitality
Make a Pleasant Passage to Your Front Door

River birch **A**

Why wait until a visitor reaches the front door to extend a cordial greeting? An entryway landscape of well-chosen plants and a revamped walkway not only make the short journey a pleasant one, they can also enhance your home's most public face and help settle it comfortably in its surroundings.

The curved walk in this design extends a helpful "Please come this way" to visitors, while creating a roomy planting area near the house. The walk bridges a grassy "inlet" created by the free-flowing lines of the beds. The flowing masses of plants, lawn, and pavement nicely complement the journey to the door.

Two handsome trees and a skirting of shrubs form a partial screen between the walk and front door and the street. A striking collection of evergreens transforms a foundation planting near the house into a shrub border. Ground covers edge the walkway with pretty foliage, flowers, and berries. A decorative screen by the stoop marks the entry. Fragrant flowers and colorful foliage cover the screen year-round, enticing visitors to linger awhile by the door.

The rest of the planting contributes to the all-season interest with flowers spring, summer, and fall (several fragrant). Colorful foliage and berries grace the autumn and winter months.

Note: All plants are appropriate for USDA Hardiness Zones 6, 7, and 8.

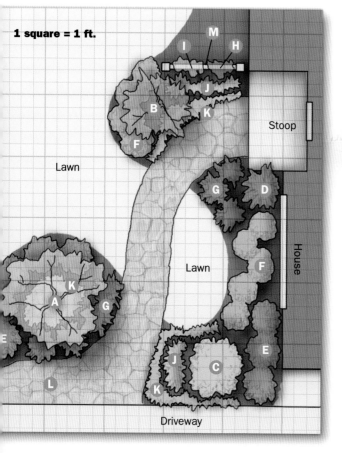

1 square = 1 ft.

Lawn

Lawn

Stoop

House

Driveway

'Otto Luyken' **E** cherry laurel

Walk **L**

Creeping willowleaf **G** cotoneaster

Plants and Projects

Preparing the planting beds and laying the walk are the main tasks in this design. Comprising mostly trees and shrubs, the planting requires only seasonal cleanup and pruning once it's installed.

A **River birch** *Betula nigra* (use 1 plant) The multiple trunks of this deciduous tree display pretty peeling bark. Leaves are glossy green in summer, colorful in fall.

B **Japanese maple** *Acer palmatum* (use 1) This small deciduous tree will thrive in the shade of the

taller birch, providing colorful delicate leaves and a graceful tracery of branches in winter.

C **Burford holly** *I. cornuta* 'Burfordii' (use 1) This evergreen shrub is easily maintained in a conical form by shearing. Its large leaves are a great backdrop for a fine show of red winter berries.

D **Heavenly bamboo** *Nandina domestica* (use 1) An evergreen shrub with leaves that change color each season, white summer flowers, and long-lasting red berries.

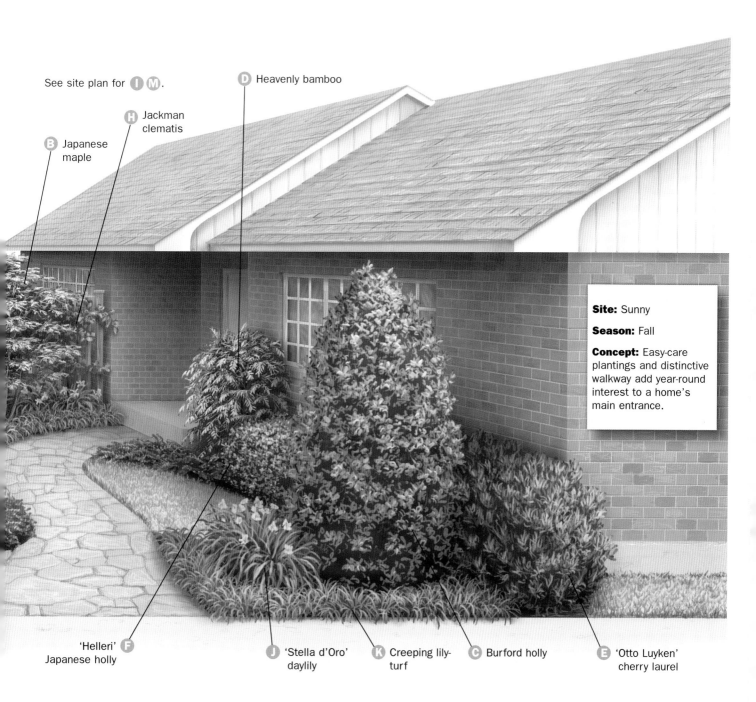

See site plan for **I** **M**.

D Heavenly bamboo

H Jackman clematis

B Japanese maple

Site: Sunny

Season: Fall

Concept: Easy-care plantings and distinctive walkway add year-round interest to a home's main entrance.

'Helleri' **F** Japanese holly

J 'Stella d'Oro' daylily

K Creeping lily-turf

C Burford holly

E 'Otto Luyken' cherry laurel

[...]o Luyken' cherry laurel [...]*us laurocerasus* (use 8) [...] low, spreading evergreen [...] fits perfectly beneath the [...] and the windows of the [...]se. Displayed against the dark [...]n leaves, spikes of fragrant [...]e flowers perfume the entry-[...] in midspring.

[...]leri' Japanese holly *I. crenata* [...] 9) This evergreen shrub [...]'t outgrow its place under the [...]dows, instead filling the space [...] mounds of small, shiny [...]es.

G **Creeping willowleaf cotoneaster** *Cotoneaster salicifolius* 'Repens' (use 7) An evergreen ground cover, this shrub displays dark purple leaves and red berries in winter and white flowers in spring.

H **Jackman clematis** *Clematis* × *jackmanii* (use 1) A graceful deciduous vine, this will cover the screen with striking violet-purple flowers in summer.

I **Carolina jasmine** *Gelsemium sempervirens* (use 1) This evergreen vine offers some-

thing year-round. Fragrant yellow trumpet-shaped flowers greet visitors in early spring. Neat green leaves complement the blooming clematis in summer, then turn maroon for the winter.

J **'Stella d'Oro' daylily** *Hemerocallis* (use 11) This cultivar is one of the longest-blooming daylilies, producing golden yellow flowers from late spring to frost. Even without the glowing flowers, this perennial's grassy light green foliage contrasts nicely with the nearby lilyturf.

K **Creeping lilyturf** *Liriope spicata* (use 44) This evergreen perennial makes a grasslike mat of dark green leaves along the walk and under the birch. Small spikes of violet, purple, or white flowers appear in summer.

L **Walk** Use flagstones of random size and shape for the ideal curved walk.

M **Screen** A simple structure with narrow vertical "pickets," this is easy to make and sturdy enough to support the vines.

A Foundation with Flair

Flowers and Foliage Dress up a Raised Entry

A home with a raised entry invites down-to-earth foundation plants that anchor the house to its surroundings and hide unattractive concrete-block underpinnings. In the hospitable climate of the South, a durable, low-maintenance planting need not mean the usual lineup of clipped junipers. As this design shows, a foundation planting can be more varied, more colorful, and more fun.

Within the graceful arc of a low boxwood hedge is a balanced arrangement of shrubs in sizes that fit under windows and hide the foundation at the same time. Larger shrubs and a small tree punctuate the planting and contribute to the variety of foliage textures and colors.

The predominantly evergreen foliage looks good year-round, and in spring and early summer it is a fine backdrop for a lovely floral display. White flowers sparkle on the trees and shrubs, with irises in blues, purples, pinks, or yellows at their feet. Twining up posts or over railings, the Confederate jasmine greets visitors with its deliciously scented creamy flowers.

Loropetalum C

Confederate jasmine I

Heavenly bamboo D

Littleleaf boxwood H

'Helleri' Japanese holly G

'Compacta' Japanese holly F

Plants and Projects

Once established, the plants in this design require little maintenance beyond seasonal cleanup and a yearly pruning to remove old, weak, or winter-damaged stems. To keep it tidy, the boxwood hedge will need trimming once or twice a year. Clean away the iris leaves when they die down in fall.

A Star magnolia *Magnolia stellata* (use 1 plant)
This small, multitrunked deciduous tree perfectly fits the corner of the house. Spring's fragrant white flowers are followed by dark green foliage that looks good all summer.

B Possumhaw *Ilex decidua* (use 1)
Brightly colored berries decorate this deciduous shrub in fall and winter. The smooth green leaves are attractive in summer. (Also called winterberry holly.)

C Loropetalum *Loropetalum chinense* (use 1)
An elegant presence next to the stoop, this evergreen shrub has layers of arching branches bearing lacy white flowers in spring and may bloom sporadically through the summer.

D Heavenly bamboo *Nandina domestica* (use 3)
A colorful evergreen shrub with straight unbranched stems and layers of lacy leaves tinged gold in spring, changing to summer green and turning orangy red in winter. White flowers in summer and months of red berries, too.

E Variegated pittosporum *Pittosporum tobira* 'Variegata' (use 8)
This evergreen shrub brings a dressy look and year-round color to the foundation with its rounded mounds of glossy gray-green leaves mottled with white. Creamy white flowers scent the air in early summer.

F 'Compacta' Japanese holly *I. crenata* (use 1)
Fill the corner next to the stoop with this handsome evergreen shrub. It can be shaped into a ball or cone by shearing.

G 'Helleri' Japanese holly *I. crenata* (use 3)
Smaller than 'Compacta', this evergreen shrub won't outgrow its place, making tidy mounds of small, rounded, dull green leaves.

H Littleleaf boxwood *Buxus microphylla* (use 32)
A classic sheared evergreen hedge defines the foundation garden; this compact shrub's small, glossy green leaves give it a fine texture.

I Confederate jasmine *Trachelospermum jasminoides* (use 2)
On early summer evenings you can sit on the stoop and enjoy the fragrance of this evergreen vine's white flowers. Twining stems of glossy dark green leaves can climb and cover the posts.

J Siberian iris *Iris sibirica* (use 8)
For graceful May flowers in shades of blue, yellow, or white, this perennial is a natural choice. After flowering, the erect grassy leaves contrast with the rounded pittosporum.

K Bearded iris *Iris* (use 12)
These perennials bear showier flowers than their Siberian cousins in a rainbow of colors. Blooms in midspring; stiff leaves are coarser and shorter than those of Siberian iris.

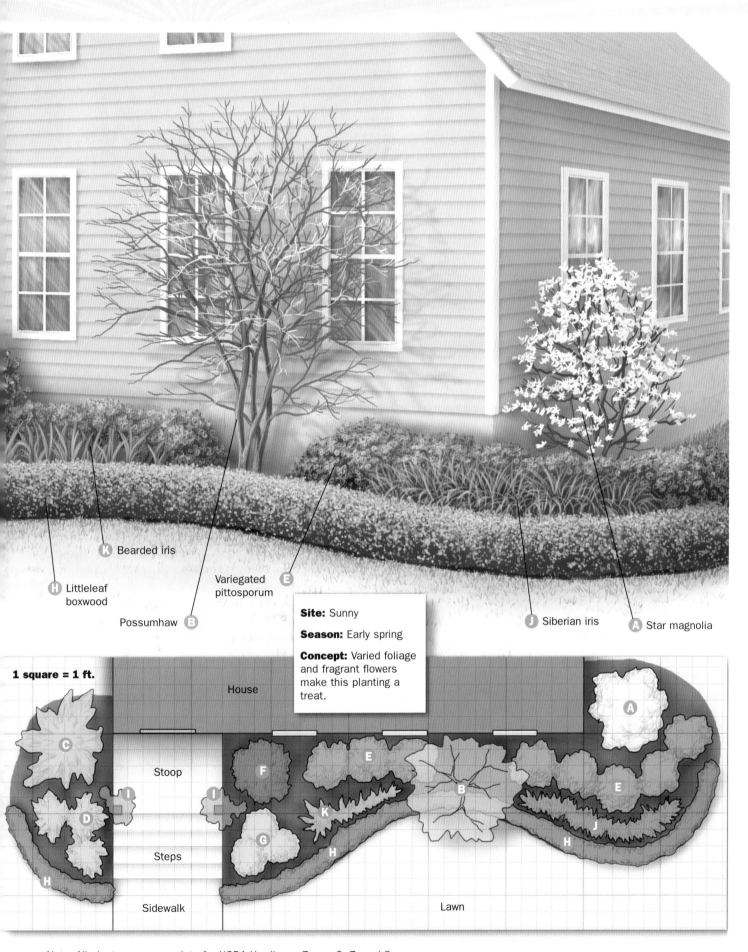

K Bearded iris

H Littleleaf boxwood

Possumhaw B

Variegated pittosporum

E

Site: Sunny

Season: Early spring

Concept: Varied foliage and fragrant flowers make this planting a treat.

J Siberian iris

A Star magnolia

1 square = 1 ft.

House

C

Stoop

I   I

D

F   E

K

B

E

Steps

G

H

J

H

Sidewalk

Lawn

Note: All plants are appropriate for USDA Hardiness Zones 6, 7, and 8.

Formal and Friendly

Mix Classic Symmetry and Comfortable Plans

A formal garden has a special appeal. Its simple geometry is soothing in a sometimes confusing world, and it never goes out of style. Traditional homes with symmetrical facades are especially suited to the elegant lines and balanced features of this design. The look is formal, but it is an easy formality featuring gentle curves, as well as straight lines, and plants whose tidy forms are produced by nature, not shears.

Unlike many formal gardens whose essentials can be taken in at a glance, this one imparts an air of mystery for visitors approaching from the street. A matching pair of crape myrtles at the corners of the property obscure that view, so that it's only when you approach the gate that the entire garden reveals itself.

A wide brick walkway creates a small courtyard with an eye-catching column of roses at its center. Neat rectangles of lawn are defined by beds of colorful annuals and perennials backed by the graceful curve of a low informal evergreen hedge. Distinctive evergreen shrubs and trees mark the corners of the design and stand guard near the front door. A picket fence reinforces the geometry of the overall design and adds a homey touch. A ground cover of low evergreen shrubs between sidewalk and fence looks good and makes this often awkward area easy to maintain.

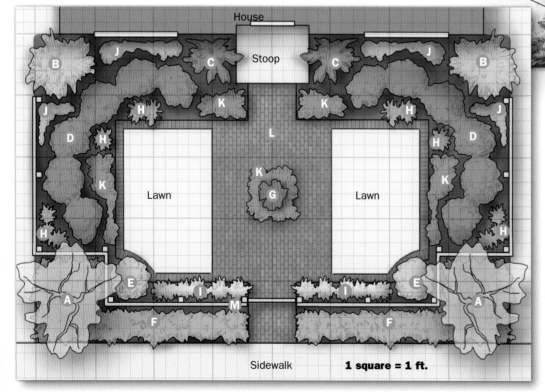

'Natchez' crape myrtle Ⓐ

See site plan for Ⓘ Ⓙ.

Dwarf pittosporum Ⓓ

Parson's juniper Ⓕ

Picket fence Ⓜ

House

Stoop

Ⓑ Ⓙ Ⓒ Ⓒ Ⓙ Ⓑ

Ⓙ Ⓗ Ⓚ Ⓚ Ⓗ Ⓙ

Ⓓ Ⓗ Ⓗ Ⓓ

Ⓛ

Ⓚ Ⓗ Ⓗ Ⓚ

Lawn Ⓚ Ⓖ Lawn

Ⓗ Ⓗ

Ⓔ Ⓔ

Ⓘ Ⓘ

Ⓐ Ⓜ Ⓐ

Ⓕ Ⓕ

Sidewalk   **1 square = 1 ft.**

Note: All plants are appropriate for USDA Hardiness Zones 6, 7, and 8.

Plants and Projects

As formal gardens go, this one is very easy to maintain. The shrubs are chosen for compact forms that need little pruning, and the perennials will bloom happily with little care—just remove the spent flowers to keep things tidy.

Ⓐ **'Natchez' crape myrtle**
Lagerstroemia indica
(use 2 plants)
These showy, multitrunked, small deciduous trees frame the garden with large clusters of crepe-papery white flowers blooming all summer, colorful leaves in fall, and handsome bark in winter.

Ⓑ **'Yoshino' Japanese cedar**

B 'Yoshino' Japanese cedar

Site: Sunny

Season: Summer

Concept: A paved "courtyard" framed by tidy shrubs and pretty perennials creates a comfortably formal look on a small lot.

Hollywood C juniper   Walk and L mowing strip   G 'Blaze' climbing rose   K Annual salvia   H Daylily   E Indian hawthorn   F Parson's juniper

Cryptomeria japonica (use 2)
A pair of these naturally cone-shaped, fine-textured evergreen trees mark the corners of the house. Foliage is rich green in summer, bronze in winter.

C Hollywood juniper *Juniperus chinensis* 'Torulosa' (use 2)
An uneven branching pattern gives this small evergreen tree an informal, sculptural look. It's narrow enough to fit on each side of the door.

D Dwarf pittosporum (use 12)
Pittosporum tobira 'Wheeleri'
This evergreen shrub makes a lush, dressy but informal hedge with shiny green leaves. Its

creamy white flowers scent the air in early summer.

E Indian hawthorn *Rhaphiolepis indica* (use 2)
Pink or white flowers cover the dark foliage of this low, spreading evergreen shrub in spring, followed by blue berries. Select any compact cultivar.

F Parson's juniper *Juniperis davurica* 'Expansa'(use 22)
Rugged, gray-green evergreen shrubs edge the sidewalk, their horizontal branches held slightly above the ground.

G 'Blaze' climbing rose *Rosa* (use 1)
This cultivar will cover the cen-

tral post with glossy green leaves and deep red flowers all summer. Buy a "rose post" at a nursery, or use an old architectural column or other post. Plant salvias around the base.

H Daylily *Hemerocallis* (use 12)
Combine early- and late-blooming cultivars of this useful perennial. Choose orange- and yellow-flowered ones here.

I 'Stella d'Oro' daylily *Hemerocallis* (use 10)
From early summer until frost, this hardy perennial's extended show of bright golden yellow flowers can't be beat. The grassy foliage is attractive, too.

J Purple verbena *Verbena bonariensis* (use 24)
This perennial's clusters of purple flowers keep blooming from early summer to frost.

K Annual salvia (use a total of 60)
Red or purple flowers greet visitors for months. Autumn sage is a good perennial substitute.

L Walk and mowing strip
A wide brick walk creates a small courtyard. The brick mowing strip eases lawn maintenance.

M Picket fence
Paint or stain the fence to complement the house.

Angle of Repose

Make a Back-Door Garden for a Sheltered Niche

Many homes offer the opportunity to tuck a garden into a protected corner. In the front yard, such spots are ideal for an entry garden or a display that showcases your house when viewed from the street. If the planting is in the backyard, as shown here, it can be a more intimate part of a comfortable outdoor room you can stroll around at leisure or enjoy from a nearby terrace or window.

This planting was designed with spring in mind, so we're showing that season here. Dozens of spring bulbs light up the corner from February through May, assisted by several early-blooming annuals, perennials, and handsome spring-flowered evergreen shrubs. Early flowers aren't the only pleasures of spring. Watch buds fatten and burst into leaf on the Japanese maple, and mark the progress of the season as new, succulent shoots of summer perennials emerge. Of course, the look of the area will change later in the season when perennials and shrubs take over the show.

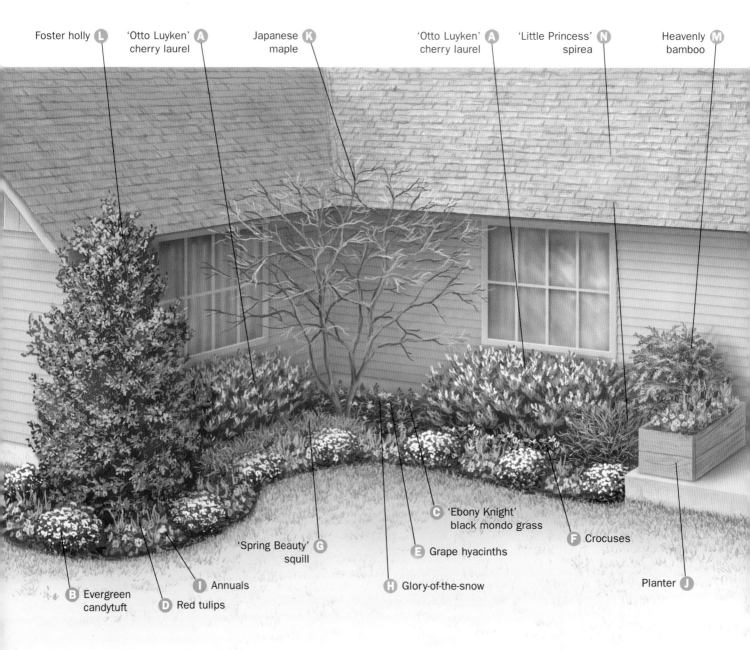

Foster holly **L**   'Otto Luyken' **A** cherry laurel   Japanese **K** maple   'Otto Luyken' **A** cherry laurel   'Little Princess' **N** spirea   Heavenly **M** bamboo

C 'Ebony Knight' black mondo grass

F Crocuses

'Spring Beauty' **G** squill

E Grape hyacinths

I Annuals

H Glory-of-the-snow

Planter **J**

B Evergreen candytuft

D Red tulips

Plants and Projects

Except for the red tulips, the bulb flowers in this planting are small, but they make a splash when blooming in masses. Their foliage will die back unnoticed among the perennial foliage that follows later in the season. Treat the tulips like pansies and other annuals—discard them after they bloom, and replant fresh tulip bulbs every fall.

A **'Otto Luyken' cherry laurel** *Prunus laurocerasus* (use 5 plants)
Glossy dark green leaves and a lovely spreading form make this a choice evergreen to dress up the walls of the house without covering the windows.

As a bonus, fragrant white flowers cover this easy-care shrub in mid-spring.

B **Evergreen candytuft** *Iberis sempervirens* (use 8)
An excellent evergreen perennial for the edge of the garden, with a low, rounded form that is not too formal, topped with white flowers in early spring. Shear off the tops of the plants after the flowers fade.

C **'Ebony Knight' black mondo grass** *Ophiopogon planiscapus* (use 28)
This evergreen grass makes an elegant carpet of thin, purple-black leaves, a striking setting for the small blue flowers of the spring bulbs sprinkled in the patch.

D **Red tulips** *Tulipa* (use about 50)
Red tulips add vibrant color to the spring garden like no other plant. Repeated along the edge of the bed and in the planter,

they look great with the yellow and blue pansies. Plant five bulbs between each clump of candytuft. Lots of different red cultivars are available; try different ones each year.

E **Grape hyacinths** *Muscari armeniacum* (use 30)
These little bulbs will spread happily beneath the maple tree, flecking the mondo-grass carpet with clusters of fragrant blue flowers.

F **Crocuses** *Crocus* (use 40)
Plant generous clumps (six to eight per square foot) of these bulbs among the sedums, and enjoy their cup-shaped flowers in February. Use yellow or purple varieties, or both.

G **'Spring Beauty' squill** *Scilla siberica* (use 10)
Clusters of bell-shaped flowers in a lovely shade of clear blue nod above the dianthus foliage in early spring.

H **Glory-of-the-snow** *Chionodoxa*

luciliae (use 60)
Starry pale blue flowers with white centers will twinkle in the mondo grass as early as February.

I **Annuals** (use about 4 dozen)
Alternating with the evergreen candytuft at the edge of the bed, yellow and blue pansies delight children (and adults) with their personable flowers.

J **Planter**
In spring this large planter offers a colorful array of tulips and pansies in a bed of blue-green dianthus foliage. You can build the 5-ft.-long, 2-ft.-wide planter yourself or purchase one.

K **Japanese maple** *Acer palmatum* (use 1)

L **Foster holly** *Ilex × attenuata* (use 1)

M **Heavenly bamboo** *Nandina domestica* (use 1)

N **'Little Princess' spirea** *Spirea japonica* (use 1)

Note: All plants are appropriate for USDA Hardiness Zones 6, 7, and 8.

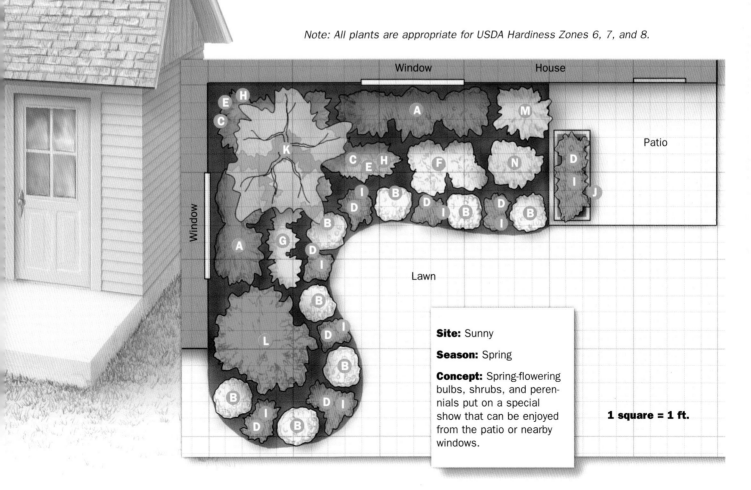

Window   House

Patio

Lawn

Site: Sunny

Season: Spring

Concept: Spring-flowering bulbs, shrubs, and perennials put on a special show that can be enjoyed from the patio or nearby windows.

1 square = 1 ft.

An Eye-Catching Corner

Dress Up the Area Between Cottage and Detached Garage

Goldflame honeysuckle **C**

Chinese abelia **B**

Germander **J**

The corner where your property meets your neighbor's and the sidewalk is often a kind of grassy no-man's-land. This design defines that boundary with a planting that can be enjoyed by both property owners, as well as by passersby. Good gardens make good neighbors, so we've used well-behaved, low-maintenance plants that won't make extra work for the person next door—or for you.

Because of its exposed location, remote from the house and close to the street, this is a less personal planting than those in other more private and frequently used parts of your property. It is meant to be appreciated from a distance. Rising from low-growing plants at the edge of the lawn to the butterfly bush near the sidewalk, the design draws the eye when viewed from the house. An existing split-rail fence along the property line serves as a backdrop for the plants without hiding them from the view of neighbors or passersby. While not intended as a barrier, the planting also provides a modest psychological, if not physical, screen from activity on the street.

There's lots of bloom summer and fall, some of it fragrant, some bearing nectar that's attractive to butterflies. Flowing grasses and the evergreen foliage of shrubs and perennials carry the planting from late fall through winter. For early-spring color, consider planting daffodils among the daylilies, coneflowers, and other perennials, whose rising leaves will quickly cover the fading bulb foliage after bloom.

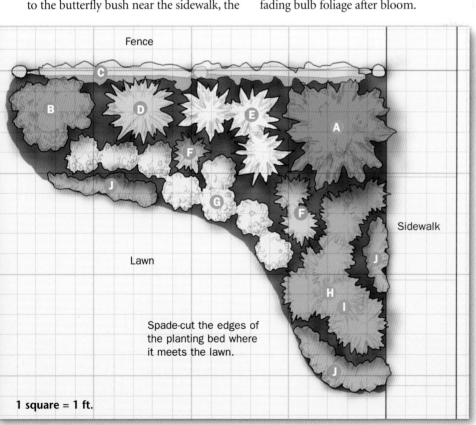

1 square = 1 ft.

Fence

Lawn

Sidewalk

Spade-cut the edges of the planting bed where it meets the lawn.

Note: All plants are appropriate for USDA Hardiness Zones 6, 7, and 8.

Plants and Projects

These rugged plants thrive on an open, sunny, dry site and require little care beyond seasonal pruning and removal of spent flowers to encourage further bloom. In spring, cut the fast-growing butterfly bush and the overwintered grasses close to the ground, shear the germander, and thin old growth out of the honeysuckle. During summer, snip off spent flowers from coneflower, daylily, and Asiatic lilies.

A **'White Profusion' butterfly bush** *Buddleia davidii* (use 1 plant)
The arching branches of this vase-shaped deciduous shrub carry long spikes of fragrant white flowers at their tips. Blooms from midsummer until fall. Butterflies love the flowers.
Chinese abelia *Abelia chinensis* (use 1)
Another favorite of butterflies, this evergreen shrub bears white flowers with a delicious

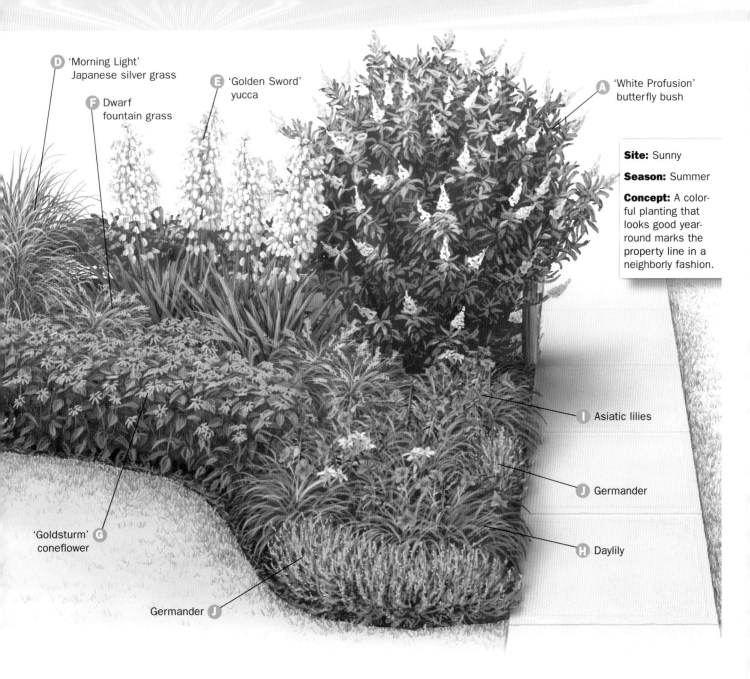

D 'Morning Light' Japanese silver grass

F Dwarf fountain grass

E 'Golden Sword' yucca

A 'White Profusion' butterfly bush

Site: Sunny

Season: Summer

Concept: A colorful planting that looks good year-round marks the property line in a neighborly fashion.

I Asiatic lilies

J Germander

H Daylily

'Goldsturm' **G** coneflower

Germander **J**

honeysuckle fragrance from early summer to frost. Its mound of glossy leaves contrasts with the grassy neighbors and turns purple-bronze in winter. If this plant isn't available, use glossy abelia (*Abelia* × *grandiflora*).

C **Goldflame honeysuckle** *Lonicera* × *heckrottii* (use 1)
Beginning in early summer, then off and on until fall, this evergreen vine covers the fence with fragrant pink-and-yellow flowers. The handsome blue-green leaves provide cover and color through the winter.

D **'Morning Light' Japanese silver grass** *Miscanthus sinensis*(use 1)
Delicate white stripes on the slender arching leaves of this ornamental grass make it glitter in the slightest breeze. Its fluffy seed heads and tawny color add fall and winter interest.

E **'Golden Sword' yucca** *Yucca filamentosa* (use 3)

This shrubby perennial's sword-shaped evergreen leaves, striped with yellow and gold, bring a strong, spiky form to the corner planting. Tall stems bearing showy clusters of creamy flowers appear in June and provide some privacy.

F **Dwarf fountain grass** *Pennisetum alopecuroides* 'Hameln' (use 3)
Near the front of the planting, this perennial grass produces spreading mounds of green leaves that turn warm shades of orange and tan in autumn. Fluffy flower spikes appear in midsummer.

G **'Goldsturm' coneflower** *Rudbeckia fulgida* (use 8)
An improved version of the reliable old black-eyed Susan. In late summer an abundance of large, gold-and-brown, daisylike flowers rise on stalks above clumps of dark green leaves.

H **Daylily** *Hemerocallis* (use 6)
For a rugged planting of grassy light green foliage and cheerful summer flowers, this hardy perennial can't be beat. Choose pink-flowered cultivars to blend with the germander and lilies. Use both early and late varieties to extend the season of bloom.

I **Asiatic lilies** *Lilium* (use 20)
The large, trumpet-shaped flowers of these regal perennials add color all summer. Plant the bulbs among the daylilies, with which they'll coexist nicely. Choose white and purple cultivars.

J **Germander** *Teucrium chamaedrys* (use 12)
A great perennial for edging the bed, forming neat mounds of small, shiny evergreen leaves. In late summer, a profusion of tiny pink flowers make a soft pink haze over the foliage.

Streetwise and Stylish

Give Your Curbside Strip a New Look

Homeowners seldom think much about the area that runs between the sidewalk and street. At best this is a tidy patch of lawn; at worst, a weed-choked eyesore. Yet this is one of the most public parts of many properties. Planting this strip with attractive perennials, shrubs, and trees can give pleasure to passersby and visitors who park next to the curb, as well as enhancing the streetscape you view from the house. (This strip is usually city-owned, so check local ordinances for restrictions before you start a remake.)

It might help to think of this curbside strip as an island bed between two defined boundaries: the street and the sidewalk. These beds are divided further by a wide pedestrian walkway, providing ample room for visitors to get in and out of front and rear car doors. A pair of handsome evergreen trees form a gateway. The diagonal skew of this design keeps the symmetry of the plantings either side from appearing staid. You can expand the beds to fill a longer strip, or plant lawn next to the beds.

This can be a difficult site. Summer drought and heat, pedestrian and car traffic, and errant dogs are the usual conditions found along the street. Plants have to be tough to perform well here, but they need not look tough. These combine colorful foliage and flowers for a dramatic impact from spring until fall. Evergreen foliage and clumps of tawny grass look good through the winter. The plantings beneath the trees won't grow tall enough to block your view of the street as you pull out of the driveway.

Japanese ligustrum **A**

'Little Princess' spirea **B**

'Crimson Pygmy' Japanese barberry **C**

Dwarf fountain grass **E**

'Stella d'Oro' daylily **F**

'Blue Pacific' shore juniper **D**

Note: All plants are appropriate for USDA Hardiness Zones 6, 7, and 8.

Sidewalk

Lawn

Driveway

Street   **1 square = 1 ft.**

Plants and Projects

Tough as they are, these plants will benefit from a generous bark mulch, which conserves moisture, helps control weeds, and makes the bed look neat in this highly visible location. In addition to seasonal cleanup, you'll need to prune the shrubs occasionally to keep them tidy and healthy. Divide the clumps of daylilies when they get crowded.

Ⓐ Japanese ligustrum *Ligustrum japonicum* (use 2 plants)
The dark green, waxy leaves of this small broad-leaved evergreen tree are a perfect background for the fragrant white flowers it bears in early summer. Dark blue berries follow in fall and winter. Grows quickly; prune lower branches as necessary to accommodate visitors using the walk.

Ⓑ 'Little Princess' spirea *Spiraea japonica* (use 6)
The small fine leaves and rosy pink flowers of this dainty deciduous shrub belie its tough nature. It will bloom happily for weeks in conditions next to the street in early summer.

Ⓒ 'Crimson Pygmy' Japanese barberry *Berberis thunbergii* (use 6)
The dark maroon leaves of this deciduous shrub turn crimson in late fall. Naturally forms a broad tidy mound.

Ⓓ 'Blue Pacific' shore juniper *Juniperus conferta* (use 2)
This low, trailing evergreen ground cover has handsome blue-green foliage that can stand up to street life. Makes a subtle carpet beneath the trees.

Ⓔ Dwarf fountain grass *Pennisetum alopecuroides* 'Hameln' (use 2)
This perennial grass is a year-round presence. Fluffy flower spikes rise above neat clumps of arching green leaves in midsummer. Flowers and foliage turn shades of gold and tan in autumn and last through the winter.

Ⓕ 'Stella d'Oro' daylily *Hemerocallis* (use 8)
This very popular perennial produces golden yellow flowers from late spring until frost; quite a feat considering that each flower lasts only a day. The grassy foliage is attractive, too.

Ⓖ Walk
This design provides interest underfoot. Set the framework of pressure-treated 2x4s on a sand-and-gravel base; position the square precast concrete pavers in the center of each cell; and fill between paver and frame with crushed rock, tamped firm.

Site: Sunny

Season: Summer

Concept: Small but varied planting transforms an often neglected area and treats visitors and passersby to a colorful display.

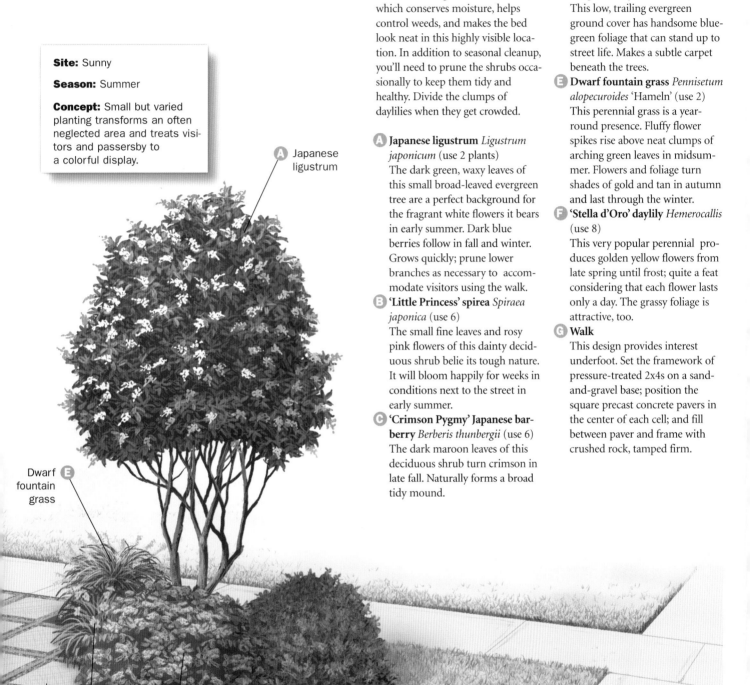

Ⓐ Japanese ligustrum

Dwarf fountain grass Ⓔ

Ⓕ 'Stella d'Oro' daylily

Ⓖ Walk

Ⓑ 'Little Princess' spirea

Ⓒ 'Crimson Pygmy' Japanese barberry

Landscaping a Low Wall

A Colorful Low-Tier Garden Replaces a Bland Slope

For some, walls are nothing more than a barrier or obstruction; for others (especially in cities) they merely represent a "canvas" for their artwork. For plants, walls offer warmth for an early start in spring and good drainage for roots. Gardeners appreciate the rich visual potential for composing a garden on two levels, as well as the practical advantage of working on two relatively flat surfaces instead of a single sloping one. If you have a wall, or have a place to put one, grasp the opportunity for some handsome landscaping.

This design places two complementary perennial borders above and below a wall bounded at one end by a set of stairs. While each bed is relatively narrow, when viewed from the lower level the two combine to form a border almost 10 ft. deep, with plants rising to eye level or more. The planting can be extended with the same or similar plants.

Building the wall that makes this impressive sight possible doesn't require the time or skill it once did. Nor is it necessary to scour the countryside for tons of fieldstone or to hire an expensive contractor. Thanks to precast retaining-wall systems, a knee-high do-it-yourself wall can be installed in as little as a weekend. More experienced or ambitious wall builders may want to tackle a natural stone wall, but anyone with a healthy back (or access to energetic teenagers) can succeed with a prefabricated system.

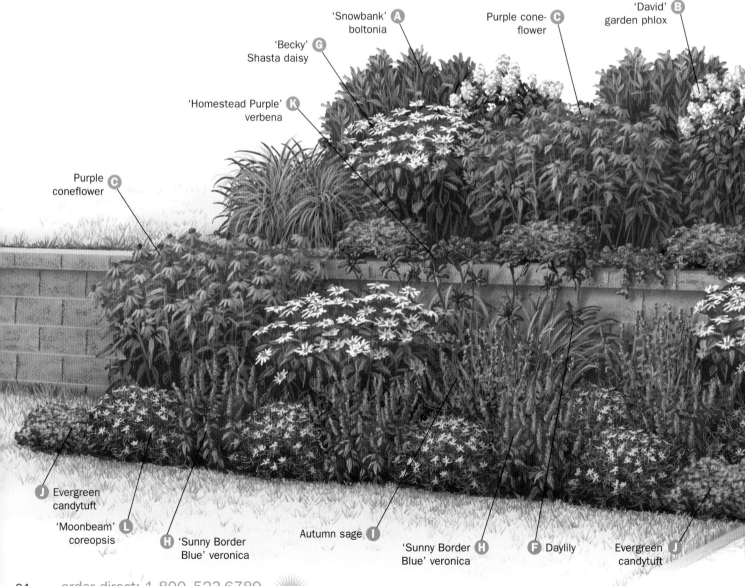

'Snowbank' boltonia **A**

'Becky' Shasta daisy **G**

'Homestead Purple' verbena **K**

Purple coneflower **C**

'David' garden phlox **B**

Purple coneflower **C**

J Evergreen candytuft

'Moonbeam' coreopsis **L**

H 'Sunny Border Blue' veronica

Autumn sage **I**

'Sunny Border Blue' veronica **H**

F Daylily

Evergreen candytuft **J**

Plants and Projects

Drifts of blues, whites, yellows, and pinks, a dash of cherry red, and the flash of butterfly wings keep the garden popping with color from summer through fall. For more color in spring, plant small bulbs like crocus or grape hyacinth throughout the beds. Care is basic: spring and fall cleanup, snipping spent flowers, and dividing a plant now and then.

A 'Snowbank' boltonia *Boltonia asteroides* (use 2 plants)
White daisylike flowers cover this tough perennial for three to five weeks in fall. An upright plant with fine blue-green leaves, it never needs staking.

B 'David' garden phlox *Phlox paniculata* (use 3)
A sturdy perennial topped with clusters of clear white, fragrant flowers in late summer. It forms a patch of upright stems clothed in healthy green leaves, a pleasing backdrop for the plants in front of it.

C Purple coneflower *Echinacea purpurea* (use 9)
Thick flower stalks rise above this perennial's clump of dark green foliage in midsummer, displaying large daisylike blossoms. Each flower has dark pink petals surrounding a dark central cone. Leave some seed heads for winter interest and the finches they attract.

D 'Caesar's Brother' Siberian iris *Iris sibirica* (use 4)
The erect grassy leaves of this perennial provide an interesting spiky look along the wall, and the graceful flowers add deep purple color in late spring.

E Gold moneywort *Lysimachia nummularia* 'Aurea' (use 4)
Planted at the feet of the irises, the bright yellow coin-shaped leaves of this creeping perennial spill over the wall. Yellow flowers in summer complement the coreopsis in the lower bed.

F Daylily *Hemerocallis* (use 5)
Grassy foliage and colorful trumpet-shaped flowers, fresh every day, make this perennial a lovely centerpiece for the lower bed. Choose a cultivar with maroon flowers to blend with the pink coneflowers, or mix several kinds to give a longer blooming period.

G 'Becky' Shasta daisy *Chrysanthemum × superbum* (use 9)
This popular perennial's big white daisies bloom all summer on sturdy stalks that never need staking. The shiny foliage looks good through the winter.

H 'Sunny Border Blue' veronica *Veronica* (use 6)
Lustrous green crinkled leaves topped with bright blue flower spikes make this perennial a cheerful recurring presence in the garden. It will bloom from early summer to frost if you clip off the spent flowers.

I Autumn sage *Salvia greggii* (use 2)
A bushy low-growing perennial with loose clusters of bright red flowers that keep coming through summer and fall.

J Evergreen candytuft *Iberis sempervirens* (use 6)
An excellent evergreen perennial for a wall, with a low, rounded form that falls loosely over the edge. It's topped with clusters of white flowers in early spring.

K 'Homestead Purple' verbena *Verbena canadensis*, (use 2)
This perennial also trails over the edge of the wall and bears purple flowers from spring to frost if you clip off the spent blossoms.

L 'Moonbeam' coreopsis *Coreopsis verticillata* (use 6)
Edging the lower bed, this perennial's tidy mound of fine foliage sparkles with small yellow flowers for months.

M Retaining wall and steps
This 2-ft.-tall wall and the steps are built from a precast concrete block system. Select a color that complements your house.

N Path
Gravel is an attractive, informal surface, easy to install and to maintain.

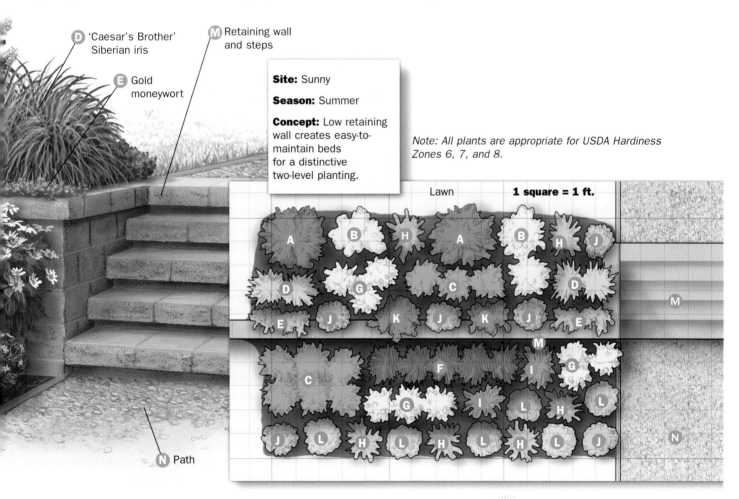

D 'Caesar's Brother' Siberian iris

E Gold moneywort

M Retaining wall and steps

Site: Sunny

Season: Summer

Concept: Low retaining wall creates easy-to-maintain beds for a distinctive two-level planting.

Note: All plants are appropriate for USDA Hardiness Zones 6, 7, and 8.

Lawn   **1 square = 1 ft.**

N Path

Images provided by designer/architect.

Plan #211069

Dimensions: 58' W x 42' D
Levels: 1½
Square Footage: 1,600
Main Level Sq. Ft.: 1,136
Upper Level Sq. Ft.: 464
Bedrooms: 3
Bathrooms: 2
Foundation: Crawl space
Materials List Available: Yes
Price Category: C

Enjoy the large front porch on this traditionally styled home when it's too sunny for the bugs, and use the screened back porch at dusk and dawn.

Features:

• Living Room: Call this the family room if you wish, but no matter what you call it, expect friends and family to gather here, especially when the fireplace gives welcome warmth.

• Kitchen: You'll love the practical layout that pleases everyone from gourmet chefs to beginning cooks.

• Master Suite: Positioned on the main floor to give it privacy, this suite has two entrances for convenience. You'll find a large walk-in closet here as well as a dressing room that includes a separate vanity and mirror makeup counter.

• Storage Space: The 462-sq.-ft. garage is roomy enough to hold two cars and still have space to store tools, out-of-season clothing, or whatever else that needs a dry, protected spot.

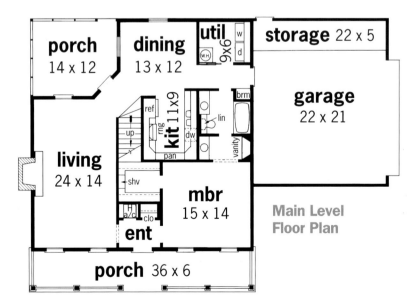

Main Level Floor Plan

Upper Level Floor Plan

Copyright by designer/architect.

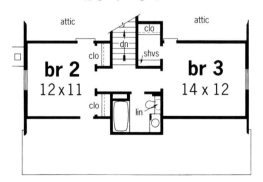

Plan #121067

Dimensions: 56' W x 59'4" D
Levels: 2
Square Footage: 2,708
Main Level Sq. Ft.: 1,860
Upper Level Sq. Ft.: 848
Bedrooms: 4
Bathrooms: 3½
Foundation: Basement
Materials List Available: Yes
Price Category: F

Images provided by designer/architect.

You'll love this home because it is such a perfect setting for a family and still has room for guests.

Features:

- **Family Room:** Expect everyone to gather in this room, near the built-in entertainment centers that flank the lovely fireplace.

- **Living Room:** The other side of the see-through fireplace looks out into this living room, making it an equally welcoming spot in chilly weather.

- **Kitchen:** This room has a large center island, a corner pantry, and a built-in desk. It also features a breakfast area where friends and family will congregate all day long.

- **Master Suite:** Enjoy the oversized walk-in closet and bath with a bayed whirlpool tub, double vanity, and separate shower.

Main Level Floor Plan

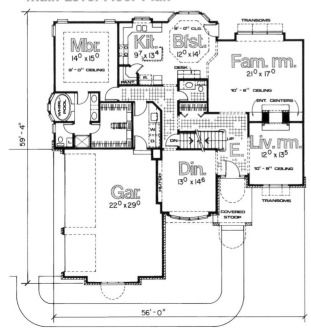

Upper Level Floor Plan

Copyright by designer/architect.

Plan #161001

Dimensions: 67'2" W x 47' D
Levels: 1
Square Footage: 1,782
Bedrooms: 3
Bathrooms: 2
Foundation: Basement
Materials List Available: Yes
Price Category: C

An all-brick exterior displays the solid strength that characterizes this gracious home.

Features:

- **Gathering Area:** A feeling of spaciousness permeates this gathering area, created by the foyer, great room, and dining room. Multiple windows provide natural light that dances along a sloped ceiling, spilling onto decorative columns and a fireplace.

- **Breakfast Area:** A continuation of the sloped ceiling leads to this breakfast area, where French doors open to a screened porch.

- **Kitchen:** An abundance of cabinets and counter space are the hallmarks of this large kitchen, with its easy access to a spacious laundry room and storage area.

- **Master Suite:** A tray ceiling and spacious walk-in closet in the master bedroom, along with a whirlpool tub and double-bowl vanity in the bathroom, enable you to pamper yourself.

Images provided by designer/architect.

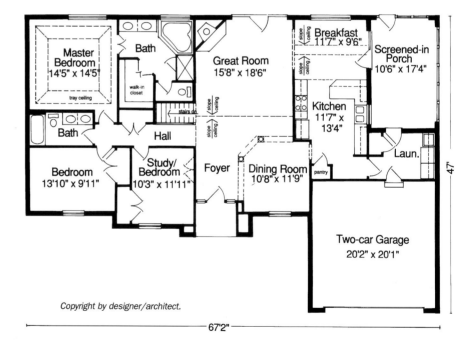

Copyright by designer/architect.

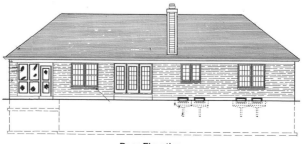

Rear Elevation

Left Side Elevation

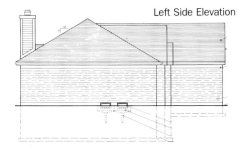

Right Side Elevation

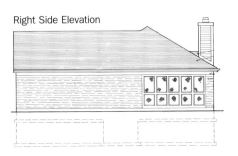

Front View

Great Room / Foyer

Plan #121066

Dimensions: 46' W x 41'5" D

Levels: 2

Square Footage: 2,078

Main Level Sq. Ft.: 1,113

Upper Level Sq. Ft.: 965

Bedrooms: 4

Bathrooms: 2½

Foundation: Basement

Materials List Available: Yes

Price Category: D

This lovely home has an unusual dignity, perhaps because its rooms are so well-proportioned and thoughtfully laid out.

Features:

• Family Room: This room is sunken, giving it an unusually cozy, comfortable feeling. Its abundance of windows let natural light stream in during the day, and the fireplace warms it when the weather's chilly.

• Dining Room: This dining room links to the parlor beyond through a cased opening.

• Parlor: A tall, angled ceiling highlights a large, arched window that's the focal point of this room.

• Breakfast Area: A wooden rail visually links this bayed breakfast area to the family room.

• Master Suite: A roomy walk-in closet adds a practical touch to this luxurious suite. The bath features a skylight, whirlpool tub, and separate shower.

Main Level Floor Plan

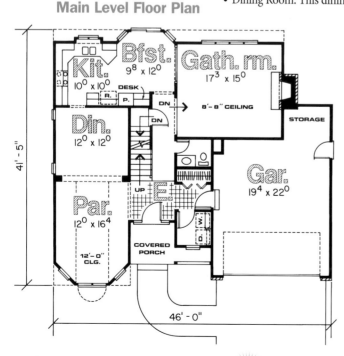

Upper Level Floor Plan

Copyright by designer/architect.

Plan #121075

Dimensions: 57'4" W x 30' D
Levels: 2
Square Footage: 2,345
Main Level Sq. Ft.: 1,000
Upper Level Sq. Ft.: 1,345
Bedrooms: 4
Bathrooms: 3½
Foundation: Basement
Materials List Available: Yes
Price Category: E

Images provided by designer/architect.

Imagine owning a home with a Colonial-styled exterior and a practical, amenity-filled interior with both formal and informal areas.

Features:

- **Family Room:** This room will be the heart of your home. A bay window lets you create a special nook for reading or quiet conversation, and a fireplace begs for a circle of comfortable chairs or soft cushions around it.

- **Living Room:** Connected to the family room by a set of French doors, you can use this room for formal entertaining or informal family fun.

- **Kitchen:** This kitchen has been designed for efficient work patterns. However, the snack bar that links it to the breakfast area beyond also invites company while the cook is working.

- **Master Suite:** Located on the second level, this suite features an entertainment center, a separate sitting area, built-in dressers, two walk-in closets, and a whirlpool tub.

Main Level Floor Plan

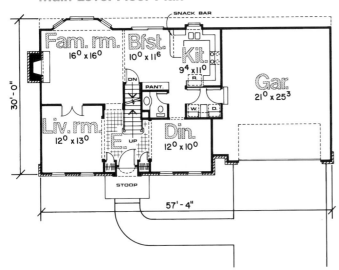

Upper Level Floor Plan

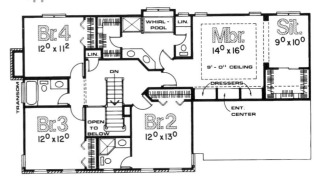

Copyright by designer/architect.

Images provided by designer/architect.

Copyright by designer/architect.

Plan #201063

Dimensions: 74'10" W x 70'10" D

Levels: 1

Square Footage: 2,697

Bedrooms: 4

Bathrooms: 3

Foundation: Crawl space, slab

Materials List Available: Yes

Price Category: F

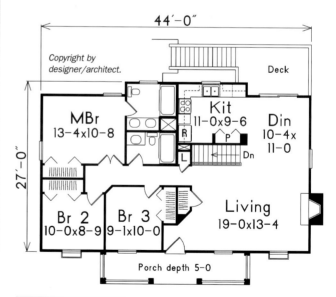

Images provided by designer/architect.

Plan #321022

Dimensions: 44' W x 27' D

Levels: 1

Square Footage: 1,140

Bedrooms: 3

Bathrooms: 2

Foundation: Basement

Materials List Available: Yes

Price Category: B

SMARTtip

Basement Moldings

Keep moldings simple in a basement with lower ceilings. Elaborate moldings around the ceiling or floor can shorten the height of the room.

Plan #351003

Dimensions: 64' W x 45'10" D

Levels: 1

Square Footage: 1,751

Bedrooms: 3

Bathrooms: 2

Foundation: Basement, crawl space, or slab

Materials List Available: Yes

Price Category: C

Images provided by designer/architect.

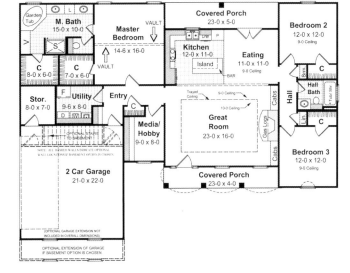

Copyright by designer/architect.

Plan #101011

Dimensions: 71'2" W x 58'1" D

Levels: 1

Square Footage: 2,184

Bedrooms: 3

Bathrooms: 3

Foundation: Slab, crawl space, or basement

Materials List Available: No

Price Category: D

Images provided by designer/architect.

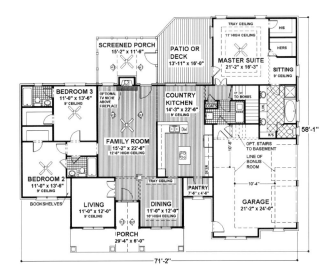

Copyright by designer/architect.

Plan #131020

Dimensions: 67'2" W x 48'10" D
Levels: 1
Square Footage: 1,735
Bedrooms: 3
Bathrooms: 2
Foundation: Basement, crawl space, or slab
Materials List Available: Yes
Price Category: C

This gorgeous ranch is designed for entertaining but is also comfortable for family living.

Features:

- Living Room: A 9-ft. stepped ceiling highlights the spaciousness of this room, which gives a view of one of the two covered porches.

- Dining Room: Also with a 9-ft. stepped ceiling and a view of the porch, this room features a bay window.

- Family Room: An 11-ft. vaulted ceiling and gliding French doors to the porch define this central gathering area.

- Kitchen: Enjoy the skylight, a fireplace that's shared with the family room, a central island cooktop, and a snack bar in this room.

- Master Suite: The tray ceiling is 9 ft. 9 in. high, and this area includes a sitting area and a bath with a whirlpool tub and dual-sink vanity.

Images provided by designer/architect.

Copyright by designer/architect.

Photos provided by designer/architect.

Kitchen

Foyer / Dining Room

Plan #151179

Dimensions: 66'4" W x 67'2" D
Levels: 1½
Square Footage: 2,405
Opt. Bonus Level Sq. Ft.: 358
Bedrooms: 4
Bathrooms: 3
Foundation: Crawl space, slab (basement or walk-out basement option for fee)
Materials List Available: Yes
Price Category: E

As beautiful inside as it is outside, this home will delight the most discerning family.

Features:

- Great Room: This room has a 10-ft. ceiling, door to the porch, fireplace, and built-ins.

- Dining Room: You'll love the way the columns set off this room from the great room and foyer.

- Kitchen: An L-shaped work area, central dining, and working island add to your efficiency.

- Hearth Room: A fireplace and computer center make this room a natural gathering spot.

- Breakfast Room: This lovely room is lit by large windows and a door that opens to the rear porch.

- Master Suite: You'll love the sitting room in the bayed area, walk-in closet, and luxury bath.

- Rear Porch: Use this porch for grilling, dining, and just relaxing—it's large enough to do it all.

Images provided by designer/architect.

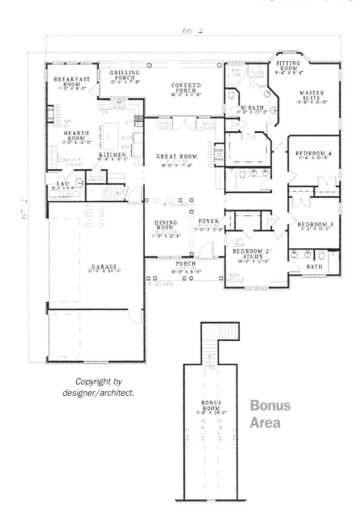

Copyright by designer/architect.

Bonus Area

Plan #121074

Dimensions: 68'8" W x 47'8" D
Levels: 2
Square Footage: 2,486
Main Level Sq. Ft.: 1,829
Upper Level Sq. Ft.: 657
Bedrooms: 4
Bathrooms: 2½
Foundation: Basement
Materials List Available: Yes
Price Category: E

Images provided by designer/architect.

Enjoy the natural light that streams through the many lovely windows in this well-designed home.

Features:

• Living Room: This room is sure to be your family's headquarters, thanks to the lovely 15-ft. ceiling, stacked windows, central location, and cozy fireplace.

• Dining Room: A boxed ceiling adds formality to this well-positioned room.

• Kitchen: The island cooktop in this kitchen is so large that it includes a snack bar area. A pantry gives ample storage space, and a built-in desk—where you can set up a computer station or a record-keeping area—adds efficiency.

• Master Suite: For the sake of privacy, this master suite is located on the opposite side of the home from the other living areas. You'll love the roomy bedroom and luxuriate in the private bath with its many amenities.

Main Level Floor Plan

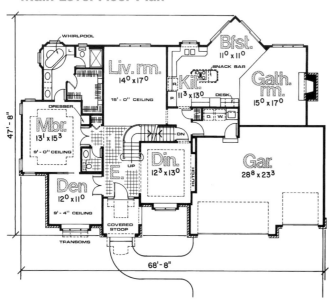

Upper Level Floor Plan

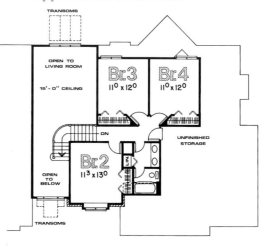

Copyright by designer/architect.

Plan #121073

Dimensions: 70' W x 52' D
Levels: 2
Square Footage: 2,579
Main Level Sq. Ft.: 1,933
Upper Level Sq. Ft.: 646
Bedrooms: 4
Bathrooms: 2½
Foundation: Basement
Materials List Available: Yes
Price Category: E

Images provided by designer/architect.

Luxury will surround you in this home with contemporary styling and up-to-date amenities at every turn.

Features:

• Great Room: This large room shares both a see-through fireplace and a wet bar with the adjacent hearth room. Transom-topped windows add both light and architectural interest to this room.

• Den: Transom-topped windows add visual interest to this private area.

• Kitchen: A center island and corner pantry add convenience to this well-planned kitchen, and a lovely ceiling treatment adds beauty to the bayed breakfast area.

• Master Suite: A built-in bookcase adds to the ambiance of this luxury-filled area, where you're sure to find a retreat at the end of the day.

Main Level Floor Plan

Upper Level Floor Plan

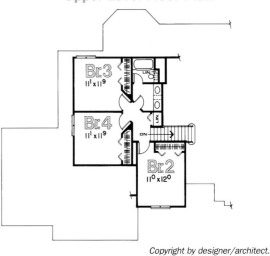

Copyright by designer/architect.

Plan #211148

Images provided by designer/architect.

Dimensions: 74'6" W x 77' D

Levels: 1

Square Footage: 2,710

Bedrooms: 4

Bathrooms: 3½

Foundation: Crawl space, slab

Materials List Available: No

Price Category: F

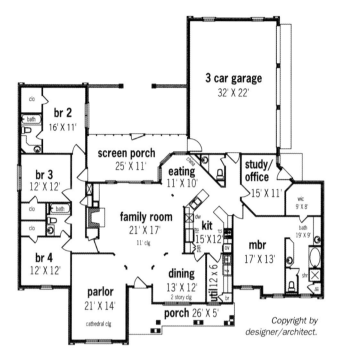

Copyright by designer/architect.

Plan #371006

Images provided by designer/architect.

Dimensions: 49'9" W x 48'6" D

Levels: 1

Square Footage: 1,374

Bedrooms: 3

Bathrooms: 2

Foundation: Slab
(crawl space option for fee)

Materials List Available: No

Price Category: B

Copyright by designer/architect.

Plan #241023

Images provided by designer/architect.

Dimensions: 56'9" W x 57'8" D
Levels: 1
Square Footage: 1,699
Bedrooms: 3
Bathrooms: 2
Foundation: Slab
Materials List Available: No
Price Category: C

Copyright by designer/architect.

Plan #361009

Images provided by designer/architect.

Dimensions: 48' W x 53' D
Levels: 2
Square Footage: 1,775
Main Level Sq. Ft.: 1,280
Upper Level Sq. Ft.: 495
Bedrooms: 3
Bathrooms: 2½
Foundation: Crawl space
Materials List Available: No
Price Category: C

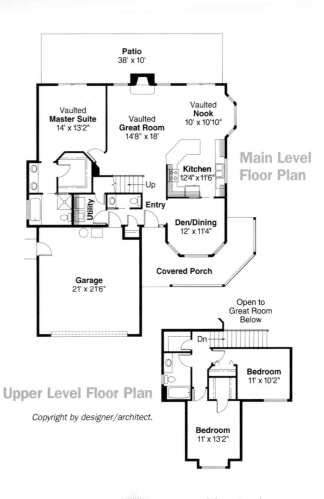

Main Level Floor Plan

Upper Level Floor Plan

Copyright by designer/architect.

Plan #151178

Dimensions: 52'6" W x 58'10" D
Levels: 1
Square Footage: 1,600
Bedrooms: 3
Bathrooms: 2
Foundation: Crawl space, slab
Materials List Available: Yes
Price Category: C

The classic styling on the exterior of this lovely home is complemented by clean lines and an open layout on the inside.

Features:

- Great Room: This spacious room has a cathedral ceiling, a fireplace surrounded by built-ins, and a door to the rear grilling porch.

- Grilling Porch: Enjoy parties on this porch in warm weather, and grill here all through the year.

- Dining Room: Boxed columns set off this room, with its 11-ft. ceiling and inset window area.

- Kitchen: A central work island adds work space, and roomy cabinets give lots of room for storage.

- Breakfast Room: A 9-ft. boxed ceiling and bank of windows highlight this lovely room.

- Master Suite: The bedroom has a 9-ft. boxed ceiling, and the bath has a walk-in closet, whirlpool tub & shower, and two vanities.

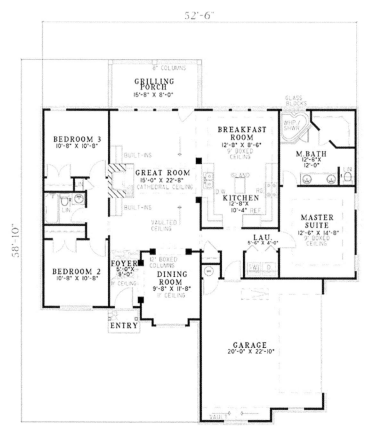

Plan #271081

Dimensions: 86' W x 54' D
Levels: 1
Square Footage: 2,539
Bedrooms: 4
Bathrooms: 2
Foundation: Slab
Materials List Available: No
Price Category: E

This traditional home is sure to impress your guests and even your neighbors.

Features:

• Living Room: This quiet space off the foyer is perfect for pleasant conversation.

• Family Room: A perfect gathering spot, this room is nicely enhanced by a fireplace.

• Kitchen: This room easily serves the bayed morning room and the formal dining room.

• Master Suite: The master bedroom overlooks a side patio, and boasts a private bath with a skylight and a whirlpool tub.

• Library: This cozy room is perfect for curling up with a good novel. It would also make a great extra bedroom.

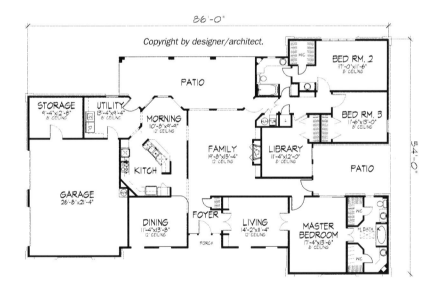

SMARTtip

Determining Curtain Length

Follow length guidelines for foolproof results, but remember that they're not rules. Go ahead and play with curtain and drapery lengths. Instead of shortening long panels at the hem, for instance, take up excess material by blousing them over tiebacks for a pleasing effect.

Plan #141023

Dimensions: 38' W x 40' D
Levels: 1½
Square Footage: 1,715
Main Level Sq. Ft.: 1,046
Upper Level Sq. Ft.: 669
Bedrooms: 3
Bathrooms: 2½
Foundation: Basement
Materials List Available: Yes
Price Category: C

Images provided by designer/architect.

A gabled front and a delightful porch join to bring added charm to this quaint, 1½-story cape with under-garage design, well-suited for a sloped lot.

Features:

• Kitchen: An angled kitchen wall to the dining room creates a sense of space, making this kitchen part of the living area without sacrificing formality. A nice surprise is a cozy breakfast nook with cathedral ceiling.

• Master Suite: You can relax at the end of the day and enjoy the maximum privacy provided by this first-floor master suite.

• Additional Bedrooms: Two spacious, second-floor bedrooms, which share a bath, complete this charming home.

• Basement: Use this functional basement for additional storage or for your family's expanding needs.

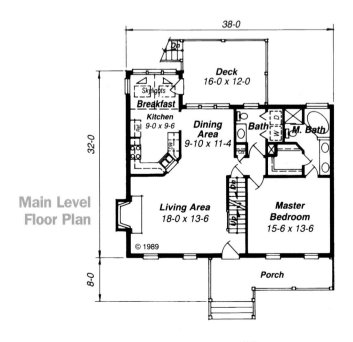

Main Level Floor Plan

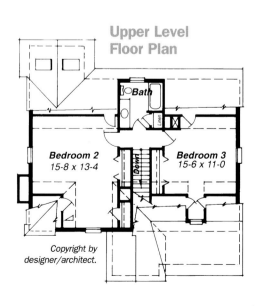

Upper Level Floor Plan

Copyright by designer/architect.

Plan #121050

Dimensions: 64' W x 50' D
Levels: 1
Square Footage: 1,996
Bedrooms: 2
Bathrooms: 2
Foundation: Basement
Materials List Available: Yes
Price Category: D

Images provided by designer/architect.

This compact design includes features usually reserved for larger homes and has styling that is typical of more-exclusive home designs.

Features:

- Entry: As you enter this home, you'll see the formal living and dining rooms—both with special ceiling detailing—on either side.

- Great Room: Located in the rear of the home for convenience, this great room is likely to be your favorite spot. The fireplace is framed by transom-topped windows, so you'll love curling up here, no matter what the weather or time of day.

- Kitchen: Ample counter and cabinet space make this kitchen a dream in which to work.

- Master Suite: A tray ceiling and lovely corner windows create an elegant feeling in the bedroom, and two walk-in closets make it easy to keep this space tidy and organized. The private bath has a skylight, corner whirlpool tub, and two separate vanities.

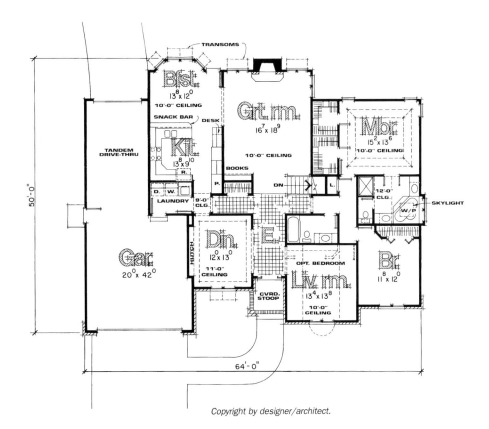

Copyright by designer/architect.

Plan #241034

Dimensions: 44'3" W x 68'3" D

Levels: 1½

Square Footage: 2,377

Main Level Sq. Ft.: 1,663

Upper Level Sq. Ft.: 714

Bedrooms: 3

Bathrooms: 2½

Foundation: Slab

Materials List Available: No

Price Category: E

Images provided by designer/architect.

Main Level Floor Plan

Upper Level Floor Plan

Copyright by designer/architect.

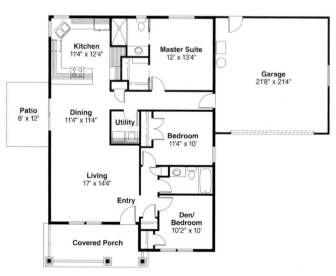

Plan #361013

Dimensions: 54' W x 46' D

Levels: 1

Square Footage: 1,321

Bedrooms: 3

Bathrooms: 2

Foundation: Crawl space

Materials List Available: No

Price Category: B

Images provided by designer/architect.

Copyright by designer/architect.

Plan #361019

Dimensions: 66' W x 47' D
Levels: 1
Square Footage: 1,619
Bedrooms: 3
Bathrooms: 2
Foundation: Basement, crawl space
Materials List Available: No
Price Category: C

Images provided by designer/architect.

Patio
24' x 12'

Master Suite
16' x 12'

Vaulted
Nook
11' x 10'8"

Vaulted
Great Room
15'6" x 18'2"

Vaulted
Kitchen
11'2" x 11'

Garage
21'6" x 23'

Utility

Vaulted
Entry

Dining
10'10" x 11'

Copyright by designer/architect.

Bedroom
12' x 10'8"

Bedroom
10' x 10'4"

Covered Porch

Alternate Basement Stairs Location

Vaulted
Great Room
15'6" x 14'6"

Dn

Utility

Entry

Plan #361021

Dimensions: 54' W x 54' D
Levels: 2
Square Footage: 1,887
Main Level Sq. Ft.: 1,369
Upper Level Sq. Ft.: 518
Bedrooms: 3
Bathrooms: 2½
Foundation: Crawl space
Materials List Available: No
Price Category: D

Images provided by designer/architect.

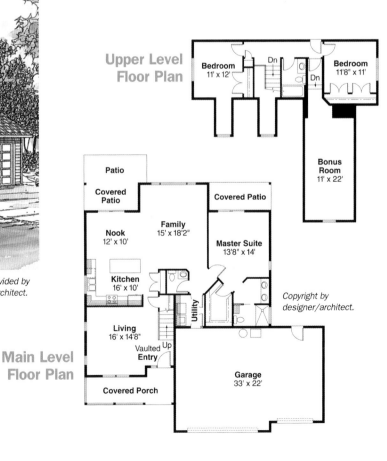

Upper Level Floor Plan

Bedroom
11' x 12'

Dn

Bedroom
11'8" x 11'

Dn

Bonus Room
11' x 22'

Main Level Floor Plan

Patio

Covered Patio

Covered Patio

Nook
12' x 10'

Family
15' x 18'2"

Master Suite
13'8" x 14'

Kitchen
16' x 10'

Utility

Copyright by designer/architect.

Living
16' x 14'8"

Vaulted Entry

Up

Garage
33' x 22'

Covered Porch

Plan #151176

Dimensions: 60' W x 77'6" D
Levels: 1½
Square Footage: 2,445
Main Level Sq. Ft.: 2,129
Upper Level Sq. Ft.: 316
Bedrooms: 4
Bathrooms: 3½
Foundation: Crawl space, slab (basement or walk-out basement option for fee)
Materials List Available: Yes
Price Category: E

Images provided by designer/architect.

You'll love the extra room and contemporary elements inside this traditional looking home.

Features:

- **Great Room:** Columns mark the sides of this large room with a fireplace, built-ins for media, and a door to the rear grilling porch.
- **Dining Room:** This spacious room is set off by columns, and is just off the foyer for convenience.

- **Kitchen:** This well-designed room includes a pantry and angled counter with a snack bar.
- **Breakfast Room:** An extended window area makes a wonderful place for a table, and you'll love the computer desk built into the wall.
- **Master Suite:** Extensive windows light the bedroom, and the bath includes a huge closet, whirlpool tub, glass shower, and dual vanity.
- **Upper Floor:** Finish the bonus space here as a playroom, media room, or home office.

Main Level Floor Plan

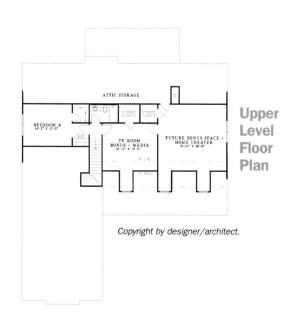

Upper Level Floor Plan

Copyright by designer/architect.

Plan #101004

Dimensions: 55'8" W x 56'6" D

Levels: 1

Square Footage: 1,787

Bedrooms: 3

Bathrooms: 2

Foundation: Slab, crawl space, or basement

Materials List Available: No

Price Category: C

Images provided by designer/architect.

This carefully designed ranch provides the feel and features of a much larger home.

Features:

- Ceiling Height: 9 ft. unless otherwise noted.

- Foyer: Guests will step up onto the inviting front porch and into this foyer, with its impressive 11-ft. ceiling.

- Dining Room: Open to the entry and to its left is this elegant dining room, perfect for entertaining or informal family gatherings.

- Family Room: This family gathering place features an 11-ft. ceiling to enhance its sense of spaciousness.

- Kitchen: This intelligently designed kitchen has an open plan. A breakfast bar and a serving bar are features that add to its convenience.

- Master Suite: This suite is loaded with amenities, including a double-step tray ceiling, direct access to the screened porch, a sitting room, deluxe bath, and his and her walk-in closets.

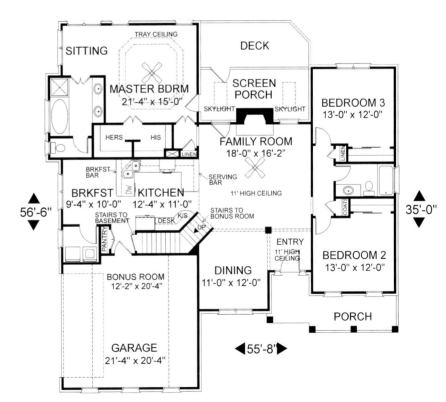

Copyright by designer/architect.

Plan #121087

Dimensions: 50' W x 40' D
Levels: 2
Square Footage: 2,103
Main Level Sq. Ft.: 1,082
Upper Level Sq. Ft.: 1,021
Bedrooms: 4
Bathrooms: 2½
Foundation: Basement
Materials List Available: Yes
Price Category: D

You'll love the comfort and the unusual design details you'll find in this home.

Features:

- Entry: A T-shaped staircase frames this two-story entry, giving both visual interest and convenience.

- Family Room: Bookcases frame the lovely fireplace here, so you won't be amiss by decorating to create a special reading nook.

- Breakfast Area: Pass through the cased opening between the family room and this breakfast area, for convenience.

- Kitchen: Combined with the breakfast area, this kitchen features an island, pantry, and desk.

- Master Suite: On the upper floor, this suite has a walk-in closet and a bath with sunlit whirlpool tub, separate shower, and double vanity. A window seat makes the bedroom especially cozy, no matter what the outside weather.

Main Level Floor Plan

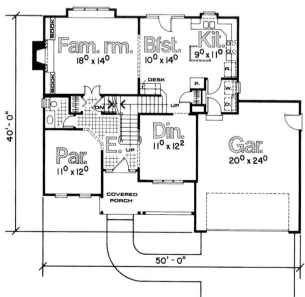

Upper Level Floor Plan

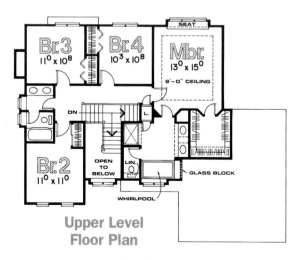

Plan #321060

Dimensions: 36' W x 46'8" D
Levels: 2
Square Footage: 1,575
Main Level Sq. Ft.: 802
Upper Level Sq. Ft.: 773
Bedrooms: 3
Bathrooms: 2½
Foundation: Basement
Materials List Available: Yes
Price Category: C

This stylish home is designed for a narrow lot but can complement any setting.

Features:

- Living Room: A masonry fireplace and large window area are the focal points in this spacious room.

- Dining Room: Open to the living room, the dining room has a large bay window that lets you enjoy the scenery as you dine.

- Breakfast Room: A bay window here lets morning sunlight help you greet the day.

- Kitchen: The center island gives extra work space as well as a snack bar. The adjacent laundry room and built-in pantry add to the convenience you'll find here.

- Master Suite: A vaulted ceiling and large walk-in closet make this room a treat, and the bath features a double vanity, tub, and separate shower.

Main Level Floor Plan

36'-0"

46'-8"

Kit 9-0x11-7
Brk fst 10-0x11-0
Dining 12-0x11-0
Living 15-7x14-4
Dn
Up
P
D W
R
Garage 19-4x20-4

Upper Level Floor Plan

MBr 12-0x14-8 — vaulted clg
Br 2 12-0x11-0
Dn
Br 3 12-0x11-3 — vaulted clg
L
plant shelf

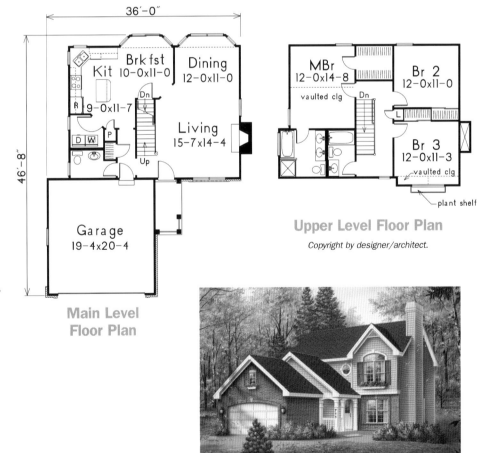

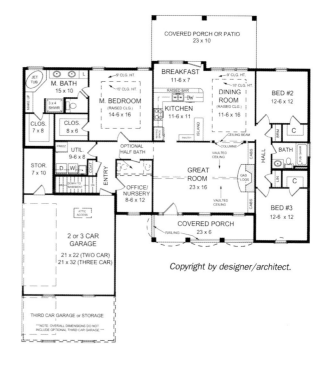

Plan #351008

Dimensions: 64'6" W x 61'4" D

Levels: 1

Square Footage: 2,002

Bedrooms: 3

Bathrooms: 2

Foundation: Basement, crawl space

Materials List Available: Yes

Price Category: D

Images provided by designer/architect.

Copyright by designer/architect.

Plan #371003

Dimensions: 61' W x 57'4" D

Levels: 2

Square Footage: 2,297

Main Level Sq. Ft.: 1,752

Upper Level Sq. Ft.: 545

Bedrooms: 3

Bathrooms: 3

Foundation: Slab
(crawl space option for fee)

Materials List Available: No

Price Category: E

Images provided by designer/architect.

Main Level Floor Plan

Upper Level Floor Plan

Copyright by designer/architect.

Plan #351011

Dimensions: 73'8" W x 53'2" D

Levels: 1

Square Footage: 2,251

Bedrooms: 3

Bathrooms: 2½

Foundation: Basement, crawl space, or slab

Materials List Available: Yes

Price Category: E

Images provided by designer/architect.

Bonus Room

Copyright by designer/architect.

Plan #371005

Dimensions: 52'6" W x 45'8" D

Levels: 1

Square Footage: 1,250

Bedrooms: 2

Bathrooms: 2

Foundation: Slab
(crawl space option for fee)

Materials List Available: No

Price Category: B

Images provided by designer/architect.

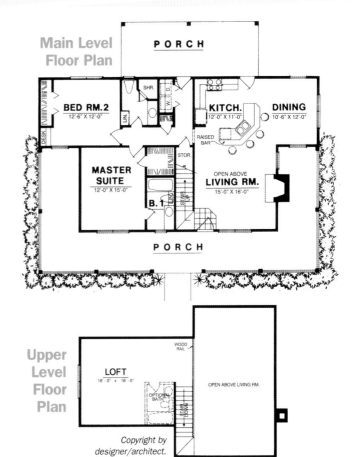

Copyright by designer/architect.

Plan #131007

Dimensions: 59'10" W x 47'8" D
Levels: 1
Square Footage: 1,595
Bedrooms: 3
Bathrooms: 2
Foundation: Crawl space, slab, basement, or walkout
Materials List Available: Yes
Price Category: D

Imagine living in this home, with its traditional country comfort and individual brand of charm.

Features:

- Exterior elements: The mixture of a front porch with a cameo front door, decorative posts, bay windows, and dormers will delight you.

- Great Room: A tray ceiling gives distinction to this large room, and a wet bar eases entertaining.

- Screened Porch: At dusk and dawn, this porch is sure to be your favorite outdoor spot.

- Kitchen: Eat any meal in this large kitchen for a touch of homey charm.

- Dining Room: Perfect for hosting a formal dinner, this bayed dining room can increase your enjoyment of simple family meals.

- Master Bedroom: For the sake of privacy, this room is somewhat secluded. Decorate to emphasize the elegant tray ceiling.

Images provided by designer/architect.

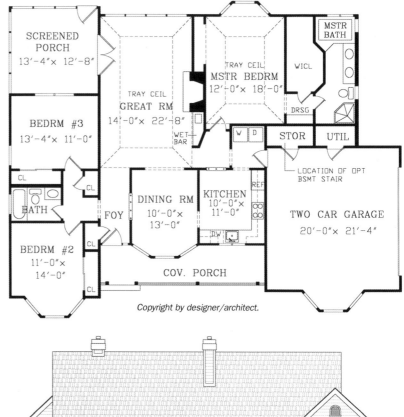

Copyright by designer/architect.

Rear Elevation

Alternate Front View

Foyer / Dining Room

Add the Extras

Simple or plain, it's the little conveniences and miscellaneous touches that push the dining experience to perfection. Here are some extra things to think about.

- You can never have too many serving trays when you entertain outside. For carrying food or drinks from the kitchen or the grill, trays are indispensable.

- A serving cart on wheels makes a perfect movable outdoor bar and provides an additional serving surface. Look for one at yard sales or buy one new.

- Chances are you won't have a sideboard, but a few small tables to hold excess items are great substitutes for one. They're also easier to position in the different places where you need them.

- For cooler weather or even a summer's evening with a bit of nip in the air, nothing beats an outdoor fireplace for comfort. You could build one into the house, but various types of stand-alone units are sold in home centers. To add a Southwest ambiance, consider a chiminea, a clay fireplace. Try burning some piñon pine, and you'll feel as if you're in Santa Fe. Be sure to follow manufacturers' instructions when using these fireplaces. You might also have to store them during the winter.

- Pots of fragrant plants—lavender, scented geraniums, flowering tobacco, or jasmine—provide a sensual aroma. Flowers such as roses climbing up an arbor or trellis are beautiful, evoke a romantic feeling, and lend a delicate scent to the atmosphere as well.

Nothing adds romance and intrigue to an evening soiree as candlelight does. Include just a few candles for an intimate dinner. Use more for a larger gathering, placing one or more on each table. Scatter luminaries around the yard. As the beautiful evening dusk begins, light candles, a few at a time, so your eyes can adjust to the dimming light. Not only do the candles illuminate the night in a magical way but they can also keep bugs at bay.

Great Room

Clutter-Cutting Tips for Your Home

One of the great things about moving into a new home is all that new, uncluttered closet space you gain. But if you are like most homeowners, storage of all types will quickly become scarce, especially in a smaller cottage home. Here are some tips for expanding and organizing storage space.

Shelving Types

Shelving is an easy and economical way to add extra storage space in almost any part of your home—along walls, inside closets, and even in the basement or garage. Building shelves doesn't usually require a lot of skill or specialized tools, so this is one project just about any do-it-yourselfer can handle. And unless you decide to use hardwood—which looks great but costs a bundle—it won't cost a lot to install them either.

Solid wood shelving is the way to go when you want to show off the wood or your work.

Plywood and particleboard offer a couple of advantages when it comes to shelving, though. They cost less than solid wood, and can be bought faced with decorative surfaces. They also come in sheets, which makes them ideal for a really wide

Home offices require a mix of storage options: open shelving, drawers, and file cabinets.

shelf. Inexpensive, manufactured storage units ready for assembly often are made from melamine-coated particleboard.

Wood trim will help match your new shelves to the rest of the room or add some interesting detail. Trim is also a handy way to hide seams, gaps, exposed edges of plywood, and other blemishes. You can get trim in either hardwood or softwood. If you plan on finishing a project with stain or sealer, make sure the trim matches the wood you used for the rest of the project.

Bracket Options

There are two basic types of ready-to-hang shelving supports: stationary shelf brackets and shelving standards. Stationary brackets come in many sizes and styles, and range from utilitarian to decorative. Shelving standards are slotted metal strips that support various types of shelf brackets.

Mounting Brackets

For maximum strength, anchor shelf supports to wall studs. If your shelf will carry a light load, you can anchor its supports between studs with mollies or toggle bolts. Attaching supports directly to the studs is always better, though, because sooner or later something heavy will wind up on the shelf. Use masonry anchors to attach shelf supports to brick or concrete. You can also attach shelf supports to a ledger attached to wall studs with 3-inch drywall screws.

Ready-made shelving, above, offers a quick alternative to building your own shelves.

Mud rooms and areas near the entrance the family uses most should have storage for coats, hats, and boots.

Shelf Standards. Metal shelf standards can be mounted directly to walls or, for a more decorative look, you can insert the standards in grooves routed into the wood itself or into hardwood strips.

Cut the standards to fit with a hacksaw, and attach them to wall studs with 3-inch drywall screws. Use a carpenter's level to make sure that both standards are plumb and that the corresponding mounting slots are level. Mount standards 6 inches from the ends of shelving to prevent sagging. For long wall shelves, install standards every 48 inches.

Many kitchen and closet storage systems use wire grids that attach to walls with molded plastic brackets. If you anticipate light loads, you can mount these brackets to drywall using the screws and expansion anchors usually included with such systems. But for heavier loads, use drywall screws to fasten the brackets directly to the wall studs.

Customized Storage

Built-in storage units are an excellent way to make the most of existing storage space in your home. Ready-made or custom-made built-in shelving units, entertainment centers, kitchen cabinets, medicine cabinets, window seats, and under-bed drawers are not only inexpensive and easy to assemble, they allow you to add a unique, personalized touch to your living spaces.

Built-in Shelving

A built-in shelving unit can create valuable storage capacity from an overlooked wall space, such as the area between windows or between a door and its adjacent corner. To construct the shelving, you'll need 1x10 or 1x12 lumber for side panels, top and base panels, and shelves; four 2x2 strips for spreaders; trim molding to conceal gaps along the top and bottom of the unit; 12d

common nails and 6d finishing nails. If the unit will be bearing heavy loads, use hardwood boards, and make sure that the shelves span no more than 36 inches. To make installation easier, cut the side pieces an inch shorter than the ceiling height. (This way, you'll be able to tilt the unit into position without scraping the ceiling.) Paint or stain the wood pieces before assembling the unit. Hang the shelves from pegs or end clips inserted into holes drilled in the side pieces.

Adding Closet Space

What homeowner, even a new homeowner, hasn't complained about having too little closet space? Fortunately, there are almost always ways to find a bit more closet space or to make the closet space you have more efficient. Often, it isn't the space that is lacking but how the space is organized that is the problem. The trick is to find ways to help you organize the space.

Ventilated closet systems help keep your belongings neat and within easy reach.

order direct: 1-800-523-6789

Organizing Systems. The easiest and most obvious solution is one of the many commercial closet organizing systems now on the market. There are a number of configurations available, and you can customize most systems to meet your needs. Constructing your own version of a commercial closet organizer is another option. With a combination of shelves and plywood partitions, you can divide a closet into storage zones, with a single clothes pole on one side for full-length garments; double clothes poles on the other side for half-length garments like jackets, skirts, or slacks; a column of narrow shelves between the two for folded items or shoes; and one or more closet-wide shelves on top.

Before design-ing a closet system, above, inventory all of the items you want to store in the closet.

Metal shelf standards can provide a quick solution for creating shelving in areas where it is needed.

Cedar Closets

Both solid cedar boards and composite cedar panels have only moderate resistance to insects, and are used more for their pleasant aroma and appearance. The sheets of pressed red and tan particles are no less aromatic than solid wood, but the panels are 40 to 50 percent less expensive, and are easier to install. Solid boards require more carpentry work, and are likely to produce a fair amount of waste unless you piece the courses and create more joints. To gain the maximum effect, every inside surface should be covered, including the ceiling and the back of the door. The simplest option is to use ¼-inch-thick panels, which are easy to cut into big sections that cover walls in one or two pieces. Try to keep cedar seams in boards or panels from falling over drywall seams. No stain, sealer, or clear finish is needed; just leave the wood raw. The cedar aroma will fade over the years as natural oils crystallize on the surface. But you can easily regenerate the

For garages and basements, you'll find a combination of shelving and hanging hooks keeps tools and equipment organized, left.

Storage for basements, garages, and workshops, opposite below, should include a cabinet that locks for storage of dangerous chemicals.

Specialized storage accessories, such as the sports storage system shown at right, not only keeps items organized but they also keep them in ready-to-play condition.

scent from the panels by scuffing the surface with fine sandpaper.

Ideas for Basements, Garages, and Workshops

Workshops and other utility areas such as garages, attics, and basements can benefit from storage upgrades as much as any other room in the home—perhaps even more so, as utility areas are prone to clutter. Convenience, flexibility, and safety are the things to keep in mind when reorganizing your work space. Try to provide storage space for tools and hardware as near as possible to where they'll be used. In addition to a sturdy workbench, utility shelving

is a mainstay in any workshop. You can buy ready-to-assemble units or make your own using ¾-inch particleboard or plywood shelves and ¾x1½-inch (1x2) hardwood stock for cleats (nailed to the wall), ribs (nailed to the front underside of the shelves), and vertical shelf supports.

DIY Utility Storage. Don't forget about pegboard. To make a pegboard tool rack, attach washers to the back of the pegboard with hot glue, spacing the washers to coincide with wall studs. Position the pegboard so that the rear washers are located over studs. Drive drywall screws through finish washers and the pegboard into studs. (Use masonry anchors for concrete walls.)

Finally, try to take advantage of any oth-

erwise wasted space. The area in your garage above your parked car is the ideal spot for a U-shaped lumber storage rack, made of 1x4 stock and connecting plates. The space in front of the car could be used for a storage cabinet or even a workbench.

Instant Storage. To utilize the overhead space in your garage, build deep storage platforms supported by ledgers screwed to wall studs and threaded rods hooked to ceiling joists or rafters. You can also hang tools from the walls by mounting pegboard. You can buy sets with a variety of hooks and brackets for tools. For small items, such as jars of nails, make shallow shelves by nailing 1x4 boards between the exposed studs.

Suit storage to your needs. The narrow pullout pantry above is located between the refrigerator and a food-preparation area. Notice how you can access the shelves from both sides of the pantry when it is extended.

Kitchen Storage

The type of storage in a kitchen is almost as important as the amount. Some people like at least a few open shelves for displaying attractive china or glassware; others want absolutely everything tucked away behind doors.

What are your storage needs? The answer depends partly on your food shopping habits and partly on how many pots, pans, and other pieces of kitchen equipment you have or would like to have. A family that goes food shopping several times a week and prepares mostly fresh foods needs more refrigerator space, less freezer capacity, and fewer cabinets than a family that prefers packaged or prepared foods and makes only infrequent forays to the local supermarket.

Planning

To help clarify your needs, mentally walk yourself through a typical meal and list the utensils used to prepare food, where you got them, and your progress throughout the work area. And don't limit yourself to full-scale meals. Much kitchen work is devoted to preparing snacks, reheating leftovers, and making lunches for the kids to take to school.

Food Preparation. During food preparation, the sink and stove come into use. Some families rely heavily on the microwave for reheating. Using water means repeated trips to the sink, so that area might be the best place to keep a steamer, salad spinner, and coffee and tea canisters, as well as glassware and cups. Near the stove you may want storage for odd-shaped items such as a fish poacher or wok. You can hang frequently used pans and utensils from a convenient rack; stow other items in cabinets so that they do not collect grease.

During the Meal. When the food is ready, you must take it to the table. If the eating space is nearby, a work counter might turn into a serving counter. If the dining space is in another room, a pass-through facilitates serving.

Storage accessories, such as the pullout pot holder above, come as options from some cabinet manufacturers, or you can install them later yourself. Notice how the side rails hold the pot lids in place. The cabinet below features space for small baskets.

After the Meal. When the meal ends, dishes must go from the table to the sink or dishwasher, and leftovers to storage containers and the refrigerator. Now the stove and counters need to be wiped down and the sink scoured. When the dishwasher finishes its cycle, everything must be put away.

Open versus Closed Storage.

Shelves, pegboards, pot racks, cup hooks, magnetic knife racks, and the like put your utensils on view, which is a good way to personalize your kitchen.

But open storage has drawbacks. Items left out in the open can look messy unless they are kept neatly arranged. Another option is to install glass doors on wall cabinets. This handily solves the dust problem but often costs more than solid doors.

Plan #131030

Dimensions: 51' W x 41'10" D
Levels: 2
Square Footage: 2,470
Main Level Sq. Ft.: 1,290
Upper Level Sq. Ft.: 1,180
Bedrooms: 4
Bathrooms: 2½
Foundation: Crawl space, slab, basement, or walk-out basement
Materials List Available: Yes
Price Category: F

Images provided by designer/architect.

Master Bedroom

Master Bathroom

Entry

If high ceilings and spacious rooms make you happy, you'll love this gorgeous home.

Features:

- **Family Room:** An 18-ft. vaulted ceiling that's open to the balcony above, a corner fireplace, and a wall of windows make this room feel special.

- **Dining Room:** This formal room, which flows into the living room, also opens to the front porch and optional backyard deck.

- **Kitchen:** A bright breakfast room joins with this kitchen and opens to the backyard deck.

- **Master Suite:** You'll smile when you see the 11-ft. vaulted ceiling, stunning arched window, and two walk-in closets in the bedroom. A skylight lets natural light into the private bath, with its spa tub, separate shower, and dual-sink vanity.

- **Bedrooms:** To reach these three charming bedrooms, you'll admire the view into the family room below as you walk along the balcony hall.

Main Level Floor Plan

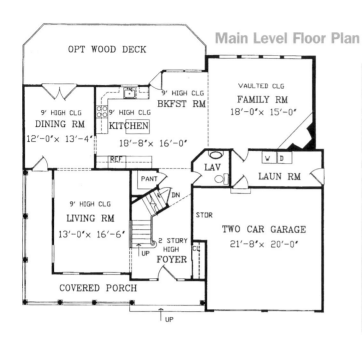

OPT WOOD DECK

9' HIGH CLG
DINING RM
12'-0" x 13'-4"

KITCHEN
18'-8" x 16'-0"
9' HIGH CLG

9' HIGH CLG
BKFST RM

VAULTED CLG
FAMILY RM
18'-0" x 15'-0"

REF

PANT

LAV

LAUN RM
W D

9' HIGH CLG
LIVING RM
13'-0" x 16'-6"

DN

UP

2 STORY
HIGH
FOYER

STOR

CL

TWO CAR GARAGE
21'-8" x 20'-0"

COVERED PORCH

UP

Upper Level Floor Plan

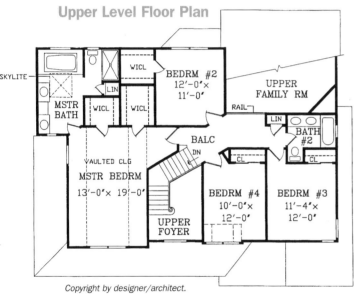

SKYLITE

MSTR BATH

WICL
LIN
WICL

WICL
LIN

BEDRM #2
12'-0" x 11'-0"

UPPER FAMILY RM

RAIL

LIN

BATH #2

VAULTED CLG
MSTR BEDRM
13'-0" x 19'-0"

BALC
DN

CL

CL

UPPER FOYER

BEDRM #4
10'-0" x 12'-0"

BEDRM #3
11'-4" x 12'-0"

Copyright by designer/architect.

Kitchen/Breakfast Area

Dining Room

Living Room

Kitchen/Breakfast Area

Plan #321057

Dimensions: 38' W x 39'4" D
Levels: 2
Square Footage: 1,524
Main Level Sq. Ft.: 951
Upper Level Sq. Ft.: 573
Bedrooms: 3
Bathrooms: 2½
Foundation: Basement
Materials List Available: Yes
Price Category: C

You'll love the comfort you'll find in this compact home, which also sports a practical design.

Features:

• Entry: This two-story entry is lit by a lovely oval window on the second-floor level.

• Living Room: A masonry fireplace sets a gracious tone, and the large windows and sliding door leading to the patio give natural lighting.

• Dining Room: The bay window here makes a perfect spot to place a table in this room.

• Kitchen: Situated between the living and dining rooms for convenience, the kitchen is designed as an efficient work area.

• Master Suite: A large walk-in closet and sliding doors to the patio are highlights of the bedroom, and the private bath features a double vanity.

• Upper Level: You'll find two walk-in closets in one bedroom and one in the other.

Upper Level Floor Plan

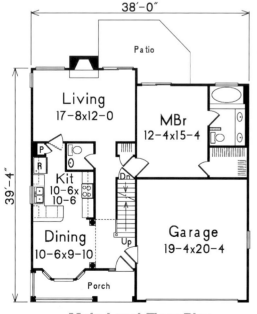

Main Level Floor Plan

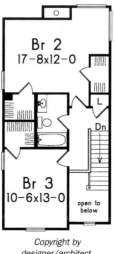

Plan #321051

Dimensions: 69'8" W x 46' D

Levels: 2

Square Footage: 2,624

Main Level Sq. Ft.: 1,774

Upper Level Sq. Ft.: 850

Bedrooms: 4

Bathrooms: 2½

Foundation: Basement

Materials List Available: Yes

Price Category: F

Images provided by designer/architect.

The dramatic exterior design allows natural light to flow into the spacious living area of this home.

Features:

- Entry: This two-story area opens into the dining room through a classic colonnade.

- Dining Room: A large bay window, stately columns, and doorway to the kitchen make this room both beautiful and convenient.

- Great Room: Enjoy light from the fireplace or the three Palladian windows in the 18-ft. ceiling.

- Kitchen: The step-saving design features a walk-in pantry as well as good counter space.

- Breakfast Room: You'll love the light that flows through the windows flanking the back door.

- Master Suite: The vaulted ceiling and bayed areas in both the bed and bath add elegance. You'll love the two walk-in closets and bath with a sunken tub, two vanities, and separate shower.

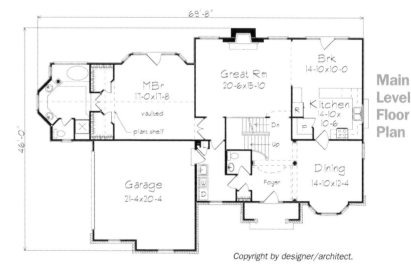

Main Level Floor Plan

Copyright by designer/architect.

Master Bath

Upper Level Floor Plan

Images provided by designer/architect.

Plan #371007

Dimensions: 72'10" W x 48'4½" D

Levels: 1

Square Footage: 1,944

Bedrooms: 4

Bathrooms: 2

Foundation: Slab
(crawl space option for fee)

Materials List Available: No

Price Category: D

Copyright by designer/architect.

Images provided by designer/architect.

Plan #371008

Dimensions: 86'4" W x 45'4" D

Levels: 2

Square Footage: 2,656

Main Level Sq. Ft.: 1,969

Upper Level Sq. Ft.: 687

Bedrooms: 4

Bathrooms: 3

Foundation: Slab
(crawl space option for fee)

Materials List Available: No

Price Category: F

Upper Level Floor Plan

Main Level Floor Plan

Copyright by designer/architect.

Main Level Floor Plan

Upper Level Floor Plan

Plan #381002

Dimensions: 68'4" W x 42'4" D
Levels: 2
Square Footage: 2,225
Main Level Sq. Ft.: 1,125
Upper Level Sq. Ft.: 1,100
Bedrooms: 3
Bathrooms: 2½
Foundation: Basement, crawl space
Materials List Available: Yes
Price Category: E

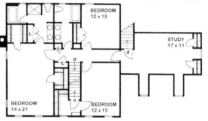

Main Level Floor Plan

Plan #381003

Dimensions: 63' W x 38'8" D
Levels: 2
Square Footage: 1,925
Main Level Sq. Ft.: 1,000
Upper Level Sq. Ft.: 925
Bedrooms: 3
Bathrooms: 2½
Foundation: Basement, crawl space
Materials List Available: Yes
Price Category: D

Upper Level Floor Plan

Plan #151172

Dimensions: 76'10" W x 53'4" D

Levels: 1½

Square Footage: 2,373

Upper Sq. Ft. (Bonus): 776

Bedrooms: 4

Bathrooms: 3

Foundation: Crawl space, slab (basement or daylight basement option for fee)

Materials List Available: Yes

Price Category: E

Images provided by designer/architect.

This lovely home easily accommodates a busy family, but it also allows expansion should you want a larger home in the future.

Features:

• **Great Room:** A wall of windows, fireplace, and media center are highlights in this spacious area.

• **Dining Room:** This lovely room is separated from the foyer by columns, and it opens to the kitchen.

• **Bedroom/Study:** Use the walk-in closet here for a computer niche if you can turn this room into a study.

• **Kitchen:** You'll love the angled snack bar in this well-designed step-saving kitchen.

• **Breakfast Room:** Large windows let natural light pour in, and a door leads to the rear grilling porch.

• **Master Suite:** The bedroom has a door to the rear porch and large corner windows, and the bath includes a corner whirlpool tub, shower with seat, two vanities, and walk-in closet.

Main Level Floor Plan

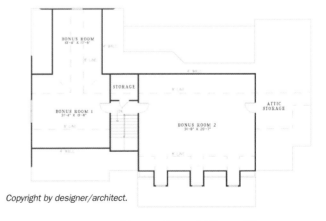

Copyright by designer/architect.

Upper Level Floor Plan

Plan #101005

Dimensions: 63' W x 57'2" D

Levels: 1

Square Footage: 1,992

Bedrooms: 3

Bathrooms: 2½

Foundation: Slab, crawl space, or basement

Materials List Available: Yes

Price Category: D

Images provided by designer/architect.

Rear View

This midsized ranch is accented with Palladian windows and inviting front porch.

Features:

- Ceiling Height: 9 ft. unless otherwise noted.

- Special Ceilings: Tray or vaulted ceilings adorn the living room, family room, dining room, and master suite.

- Kitchen: This bright and airy kitchen is designed to be a pleasure in which to work. It shares a big bay window with the contiguous breakfast room.

- Breakfast Room: The light streaming in from the bay window makes this the perfect place to linger with coffee and the Sunday paper.

- Master Suite: This exceptional suite has a sitting area and direct access to the deck, as well as a sitting area, full-featured bath, and spacious walk-in closet.

- Secondary Bedrooms: The other bedrooms each measure about 13 ft. x 11 ft. They have walk-in closets and share a "Jack-and-Jill" bath.

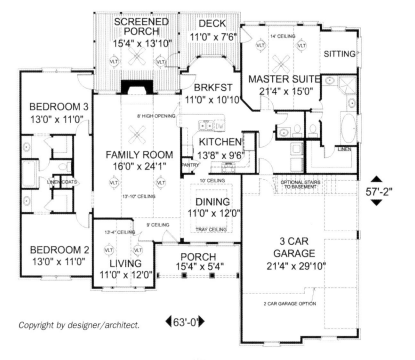

Copyright by designer/architect.

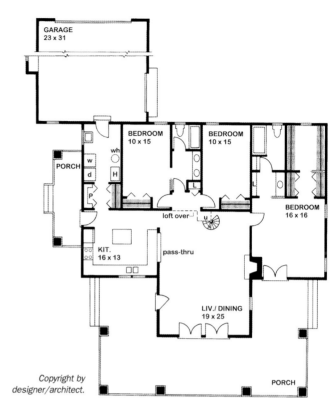

Plan #381010

Dimensions: 62' W x 87'6" D

Levels: 1

Square Footage: 1,905

Main Level Sq. Ft.: 1,905

Opt. Bonus Level Sq. Ft.: 320

Bedrooms: 3

Bathrooms: 2

Foundation: Crawl space

Materials List Available: Yes

Price Category: D

Images provided by designer/architect.

Copyright by designer/architect.

Main Level Floor Plan

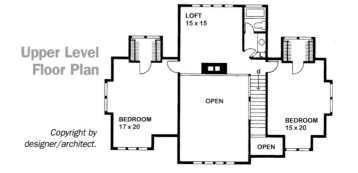

Upper Level Floor Plan

Plan #381019

Dimensions: 62' W x 49'6" D

Levels: 2

Square Footage: 2,535

Main Level Sq. Ft.: 1,740

Upper Level Sq. Ft.: 795

Bedrooms: 3

Bathrooms: 2½

Foundation: Crawl space

Materials List Available: Yes

Price Category: E

Images provided by designer/architect.

Copyright by designer/architect.

Plan #371004

Dimensions: 49'10" W x 53'6" D
Levels: 2
Square Footage: 1,815
Main Level Sq. Ft.: 1,245
Upper Level Sq. Ft.: 570
Bedrooms: 3
Bathrooms: 2
Foundation: Slab
(crawl space option for fee)
Materials List Available: No
Price Category: D

Images provided by designer/architect.

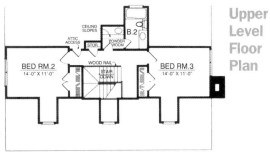

Main Level Floor Plan

Upper Level Floor Plan

Copyright by designer/architect.

Plan #381020

Dimensions: 69' W x 52' D
Levels: 1
Square Footage: 2,000
Bedrooms: 3
Bathrooms: 2
Foundation: Crawl space
Materials List Available: Yes
Price Category: D

Images provided by designer/architect.

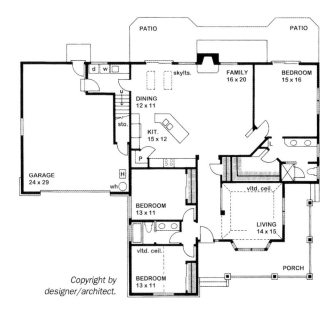

Copyright by designer/architect.

Plan #141038

Dimensions: 40'4" W x 38' D
Levels: 2
Square Footage: 1,668
Main Level Sq. Ft.: 1,057
Upper Level Sq. Ft.: 611
Bedrooms: 3
Bathrooms: 2½
Foundation: Basement with drive-under garage
Materials List Available: No
Price Category: C

If you're looking for the ideal plan for a sloping site, this could be the home of your dreams.

Features:

- Porch: Set a couple of rockers on this large porch so you can enjoy the evening views.
- Living Room: A handsome fireplace makes a lovely focal point in this large room.
- Dining Room: Three large windows over looking the sundeck flood this room with natural light.
- Kitchen: The U-shaped, step-saving layout makes this kitchen a cook's dream.
- Breakfast Room: With an expansive window area and a door to the sundeck, this room is sure to be a family favorite in any season of the year.
- Master Suite: A large walk-in closet and a private bath with tub, shower, and double vanity complement this suite's spacious bedroom.

Main Level Floor Plan

Upper Level Floor Plan

Copyright by designer/architect.

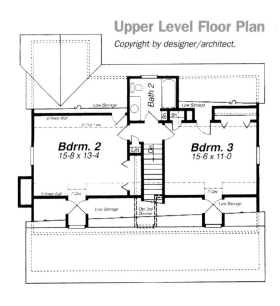

Plan #141037

Dimensions: 40'4" W x 44' D
Levels: 2
Square Footage: 1,735
Main Level Sq. Ft.: 1,045
Upper Level Sq. Ft.: 690
Bedrooms: 3
Bathrooms: 2½
Foundation: Basement with drive under garage
Materials List Available: No
Price Category: C

The contemporary design features inside this traditional-looking home will delight you.

Features:

- Living Room: The open floor plan adds an airy feeling to this spacious room, but you'll be cozy by the handsome fireplace.

- Dining Room: Natural light pours into this room, which looks out to the sundeck.

- Kitchen: The angled bar adds to the convenient layout here that speeds your tasks.

- Breakfast Room: With large windows and a door to the deck, this room will be a gathering spot.

- Master Suite: The large bedroom is complemented by a walk-in closet and bath with corner tub, separate shower, and double vanity.

- Upper Floor: The sitting area is a lovely feature on this floor, which has two large bedrooms, a bath, extra storage space, and a linen closet.

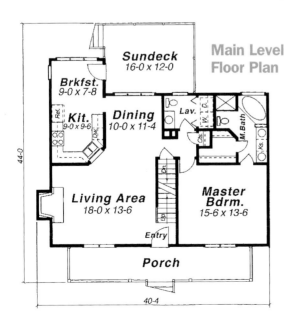

Main Level Floor Plan

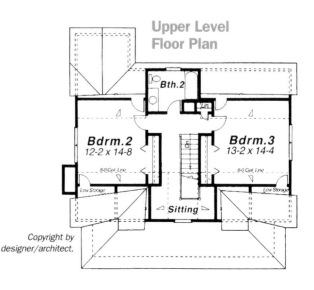

Upper Level Floor Plan

Copyright by designer/architect.

Plan #151170

Dimensions: 57' W x 64'4" D

Levels: 1

Square Footage: 1,965

Bedrooms: 4

Bathrooms: 2

Foundation: Crawl space, slab (basement or daylight basement option for fee)

Materials List Available: Yes

Price Category: D

The clean lines of the open floor plan and high ceilings match the classic good looks of this home's exterior.

Features:

- Foyer: The 10-ft. ceiling here sets the stage for the open, airy feeling of this lovely home.

- Dining Room: Set off by columns from the foyer and great room, this area is ideal for entertaining.

- Great Room: Open to the breakfast room beyond, this great room features a masonry fireplace and a door to the rear grilling porch.

- Breakfast Room: A deep bay overlooking the porch is the focal point here.

- Kitchen: Planned for efficiency, the kitchen has an angled island with storage and snack bar.

- Master Suite: A boxed ceiling adds elegance to the bedroom, and the bath features a whirlpool tub, double vanity, and separate shower.

Images provided by designer/architect.

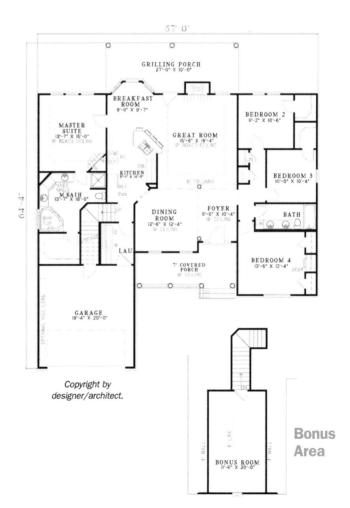

Copyright by designer/architect.

Bonus Area

Plan #151168

Dimensions: 66' W x 65'2" D
Levels: 1
Square Footage: 2,261
Bedrooms: 4
Bathrooms: 2½
Foundation: Basement, daylight basement, crawl space, or slab
Materials List Available: Yes
Price Category: E

The well-planned layout of this home will delight your family if you want plenty of space for group activities, as well as private times.

Features:

- **Great Room:** Natural light flows into this room, with its door to the covered porch and fireplace.

- **Outdoor Areas:** Relax and enjoy the rear covered porch, the patio, and the front covered porch.

- **Dining Room:** An 11-ft. boxed ceiling and entry columns let you decorate for formality here.

- **Kitchen:** The central island has space for working as well as a snack bar, and you'll love the pantry.

- **Breakfast Room:** Set the table in the deep bay to enjoy the morning light.

- **Master Suite:** A 9-ft. boxed ceiling and door to the rear porch make the bedroom luxurious, and the bath has two walk-in closets and a whirlpool tub, separate shower, and dual vanity.

Images provided by designer/architect.

Bonus Area

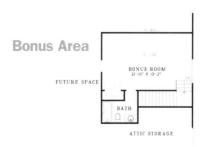

Plan #241025

Dimensions: 59'9" W x 44'3" D

Levels: 1

Square Footage: 1,487

Bedrooms: 3

Bathrooms: 2

Foundation: Slab

Materials List Available: No

Price Category: B

Images provided by designer/architect.

Copyright by designer/architect.

Plan #311026

Dimensions: 74' W x 49'8" D

Levels: 1

Square Footage: 1,916

Main Level Sq. Ft.: 1,916

Opt. Bonus Sq. Ft.: 1,245

Bedrooms: 3

Bathrooms: 2½

Foundation: Basement, crawl space, or slab

Materials List Available: Yes

Price Category: D

Images provided by designer/architect.

Rear View

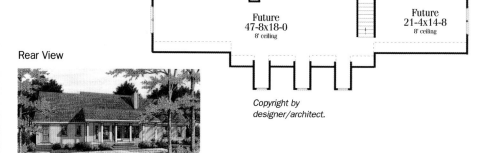

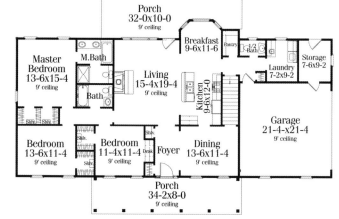

Bonus Area

Copyright by designer/architect.

Plan #241026

Dimensions: 59'11" W x 50'2" D
Levels: 1
Square Footage: 1,660
Bedrooms: 3
Bathrooms: 2
Foundation: Slab
Materials List Available: No
Price Category: C

Images provided by designer/architect.

Bonus Area

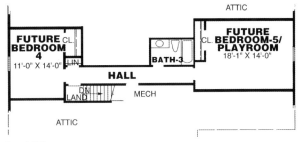

Copyright by designer/architect.

Plan #241029

Dimensions: 70' W x 53'5" D
Levels: 1
Square Footage: 2,074
Bedrooms: 3
Bathrooms: 2½
Foundation: Slab
Materials List Available: No
Price Category: D

Images provided by designer/architect.

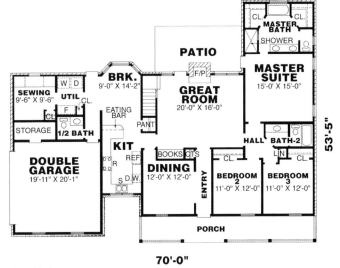

Copyright by designer/architect.

Plan #321041

Dimensions: 64' W x 34' D
Levels: 2
Square Footage: 2,286
Main Level Sq. Ft.: 1,283
Upper Level Sq. Ft.: 1,003
Bedrooms: 4
Bathrooms: 2½
Foundation: Basement
Materials List Available: Yes
Price Category: E

If you love the way these gorgeous windows look from the outside, you'll be thrilled with the equally gracious interior of this home.

Features:

- Entryway: This two-story entryway shows off the fine woodworking on the railing and balustrades.

- Living Room: The large front windows form a glamorous background in this spacious room.

- Family Room: A handsome fireplace and a sliding glass door to the backyard enhance the open design of this room.

- Breakfast Room: Large enough for a crowd, this room makes a perfect dining area.

- Kitchen: The angled bar and separate pantry are highlights in this step-saving design.

- Master Suite: Enjoy this suite's huge walk-in closet, vaulted ceiling, and private bath, which features a double vanity, tub, and shower stall.

Images provided by designer/architect.

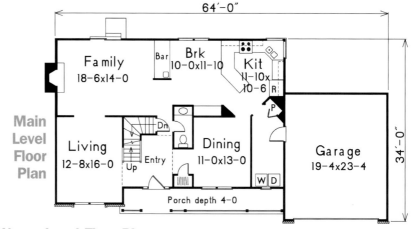

Main Level Floor Plan

Upper Level Floor Plan

Copyright by designer/architect.

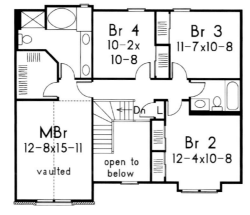

Plan #311003

Dimensions: 70'10" W x 65'4" D
Levels: 2
Square Footage: 2,428
Main Level Sq. Ft.: 2,348
Upper Level Sq. Ft.: 80
Bedrooms: 3
Bathrooms: 2½
Foundation: Crawl space, slab
Materials List Available: Y
Price Category: E

If you admire the gracious colonnaded porch, curved brick steps, and stunning front windows, you'll fall in love with the interior of this home.

Features:

- Great Room: Enjoy the vaulted ceiling, balcony from the upper level, and fireplace with flanking windows that let you look out to the patio.

- Dining Room: Columns define this formal room, which is adjacent to the breakfast room.

- Kitchen: A bayed sink area and extensive curved bar provide visual interest in this well-designed kitchen, which every cook will love.

- Breakfast Room: Huge windows let the sun shine into this room, which is open to the kitchen.

- Master Suite: The sitting area is open to the rear porch for a special touch in this gorgeous suite. Two walk-in closets and a vaulted ceiling and double vanity in the bath will make you feel completely pampered.

Main Level Floor Plan

- Patio
- Garage 24-6x21-2
- Bath 16-2x16-1
- Sitting 12-10x9-8
- Porch 20-2x10-0
- Owner's Bedroom 16-2x15-3
- Greatroom 18-0x17-2
- Laun. 7-3x6-0
- Kitchen 17-0x11-8
- Bedroom 11-3x14-3
- Bedroom 11-7x12-3
- Foyer
- Dining 14-0x12-6
- Brkfst 11-3x10-0
- Porch 36-0x8-2

Copyright by designer/architect.

Upper Level Floor Plan

- Open to Below
- Future 21-8x12-0
- Future 13-5x12-0
- Balcony
- Future 35-5x11-4

Plan #101025

Dimensions: 38' W x 34' D
Levels: 1½
Square Footage: 1,643
Main Level Sq. Ft.: 1,064
Upper Level Sq. Ft.: 579
Bedrooms: 3
Bathrooms: 2½
Foundation: Basement, crawl space
Materials List Available: No
Price Category: C

Images provided by designer/architect.

The layout of this home creates a beautiful interior while also making great use of the space.

Features:

• Family Room: A fireplace creates a cozy feeling in this central room, where the whole family is sure to gather.

• Dining Room: The wide windows let light pour into this room, and the door to the large rear deck makes it easy to dine outside.

• Kitchen: Steps into the kitchen and a skylight in the vaulted ceiling add an elegant touch to this step-saving design.

• Master Suite: The spacious bedroom is well matched to the luxury bath with a walk-in closet, tub, separate shower, and dual vanity.

• Upper Floor: Each bedroom has a lovely dormer that makes a play area or spot for quiet time, and both bedrooms feature large closets and easy access to a comfortable bath.

Main Level Floor Plan

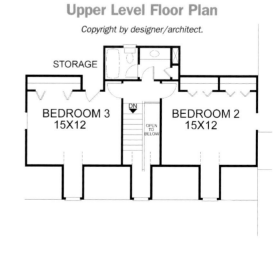

Upper Level Floor Plan

Copyright by designer/architect.

Plan #211011

Dimensions: 84' W x 54' D
Levels: 1
Square Footage: 2,791
Bedrooms: 3 or 4
Bathrooms: 2
Foundation: Slab or crawl space
Materials List Available: Yes
Price Category: F

Plenty of room plus an open, flexible floor plan make this a home that will adapt to your needs.

Features:

- Ceiling Height: 8 ft. unless otherwise noted.

- Living Room: This distinctive room features a 12-ft. ceiling and is designed so that it can also serve as a master suite with a sitting room.

- Family Room: The whole family will want to gather in this large, inviting family room.

- Morning Room: The family room blends into this sunny spot, which is perfect for informal family meals.

- Kitchen: This spacious kitchen offers a smart layout. It is also contiguous to the family room.

- Master Suite: You'll look forward to the end of the day when you can enjoy this master suite. It includes a huge, luxurious master bath with two large walk-in closets and two vanity sinks.

- Optional Bedroom: This optional fourth bedroom is located so that it can easily serve as a library, den, office, or music room.

SMARTtip

Types of Decks

Ground-level decks resemble a low platform and are best for flat locations. They can be the most economical type to build because they don't require stairs.

Raised decks can rise just a few steps up or meet the second story of a house. Lifted high on post supports, they adapt well to uneven or sloped locations.

Multilevel decks feature two or more stories and are connected by stairways or ramps. They can follow the contours of a sloped lot, unifying the deck with the outdoors.

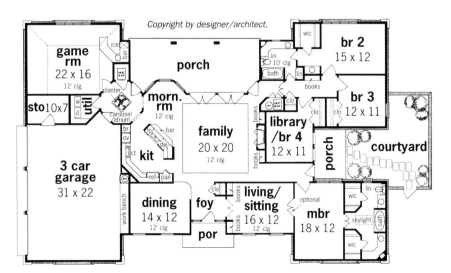

Plan #241033

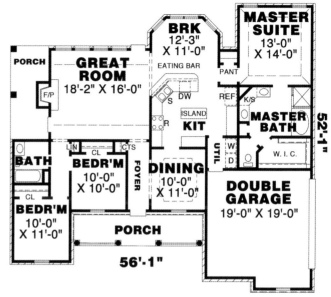

Images provided by designer/architect.

Dimensions: 56'1" W x 52'1" D

Levels: 1

Square Footage: 1,686

Bedrooms: 3

Bathrooms: 2

Foundation: Slab

Materials List Available: No

Price Category: C

Copyright by designer/architect.

Plan #311020

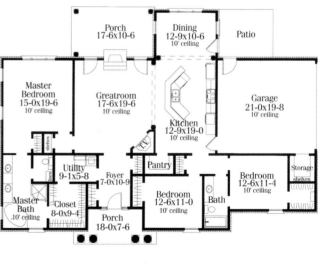

Main Level Floor Plan

Images provided by designer/architect.

Dimensions: 68' W x 49'5" D

Levels: 1

Square Footage: 1,833

Bedrooms: 3

Bathrooms: 2

Foundation: Basement, crawl space, or slab

Materials List Available: Yes

Price Category: D

Optional Stairs Location

Copyright by designer/architect.

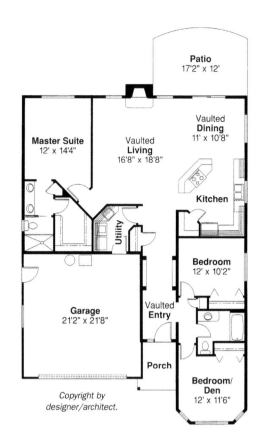

Plan #361011

Dimensions: 41' W x 60' D

Levels: 1

Square Footage: 1,632

Bedrooms: 3

Bathrooms: 2

Foundation: Crawl space

Materials List Available: No

Price Category: C

Images provided by designer/architect.

Copyright by designer/architect.

Plan #381021

Dimensions: 30' W x 30'8" D

Levels: 2

Square Footage: 1,425

Main Level Sq. Ft.: 1,025

Upper Level Sq. Ft.: 400

Bedrooms: 3

Bathrooms: 2

Foundation: Basement

Materials List Available: Yes

Price Category: B

Images provided by designer/architect.

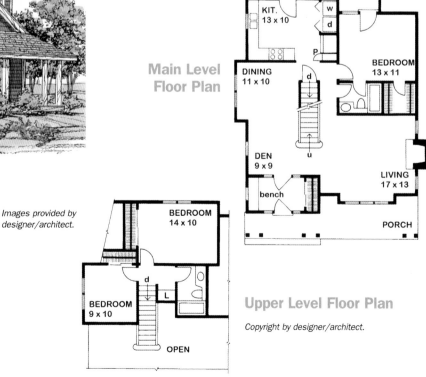

Main Level Floor Plan

Upper Level Floor Plan

Copyright by designer/architect.

Plan #161016

Dimensions: 59'4" W x 58'8" D
Levels: 2
Square Footage: 2,101
Main Level Sq. Ft.: 1,626
Upper Level Sq. Ft.: 475
Bedrooms: 3
Bathrooms: 2½
Foundation: Basement
Materials List Available: Yes
Price Category: D

Images provided by designer/architect.

You'll love the exciting roofline that sets this elegant home apart from its neighbors as well as the embellished, solid look that declares how well-designed it is—from the inside to the exterior.

Features:

- **Great Room:** Made for relaxing and entertaining, the great room is sunken to set it off from the rest of the house. A balcony from the second floor looks down into this spacious area, making it easy to keep track of the kids while they are playing.

- **Kitchen:** Convenience marks this well laid-out kitchen where you'll love to cook for guests and for family.

- **Master Bedroom:** A vaulted ceiling complements the unusual octagonal shape

of the master bedroom. Located on the first floor, this room allows some privacy from the second floor bedrooms. It is also ideal for anyone who no longer wishes to climb stairs to reach a bedroom.

Rear Elevation

Main Level Floor Plan

Upper Level Floor Plan

Plan #151004

Dimensions: 64'8" W x 62'1" D

Levels: 1

Square Footage: 2,158

Bedrooms: 4

Bathrooms: 2½

Foundation: Basement, slab, crawl space

Materials List Available: Yes

Price Category: D

Images provided by designer/architect.

You'll love the spacious feeling in this comfortable home designed for a family.

Features:

• Foyer: A 10-ft. ceiling greets you in this home.

• Great Room: A 10-ft. ceiling complements this large room, with its fireplace, built-in cabinets, and easy access to the rear covered porch.

• Dining Room: The 9-ft. boxed ceiling in this large room helps to create a beautiful formal feeling.

• Kitchen: The island in this kitchen is open to the breakfast room for true convenience.

• Breakfast Room: Morning light will stream through the bay window here.

• Master Suite: A 9-ft. pan ceiling adds a distinctive note to this room with access to the rear porch. In the bath, you'll find a whirlpool tub, separate shower, double vanities, and two walk-in closets.

Copyright by designer/architect.

Porch 31-4x7-8 9' ceiling

Master Bedroom 16-6x13-2 9' ceiling

Closet 6-6x8-0

Bedroom 11-4x11-4 9' ceiling

Kitchen/Dining 19-11x11-4 9' ceiling

Snack Bar

Laundry 6-7x5-10

M.Bath 12-4x11-0 9' ceiling

Bath

Greatroom 16-11x19-0 11' ceiling

Garage 21-3x19-2 9' ceiling

Storage

Bedroom 11-4x11-4 9' Ceiling

Porch 32-0x5-4 9' ceiling

Images provided by designer/architect.

Plan #311024

Dimensions: 56' W x 45' D

Levels: 1

Square Footage: 1,492

Bedrooms: 3

Bathrooms: 2

Foundation: Basement, crawl space, or slab

Materials List Available: Yes

Price Category: B

Rear View

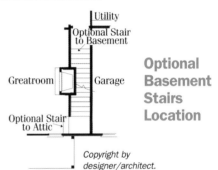

Utility

Optional Stair to Basement

Greatroom

Garage

Optional Stair to Attic

Optional Basement Stairs Location

Copyright by designer/architect.

OPTIONAL DECK 17 x 13

REAR PORCH 12 x 9

LOUNGE/OFFICE 8 x 13

MASTER BEDROOM 14 x 17

MSTR BATH 10 x 13

TUB

REAR PORCH 17 x 6

BREAKFAST 12 x 15

BEDROOM #3 13 x 14 9' CLG. HT. (TYP.)

CLOS.

HALL BATH

GREAT ROOM 17 x 20 12' CLG. HT.

ENTRY

TO BONUS UP

STORAGE

DOWN TO OPTIONAL BASEMENT

CLOSET 10 x 8

STORAGE

HALL

KITCHEN 12 x 15

UTILITY 8 x 10

TWO CAR GARAGE 24 x 26

ARCH ABOVE

COLUMN

BEAM

FOYER 14 x 6

HALF COLUMNS

NOTE: DASHED WALLS INDICATE OPTIONAL WALLS IF BASEMENT OPTION IS CHOSEN.

BEDROOM #2 13 x 14

CLOS.

FRONT PORCH 14 x 5

DINING 12 x 14 (VAULTED)

Images provided by designer/architect.

Plan #351007

Dimensions: 73'8" W x 53'2" D

Levels: 1

Square Footage: 2,251

Bedrooms: 3

Bathrooms: 2½

Foundation: Basement, crawl space, or slab

Materials List Available: Yes

Price Category: E

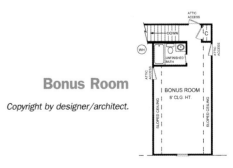

ATTIC ACCESS

DOWN

WH

UNFINISHED BATH

BONUS ROOM 8' CLG. HT.

Bonus Room

Copyright by designer/architect.

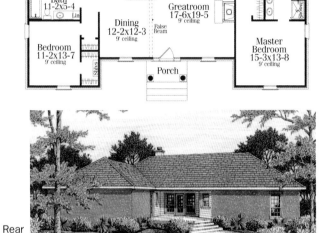

Copyright by designer/architect.

Plan #311028

Images provided by designer/architect.

Dimensions: 65' W x 56'8" D
Levels: 1
Square Footage: 1,847
Bedrooms: 3
Bathrooms: 2½
Foundation: Crawl space, slab
Materials List Available: Yes
Price Category: D

Rear View

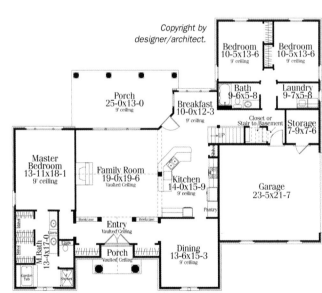

Plan #311023

Images provided by designer/architect.

Dimensions: 72'8" W x 61'4" D
Levels: 1
Square Footage: 2,339
Bedrooms: 3
Bathrooms: 2
Foundation: Basement, crawl space, or slab
Materials List Available: Yes
Price Category: E

Copyright by designer/architect.

Rear View

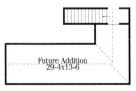

Future Addition
29-4x13-6

Bonus Area

Plan #151007

Dimensions: 54'2" W x 56'2" D

Levels: 1

Square Footage: 1,787

Bedrooms: 3

Bathrooms: 2

Foundation: Basement, crawl space, or slab

Materials List Available: Yes

Price Category: C

Images provided by designer/architect.

This compact, well-designed home is graced with amenities usually reserved for larger houses.

Features:

- Foyer: A 10-ft. ceiling creates unity between the foyer and the dining room just beyond it.

- Dining Room: 8-in. boxed columns welcome you to this dining room, with its 10-ft. ceilings.

- Great Room: The 9-ft. boxed ceiling suits the spacious design. Enjoy the fireplace in the winter and the rear-grilling porch in the summer.

- Breakfast Room: This bright room is a lovely spot for any time of day.

- Master Suite: Double vanities and a large walk-in closet add practicality to this quiet room with a 9-ft. pan ceiling. The master bath includes whirlpool tub with glass block and a separate shower.

- Bedrooms: Bedroom 2 features a bay window, and both rooms are convenient to the bathroom.

Copyright by designer/architect.

Plan #151010

Dimensions: 38'4" W x 68'6" D
Levels: 1
Square Footage: 1,379
Bedrooms: 3
Bathrooms: 2
Foundation: Crawl, slab
Materials List Available: Yes
Price Category: B

Images provided by designer/architect.

This French Country home has a spacious great room for friends and family to gather, but you can sneak away to the covered rear porch or patio off the master suite for cozy tête-à-têtes.

Features:

- **Entry:** Take advantage of the marvelous 10-ft. ceilings to hang groups of potted flowering plants.

- **Great Room:** This spacious room, with an optional 10-ft. boxed ceiling, is the place to curl up by the gas fireplace on a cold winter night.

- **Kitchen:** The kitchen includes a bar for casual meals, and is open to the breakfast room.

- **Rear Porch:** Enjoy leisurely meals on the covered rear porch that you can access from both the master suite and the breakfast room.

- **Master Suite:** The 10-ft. boxed ceiling in the bedroom and the master bath with a whirlpool tub and separate shower make this suite a luxurious place to end a long day.

Copyright by designer/architect.

Plan #101022

Dimensions: 66'2" W x 62' D

Levels: 1

Square Footage: 1,992

Bedrooms: 3

Bathrooms: 3

Foundation: Basement, crawl space, or slab

Materials List Available: Yes

Price Category: D

Images provided by designer/architect.

The exterior of this lovely home is traditional, but the unusually shaped rooms and amenities are contemporary.

Features:

- Foyer: This two-story foyer is open to the family room, but columns divide it from the dining room.

- Family Room: A gas fireplace and TV niche, flanked by doors to the covered porch, sit at the rear of this seven-sided, spacious room.

- Breakfast Room: Set off from the family room by columns, this area shares a snack bar with the kitchen and has windows looking over the porch.

- Bedroom 3: Use this room as a living room if you wish, and transform the guestroom to a media room or a family bedroom.

- Master Suite: The bedroom features a tray ceiling, has his and her dressing areas, and opens to the porch. The bath has a large corner tub, separate shower, linen closet, and two vanities.

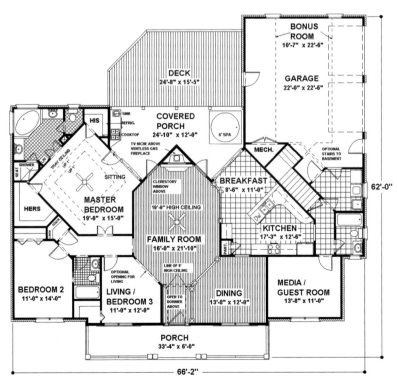

Copyright by designer/architect.

Plan #131046

Dimensions: 68' W x 57'6" D
Levels: 2
Square Footage: 2,245
Main Level Sq. Ft.: 1,720
Upper Level Sq. Ft.: 525
Bedrooms: 3
Bathrooms: 2½
Foundation: Crawl space, slab, or basement
Materials List Available: Yes
Price Category: F

You'll love the mixture of country charm and contemporary amenities in this lovely home.

Features:

- **Porch:** The covered wraparound porch spells comfort, and the arched windows spell style.

- **Great Room:** Look up at the 18-ft. vaulted ceiling and the balcony that looks over this room from the upper level, and then notice the wall of windows and the fireplace that's set into a media wall for decorating ease.

- **Kitchen:** This roomy kitchen is also designed for convenience, thanks to its ample counter space and work island.

- **Breakfast Room:** The kitchen looks out to this lovely room, with its vaulted ceiling and sliding French doors that open to the rear covered porch.

- **Master Bedroom:** A 10-ft-ceiling and a dramatic bay window give character to this charming room.

Images provided by designer/architect.

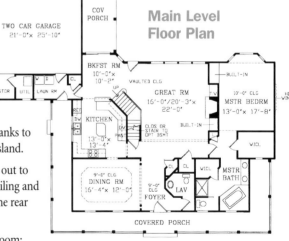

Main Level Floor Plan

Copyright by designer/architect.

Upper Level Floor Plan

Plan #221001

Dimensions: 87' W x 60' D

Levels: 1

Square Footage: 2,600

Bedrooms: 2

Bathrooms: 2½

Foundation: Basement

Materials List Available: No

Price Category: F

Images provided by designer/architect.

You'll love this traditional ranch for its unusual spaciousness and many comfortable amenities.

Features:

- **Great Room:** As you enter the home, you'll have a clear view all the way to the backyard through the many windows in this huge room. Built-ins here provide a practical touch, and the fireplace makes this room cozy when the weather's cool.

- **Kitchen:** This large kitchen has been thoughtfully designed to make cooking a pleasure. It flows into a lovely dining nook, so it's also a great place to entertain.

- **Master Suite:** Relaxing will come naturally in this lovely suite, with its two walk-in ` closets, private sitting area, and large, sumptuous bathroom that features a Jacuzzi tub.

- **Additional Bedrooms:** Located on the opposite side of the house from the master

suite, these bedrooms are both convenient to a full bath. You can use one room as a den if you wish.

Copyright by designer/architect.

Rear Elevation

Kitchen

Plan #151003

Dimensions: 51'6" W x 52'4" D

Levels: 1

Square Footage: 1,680

Bedrooms: 3

Bathrooms: 2

Foundation: Basement, slab, or daylight basement.

Materials List Available: Yes

Price Category: C

Images provided by designer/architect.

A lovely front porch, bay windows, and dormers add sparkle to this country-style home.

Features:

- Great Room: Perfect for entertaining, this room features a tray ceiling, wet bar, and a quiet screened porch nearby.

- Dining Room: This bayed dining room facing the front porch is cozy yet roomy enough for family parties during the holidays.

- Kitchen: This eat-in kitchen also faces the front and is ideal for preparing meals for any occasion.

- Master Suite: The tray ceiling here gives an added feeling of space, while the distance from the other bedrooms allows for all the privacy you'll need.

Copyright by designer/architect.

Plan #311031

Dimensions: 76' W x 63'6" D
Levels: 1
Square Footage: 2,034
Bedrooms: 3
Bathrooms: 2½
Foundation: Basement, crawl space, or slab
Materials List Available: Yes
Price Category: D

Images provided by designer/architect.

Rear View

Bonus Area

Plan #341037

Dimensions: 48' W x 62'4" D
Levels: 1
Square Footage: 1,784
Bedrooms: 3
Bathrooms: 2
Foundation: Crawl space, slab (basement option for fee)
Materials List Available: Yes
Price Category: C

Images provided by designer/architect.

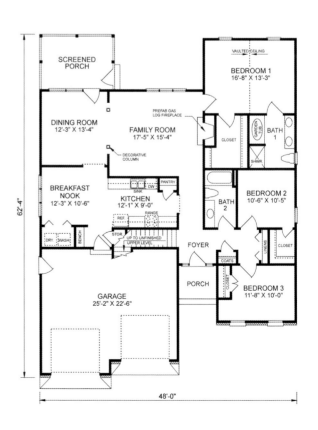

Plan #341040

Dimensions: 74'6" W x 50'6" D
Levels: 2
Square Footage: 2,624
Main Level Sq. Ft.: 1,800
Upper Level Sq. Ft.: 824
Bedrooms: 3
Bathrooms: 2½
Foundation: Crawl space, slab (basement option for fee)
Materials List Available: Yes
Price Category: F

Images provided by designer/architect.

Upper Level Floor Plan

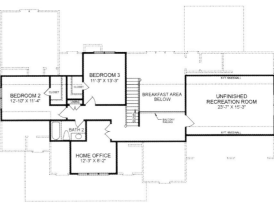

Copyright by designer/architect.

Plan #351001

Dimensions: 78'8" W x 51' D
Levels: 1
Square Footage: 1,855
Bedrooms: 3
Bathrooms: 2½
Foundation: Basement, crawl space, or slab
Materials List Available: Yes
Price Category: D

Images provided by designer/architect.

Kitchen/Great Room

Bonus Area

Copyright by designer/architect.

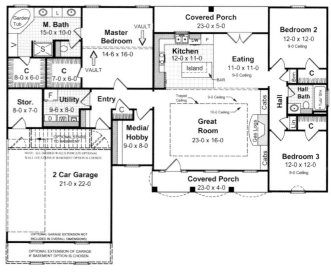

Images provided by designer/architect.

Copyright by designer/architect.

Plan #351002

Dimensions: 64' W x 45'10" D
Levels: 1
Square Footage: 1,751
Bedrooms: 3
Bathrooms: 2
Foundation: Basement, crawl space, or slab
Materials List Available: Yes
Price Category: C

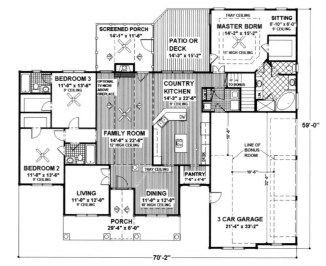

Images provided by designer/architect.

Copyright by designer/architect.

Plan #101009

Dimensions: 70'2" W x 59' D
Levels: 1
Square Footage: 2,097
Bedrooms: 3
Bathrooms: 3
Foundation: Slab
Materials List Available: No
Price Category: D

SMARTtip

Single-Level Decks

A single-level deck can use a strong vertical element, such as a pergola or a gazebo, to make it interesting. A simple and less-expensive option is a potted conical shrub or a clematis growing on a trellis.

Plan #301005

Dimensions: 71' W x 42' D

Levels: 1

Square Footage: 1,930

Bedrooms: 3

Bathrooms: 2

Foundation: Crawl space, slab

Materials List Available: Yes

Price Category: D

Images provided by designer/architect.

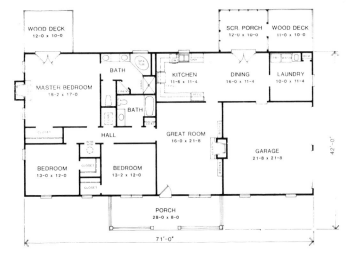

Copyright by designer/architect.

Plan #251001

Dimensions: 61'3" W x 40'6" D

Levels: 1

Square Footage: 1,253

Bedrooms: 3

Bathrooms: 2

Foundation: Crawl space, basement

Materials List Available: Yes

Price Category: B

Images provided by designer/architect.

Copyright by designer/architect.

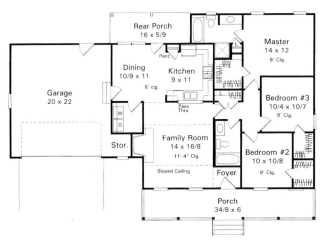

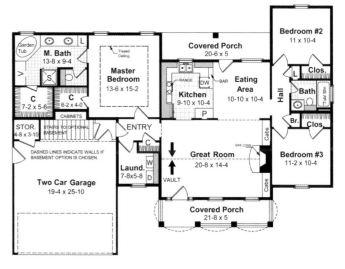

Plan #351005

Dimensions: 61' W x 47'4" D

Levels: 1

Square Footage: 1,501

Bedrooms: 3

Bathrooms: 2

Foundation: Basement, crawl space, or slab

Materials List Available: Yes

Price Category: C

Images provided by designer/architect.

Copyright by designer/architect.

Plan #351006

Dimensions: 72'10" W x 41' D

Levels: 1

Square Footage: 1,638

Bedrooms: 3

Bathrooms: 2

Foundation: Basement, crawl space, or slab

Materials List Available: Yes

Price Category: C

Images provided by designer/architect.

Stair Location for Basement Option

Copyright by designer/architect.

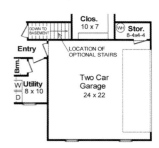

Plan #131050

Dimensions: 72'8" W x 47' D
Levels: 2
Square Footage: 2,874
Main Level Sq. Ft.: 2,146
Upper Level Sq. Ft.: 728
Bedrooms: 4
Bathrooms: 3
Foundation: Crawl space, slab, or basement
Materials List Available: Yes
Price Category: G

Images provided by designer/architect.

A gazebo and long covered porch at the entry let you know that this is a spectacular design.

Features:

- **Foyer:** This vaulted foyer divides the formal living room and dining room, setting the stage for guests to feel welcome in your home.

- **Great Room:** This large room is defined by several columns; a corner fireplace and vaulted ceiling add to its drama.

- **Kitchen:** An island work space

separates this area from the bayed breakfast nook.

- **Master Suite:** You'll have privacy in this main-floor suite, which features two walk-in closets and a compartmented bath with a dual-sink vanity.

- **Upper Level:** The two large bedrooms share a bath and a dramatic balcony.

- **Bonus Room:** Walk down a few steps into this large bonus room over the 3-car garage.

Main Level Floor Plan

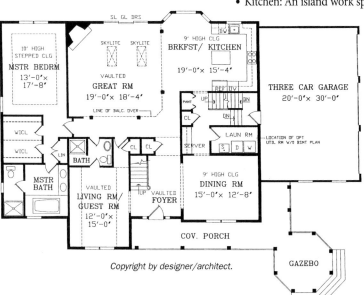

Copyright by designer/architect.

Upper Level Floor Plan

Rear Elevation

Plan #361001

Dimensions: 81' W x 68'11" D
Levels: 1
Square Footage: 3,055
Bedrooms: 3
Bathrooms: 3
Foundation: Basement, crawl space
Materials List Available: No
Price Category: G

Images provided by designer/architect.

You'll love the design elements that make it a joy to relax or entertain in this luxurious home.

Features:

- **Family Room:** This spacious room has a vaulted ceiling and a fireplace flanked by windows.

- **Living Room:** You'll find a fireplace here, too, and columns to set off the space from the foyer.

- **Den:** Enjoy the quiet in this isolated room.

- **Dining Room:** The angled wall adds interest, and the windows let light pour in during the day.

- **Dining Nook:** A door to the covered patio lets you serve meals outside or simply relax here.

- **Patio:** A door to a bath is ideal when you're having a party on this lovely covered patio.

- **Master Suite:** Double doors lead to the patio, and two walk-in closets and a bath with two vanities, a garden tub, and glass shower pamper you.

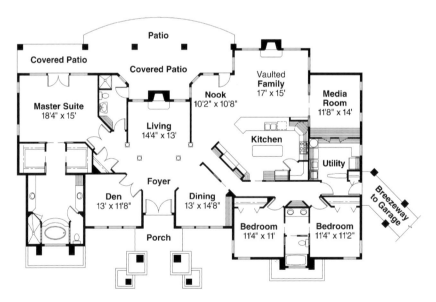

Copyright by designer/architect.

Plan #101024

Dimensions: 53' W x 57' D
Levels: 2
Square Footage: 3,135
Main Level Sq. Ft.: 1,600
Upper Level Sq. Ft.: 1,535
Bedrooms: 5
Bathrooms: 4
Foundation: Basement
Materials List Available: No
Price Category: G

Images provided by designer/architect.

The amenities and conveniences inside this elegant home are perfect for an active family.

Features:

- Family Room: A fireplace, 18-ft ceiling, and door to the rear deck attract everyone to this room.
- Dining Room: Columns separate this room and the living room from the foyer, adding formality.

- Kitchen: A central island, walk-in pantry, and door to the deck will delight the whole family.
- Media Room: A large closet and door to the adjoining bath allow real versatility here.
- Master Suite: You'll love the corner fireplace and doors to the upper rear deck that open from the sitting room, the tray ceiling in the bedroom, and the luxury bath that leads to the spacious exercise room, walk-in closet, and storage room.
- Additional Bedrooms: Huge closets and doors to adjacent baths make each room a pleasure.

Main Level Floor Plan

Copyright by designer/architect.

Upper Level Floor Plan

Plan #161030

Dimensions: 98'6" W x 61'5" D
Levels: 2
Square Footage: 4,562
Main Level Sq. Ft.: 3,364
Upper Level Sq. Ft.: 1,198
Bedrooms: 4
Bathrooms: 3½
Foundation: Basement
Materials List Available: Yes
Price Category: I

Images provided by designer/architect.

You'll be charmed by this impressive home, with its stone-and-brick exterior.

Features:

- Great Room: The two-story ceiling here adds even more dimension to this expansive space.

- Hearth Room: A tray ceiling and molding help to create a cozy feeling in this room, which is located so your guests will naturally gravitate to it.

- Dining Room: This formal room features columns at the entry and a butler's pantry for entertaining.

- Master Suite: A walk-in closet, platform whirlpool tub, and 2-person shower are only a few of the luxuries in the private bath, and tray ceilings and moldings give extra presence to the bedroom.

- Upper Level: A balcony offers a spectacular view of the great room and leads to three large bedrooms, each with a private bath.

Main Level Floor Plan

Upper Level Floor Plan

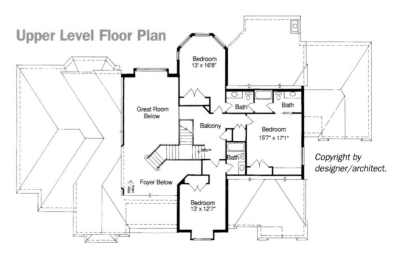

Copyright by designer/architect.

Plan #121069

Dimensions: 58' W x 59'4" D

Levels: 2

Square Footage: 2,914

Main Level Sq. Ft.: 1,583

Upper Level Sq. Ft.: 1,331

Bedrooms: 4

Bathrooms: 3½

Foundation: Basement

Materials List Available: Yes

Price Category: F

Images provided by designer/architect.

You'll love this design if you're looking for a home to complement a site with a lovely rear view.

Features:

- **Great Room:** A trio of lovely windows looks out to the front entry of this home. The French doors in this room open to the breakfast area for everyone's convenience.

- **Kitchen:** Designed to suit a gourmet cook, this kitchen includes a roomy pantry and an island with a snack bar.

- **Breakfast Area:** The boxed window here is perfect for houseplants or a collection of culinary herbs. A door leads to the rear porch, where you'll love to dine in good weather.

- **Master Suite:** On the upper level, the bedroom features a cathedral ceiling, two walk-in closets, and a window seat. The bath also has a cathedral ceiling and includes dual lavatories, a large dressing area, and a sunlit whirlpool tub.

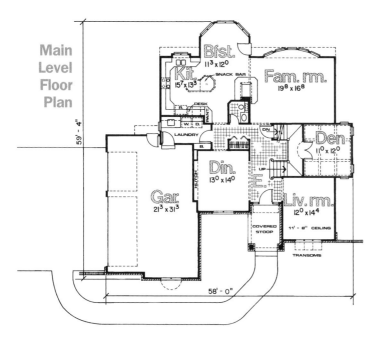

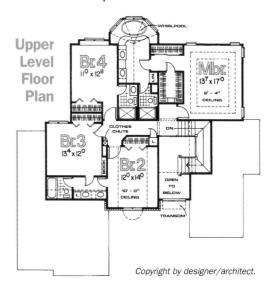

Copyright by designer/architect.

Images provided by designer/architect.

Plan #121061

Dimensions: 56' W x 52' D
Levels: 2
Square Footage: 3,025
Main Level Sq. Ft.: 1,583
Upper Level Sq. Ft.: 1,442
Bedrooms: 4
Bathrooms: 3 ½
Foundation: Basement
Materials List Available: Yes
Price Category: G

This large home with a contemporary feeling is ideal for the family looking for comfort and amenities.

Features:

• Entry: Stacked windows bring sunlight into this two-story entry, with its stylish curved staircase.

• Library: French doors off the entry lead to this room, with its built-in bookcases flanking a large, picturesque window.

• Family Room: Located in the rear of the home, this family room is sunken to set it apart. A spider-beamed ceiling gives it a contemporary feeling, and a bay window, wet bar, and pass-through fireplace add to this impression.

• Kitchen: The island in this kitchen makes working here a pleasure. The corner pantry joins a breakfast area and hearth room to this space.

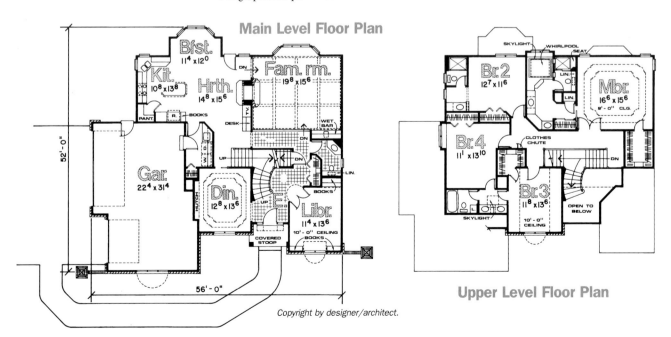

Main Level Floor Plan

Upper Level Floor Plan

Copyright by designer/architect.

Plan #161018

Dimensions: 74'4" W x 69'11" D

Levels: 2

Square Footage: 2,816
+ 325 Sq. Ft. bonus room

Main Level Sq. Ft.: 2,231

Upper Level Sq. Ft.: 624

Bedrooms: 3

Bathrooms: 3 full, 2 half

Foundation: Basement

Materials List Available: No

Price Category: F

If you love classic European designs, look closely at this home with its multiple gables and countless conveniences and luxuries.

Features:

- Foyer: Open to the great room, the 2-story foyer offers a view all the way to the rear windows.

- Great Room: A fireplace makes this room cozy in any kind of weather.

- Kitchen: This large room features an island with a sink, and an angled wall with French doors to the back yard.

- Dining Room: The furniture alcove and raised ceiling make this room both formal and practical.

- Master Suite: You'll love the quiet in the bedroom and the luxuries—a whirlpool tub, separate shower, and double vanities—in the bath.

- Basement: The door from the basement to the side yard adds convenience to outdoor work.

Rear View

Main Level Floor Plan

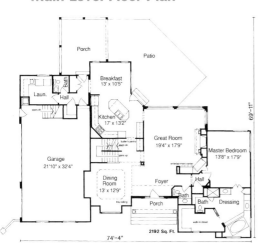

Upper Level Floor Plan

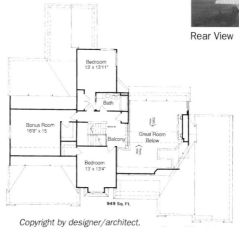

Copyright by designer/architect.

Foyer/Dining Room

Plan #121071

Dimensions: 72'8" W x 51'4" D
Levels: 2
Square Footage: 2,957
Main Level Sq. Ft.: 2,063
Upper Level Sq. Ft.: 894
Bedrooms: 4
Bathrooms: 4½
Foundation: Basement
Materials List Available: Yes
Price Category: F

Images provided by designer/architect.

You'll appreciate the mix of open public areas and private quarters that the layout of this home guarantees.

Features:

- Entry: From this entry, the formal living and dining rooms, as well as the great room, are all visible.

- Great Room: A soaring cathedral ceiling sets an elegant tone for this room, and the fireplace that's flanked with lovely transom-topped windows adds to it.

- Den: French doors from the great room lead to this den, where you'll find a generous bay window, a wet bar, and a decorative ceiling.

- Master Suite: On the main floor to give it needed privacy, this master suite will make you feel at home the first time you walk into it. The private bath has an angled ceiling and a whirlpool tub.

Main Level Floor Plan

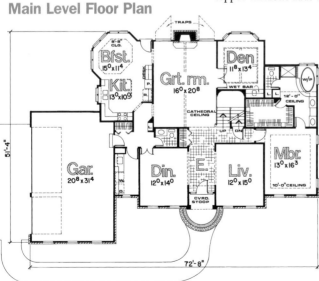

Upper Level Floor Plan

Copyright by designer/architect.

Plan #121062

Dimensions: 70' W x 62' D
Levels: 2
Square Footage: 3,448
Main Level Sq. Ft.: 2,375
Upper Level Sq. Ft.: 1,073
Bedrooms: 4
Bathrooms: 3½
Foundation: Basement
Materials List Available: Yes
Price Category: G

Images provided by designer/architect.

You'll love this design if you're looking for a comfortable home with dimensions and details that create a sense of grandeur.

Features:

• Entry: A soaring ceiling, curved staircase, and balcony that overlooks a tall plant shelf combine to create your first impression of grandeur in this home.

• Great Room: A transom-topped bowed window highlights this room, with its 11-ft., beamed ceiling, built-in wet bar, and see-through fireplace.

• Kitchen: Designed for the gourmet cook, this kitchen has every amenity you could desire.

• Breakfast Room: Adjacent to the great room and the kitchen, this gazebo-shaped breakfast area lights both the kitchen and hearth room.

Main Level Floor Plan

Upper Level Floor Plan

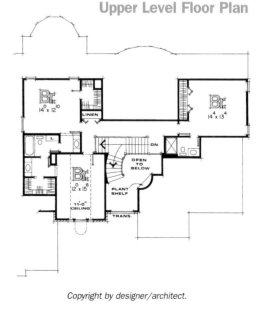

Copyright by designer/architect.

Plan #221022

Dimensions: 79' W x 55' D

Levels: 2

Square Footage: 3,382

Main Level Sq. Ft.: 2,376

Upper Level Sq. Ft.: 1,006

Bedrooms: 4

Bathrooms: 3½

Foundation: Basement

Materials List Available: No

Price Category: G

Images provided by designer/architect.

The traditional-looking facade of stone, brick, and siding opens into a home you'll love for its spaciousness, comfort, and great natural lighting.

Features:

- Ceiling Height: 9 ft.

- Great Room: The two-story ceiling here emphasizes the dimensions of this large room, and the huge windows make it bright and cheery.

- Sunroom: Use this area as a den or an indoor conservatory where you can relax in the midst of health-promoting and beautiful plants.

- Kitchen: This well-planned kitchen features a snacking island and opens into a generous dining nook where everyone will gather.

- Master Suite: Located on the main floor for privacy, this area includes a walk-in closet and a deluxe full bathroom.

- Upper Level: Look into the great room and entryway as you climb the stairs to the three large bedrooms and full bath on this floor.

Main Level Floor Plan

Upper Level Floor Plan

Plan #141022

Dimensions: 90' W x 93' D
Levels: 1
Square Footage: 2,911
Bedrooms: 3
Bathrooms: 2½
Foundation: Basement
Materials List Available: Yes
Price Category: F

Second-floor dormers accent this charming country ranch, which features a gracious porch that spans its entire front. A detached garage, connected by a covered extension, creates an impressive, expansive effect.

Features:

- **Living Room:** As you enter the foyer, you are immediately drawn to this dramatic, bayed living room.

- **Study:** Flanking the foyer, this cozy study features built-in shelving and a direct-vent fireplace.

- **Kitchen:** From a massive, partially covered deck, a wall of glass floods this spacious kitchen, breakfast bay, and keeping room with light.

- **Master Suite:** Enjoy the complete privacy provided by this strategically located master suite.

- **Guest Quarters:** You can convert the bonus room, above the garage, into a guest apartment.

Images provided by designer/architect.

Rear View

Copyright by designer/architect.

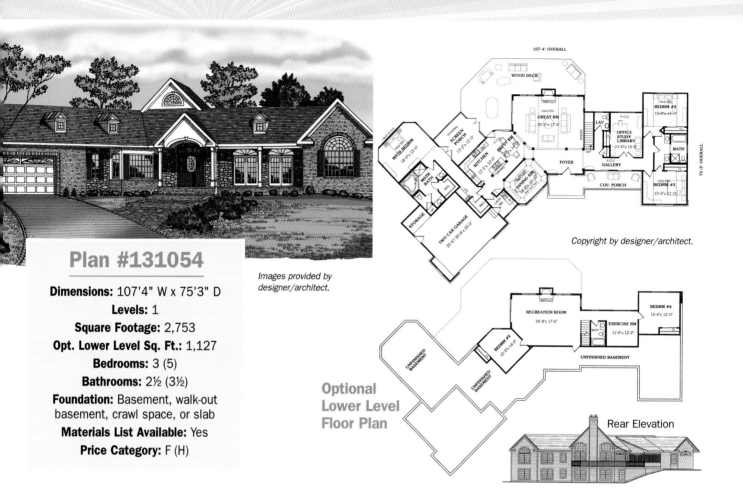

Plan #131054

Dimensions: 107'4" W x 75'3" D
Levels: 1
Square Footage: 2,753
Opt. Lower Level Sq. Ft.: 1,127
Bedrooms: 3 (5)
Bathrooms: 2½ (3½)
Foundation: Basement, walk-out basement, crawl space, or slab
Materials List Available: Yes
Price Category: F (H)

Images provided by designer/architect.

Copyright by designer/architect.

Optional Lower Level Floor Plan

Rear Elevation

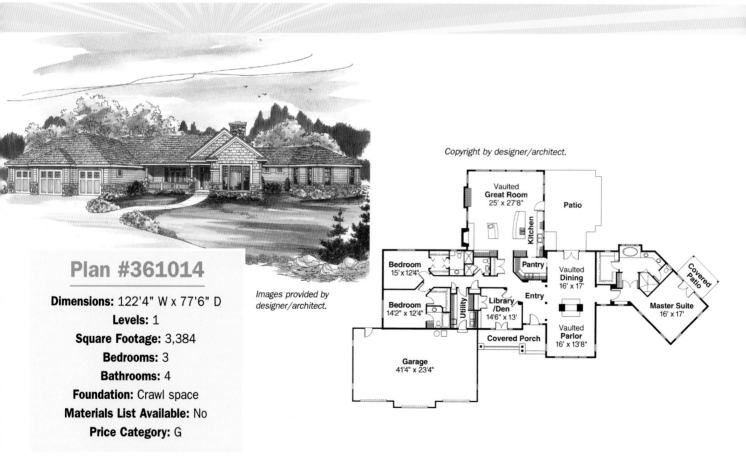

Plan #361014

Dimensions: 122'4" W x 77'6" D
Levels: 1
Square Footage: 3,384
Bedrooms: 3
Bathrooms: 4
Foundation: Crawl space
Materials List Available: No
Price Category: G

Images provided by designer/architect.

Copyright by designer/architect.

FIRST FLOOR PLAN

Copyright by designer/architect.

Images provided by designer/architect.

Plan #161062

Dimensions: 76' W x 68'1" D
Levels: 1
Square Footage: 2,904
Opt. Finished Basement Sq. Ft.: 1,905
Bedrooms: 3
Bathrooms: 2½
Foundation: Basement, walk-out basement
Materials List Available: Yes
Price Category: F

Rear Elevation

Optional Basement Level Floor Plan

Copyright by designer/architect.

Images provided by designer/architect.

Plan #311027

Dimensions: 79' W x 65'4" D
Levels: 1
Square Footage: 3,175
Bedrooms: 4
Bathrooms: 2½
Foundation: Basement, crawl space, or slab
Materials List Available: Yes
Price Category: G

Rear View

Main Level Floor Plan

Copyright by designer/architect.

Images provided by designer/architect.

Rear Elevation

Upper Level Floor Plan

Plan #161063

Dimensions: 81'8" W x 51' D
Levels: 2
Square Footage: 3,168
Main Level Sq. Ft.: 2,144
Upper Level Sq. Ft.: 1,024
Bedrooms: 5
Bathrooms: 3½
Foundation: Basement, walk-out basement
Materials List Available: Yes
Price Category: G

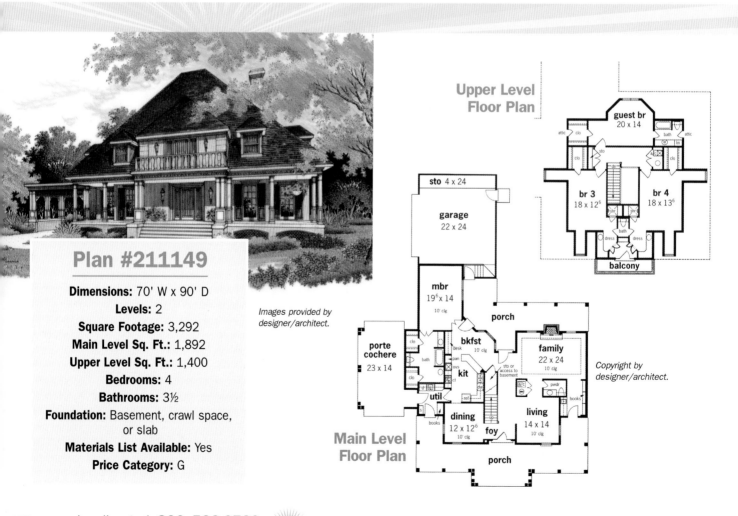

Upper Level Floor Plan

Main Level Floor Plan

Images provided by designer/architect.

Copyright by designer/architect.

Plan #211149

Dimensions: 70' W x 90' D
Levels: 2
Square Footage: 3,292
Main Level Sq. Ft.: 1,892
Upper Level Sq. Ft.: 1,400
Bedrooms: 4
Bathrooms: 3½
Foundation: Basement, crawl space, or slab
Materials List Available: Yes
Price Category: G

Plan #151191

Dimensions: 112' W x 81'8" D

Levels: 1½

Square Footage: 3,342

Opt. Bonus Sq. Ft.: 713

Bedrooms: 3

Bathrooms: 4½

Foundation: Crawl space, slab (basement or walk-out basement option for fee)

Materials List Available: Yes

Price Category: G

Images provided by designer/architect.

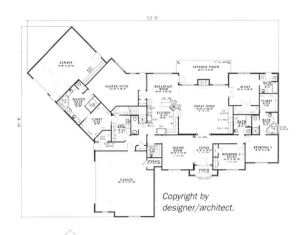

Copyright by designer/architect.

Bonus Area

Plan #241020

Dimensions: 82'6" W x 78'7" D

Levels: 2

Square Footage: 4,058

Main Level Sq. Ft.: 2,570

Upper Level Sq. Ft.: 1,488

Bedrooms: 4

Bathrooms: 3 full, 2 half

Foundation: Slab

Materials List Available: No

Price Category: I

Images provided by designer/architect.

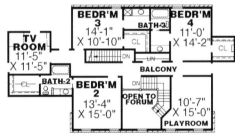

Upper Level Floor Plan

Copyright by designer/architect.

Main Level Floor Plan

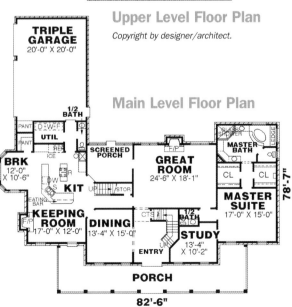

Plan #151190

Dimensions: 71' W x 75'10" D
Levels: 1
Square Footage: 3,033
Opt. Bonus Sq. Ft.: 572
Bedrooms: 4
Bathrooms: 3
Foundation: Crawl space, slab (basement or walk-out basement option for fee)
Materials List Available: Yes
Price Category: G

Images provided by designer/architect.

Bonus Area

Copyright by designer/architect.

Plan #241024

Dimensions: 54'8" W x 63' D
Levels: 2
Square Footage: 2,867
Main Level Sq. Ft.: 2,163
Upper Level Sq. Ft.: 704
Bedrooms: 4
Bathrooms: 3
Foundation: Slab
Materials List Available: No
Price Category: F

Images provided by designer/architect.

Main Level Floor Plan

Upper Level Floor Plan

Copyright by designer/architect.

Plan #151183

Dimensions: 67'8" W x 60' D
Levels: 2
Square Footage: 2,952
Main Level Sq. Ft.: 2,266
Upper Level Sq. Ft.: 686
Bedrooms: 4
Bathrooms: 3
Foundation: Crawl space, slab (basement or walk-out basement option for fee)
Materials List Available: Yes
Price Category: F

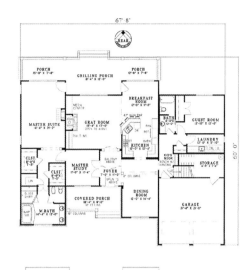

Main Level Floor Plan

Images provided by designer/architect.

Upper Level Floor Plan

Copyright by designer/architect.

Plan #151185

Dimensions: 58'10" W x 57' D
Levels: 2
Square Footage: 2,955
Main Level Sq. Ft.: 2,245
Upper Level Sq. Ft.: 710
Bedrooms: 4
Bathrooms: 3
Foundation: Crawl space, slab (basement or walk-out basement option for fee)
Materials List Available: Yes
Price Category: F

Images provided by designer/architect.

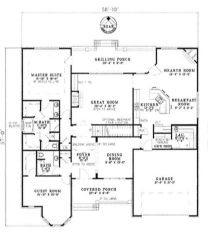

Main Level Floor Plan

Upper Level Floor Plan

Copyright by designer/architect.

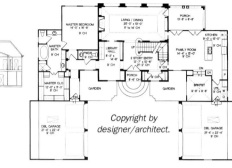

Rear
Elevation

*Images provided by
designer/architect.*

*Copyright by
designer/architect.*

Plan #121049

Dimensions: 82' W x 60'8" D
Levels: 2
Square Footage: 3,335
Main Level Sq. Ft.: 2,054
Upper Level Sq. Ft.: 1,281
Bedrooms: 4
Bathrooms: 3½
Foundation: Slab
Materials List Available: Yes
Price Category: G

Upper Level
Floor Plan

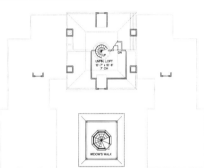

Plan #151180

Dimensions: 67'3" W x 68'6" D
Levels: 2
Square Footage: 3,167
Main Level Sq. Ft.: 2,486
Upper Level Sq. Ft.: 681
Bedrooms: 4
Bathrooms: 3
Foundation: Crawl space, slab
(basement or walk-out basement
option for fee)
Materials List Available: Yes
Price Category: G

Main Level
Floor Plan

*Images provided by
designer/architect.*

Upper Level
Floor Plan

*Copyright by
designer/architect.*

Plan #121072

Dimensions: 64' W x 53'4" D
Levels: 2
Square Footage: 3,031
Main Level Sq. Ft.: 1,640
Upper Level Sq. Ft.: 1,391
Bedrooms: 4
Bathrooms: 3½
Foundation: Basement
Materials List Available: Yes
Price Category: G

Images provided by designer/architect.

Main Level Floor Plan

Upper Level Floor Plan

Copyright by designer/architect.

Plan #321054

Dimensions: 70'6" W x 55'6" D
Levels: 2
Square Footage: 2,828
Main Level Sq. Ft.: 2,006
Upper Level Sq. Ft.: 822
Bedrooms: 5
Bathrooms: 3½
Foundation: Basement
Materials List Available: Yes
Price Category: F

Images provided by designer/architect.

Main Level Floor Plan

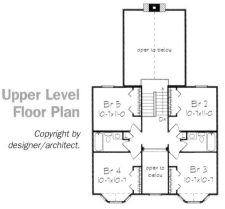

Upper Level Floor Plan

Copyright by designer/architect.

Plan #121065

Dimensions: 62' W x 55'4" D

Levels: 2

Square Footage: 3,407

Main Level Sq. Ft.: 1,719

Upper Level Sq. Ft.: 1,688

Bedrooms: 4

Bathrooms: 2½

Foundation: Basement

Materials List Available: Yes

Price Category: G

If you love contemporary design, the unusual shapes of the rooms in this home will delight you.

Features:

- **Entry:** You'll see a balcony from the upper level that overlooks this entryway, as well as the lovely curved staircase to this floor.

- **Great Room:** This room is sunken to set it apart. A fireplace, wet bar, spider-beamed ceiling, and row of arched windows give it character.

- **Dining Room:** Columns define this lovely octagon room, where you'll love to entertain guests or create lavish family dinners.

- **Master Suite:** A multi-tiered ceiling adds a note of grace, while the fireplace and private library create a real retreat. The gracious bath features a gazebo ceiling and a skylight.

Main Level Floor Plan

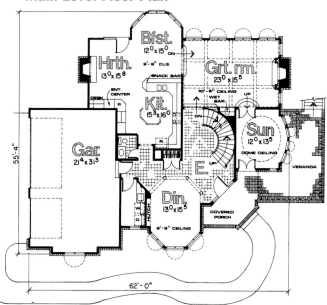

Upper Level Floor Plan

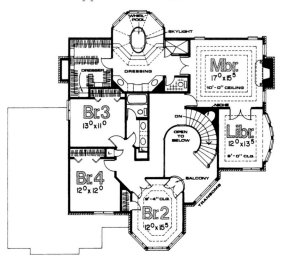

Plan #121081

Dimensions: 76'8" W x 68' D
Levels: 2
Square Footage: 3,623
Main Level Sq. Ft.: 2,603
Upper Level Sq. Ft.: 1,020
Bedrooms: 4
Bathrooms: 4½
Foundation: Basement
Materials List Available: Yes
Price Category: G

You'll love this impressive home if you're looking for perfect spot for entertaining as well as a home for comfortable family living.

Features:

- Entry: Walk into this grand two-story entryway through double doors, and be greeted by the sight of a graceful curved staircase.

- Great Room: This two-story room features stacked windows, a fireplace flanked by an entertainment center, a bookcase, and a wet bar.

- Dining Room: A corner column adds formality to this room, which is just off the entryway for the convenience of your guests.

- Hearth Room: Connected to the great room by a lovely set of French doors, this room features another fireplace as well as a convenient pantry.

Main Level Floor Plan

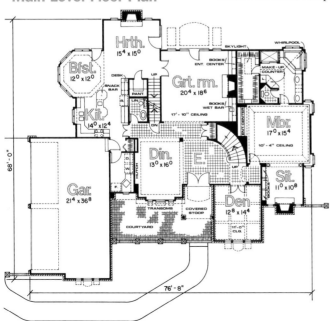

Upper Level Floor Plan

Plan #221023

Dimensions: 90'3" W x 65'8" D
Levels: 2
Square Footage: 3,511
Main Level Sq. Ft.: 1,931
Upper Level Sq. Ft.: 1,580
Bedrooms: 4
Bathrooms: 3½
Foundation: Basement
Materials List Available: No
Price Category: H

The curb appeal of this traditional two-story home, with its brick-and-stucco facade, is well matched by the luxuriousness you'll find inside.

Images provided by designer/architect.

Features:

- Ceiling Height: 9 ft.

- Family Room: This large room is open to the kitchen and the dining nook, making it an ideal spot in which to entertain.

- Living Room: The high ceiling in this room contributes to its somewhat formal feeling, and the fireplace and built-in bookcase allow you to decorate for a classic atmosphere.

- Master Suite: The bedroom in this suite has a luxurious feeling, partially because of the double French doors that are flanked by niches for displaying small art pieces or

collectables. The bathroom here is unusually large and features a walk-in closet.

- Upper Level: You'll find four bedrooms, three bathrooms, and a large bonus room to use as a study or play room on this floor.

Rear View

Main Level Floor Plan

Upper Level Floor Plan

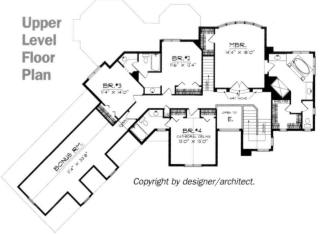

Copyright by designer/architect.

Plan #121082

Dimensions: 68'8" W x 60' D
Levels: 2
Square Footage: 2,932
Main Level Sq. Ft.: 2,084
Upper Level Sq. Ft.: 848
Bedrooms: 4
Bathrooms: 3½
Foundation: Basement
Materials List Available: Yes
Price Category: F

Images provided by designer/architect.

Enjoy the spacious covered veranda that gives this house so much added charm.

Features:

• Great Room: A volume ceiling enhances the spacious feeling in this room, making it a natural gathering spot for friends and family. Transom-topped windows look onto the veranda, and French doors open to it.

• Den: French doors from the entry lead to this room, with its unusual ceiling detail, gracious fireplace, and transom-topped windows.

• Hearth Room: Three skylights punctuate the cathedral ceiling in this room, giving it an extra measure of light and warmth.

• Kitchen: This kitchen is a delight, thanks to its generous working and storage space.

Main Level Floor Plan

Upper Level Floor Plan

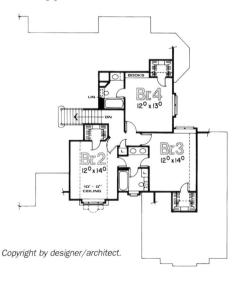

Copyright by designer/architect.

Outdoor Living

Many homeowners treat their decks and patios as another room of the house. To gain the fullest use of these areas, homeowners often add cooking areas, outdoor lighting centers, and other features to their outdoor living areas.

Cooking Centers

As the trend toward outdoor entertaining gains popularity, many people are setting up complete, permanent outdoor cooking centers, which often become the focus of their decks. Others content themselves with a simple grill. In either case, practical planning makes outdoor cooking efficient and more enjoyable, whether it is for everyday family meals or for a host of guests.

Decide exactly what features you want in the outdoor kitchen area. If you prefer to keep it simple with just a grill, you'll still have some decisions to make. Do you want a charcoal, gas, or electric unit? A charcoal grill is the least expensive option; a natural gas grill will cost you the most because it must be professionally installed. (Check with your local building department beforehand. Some localities will require a permit or may not allow this installation.) Extra features and accessories, such as rotisseries, woks, burners, smoke ovens, and warming racks increase the cost, too. Just remember: if you intend to locate the grill in a wooden enclosure, choose a model designed for this application.

In addition to a grill, do you want an elaborate setup with a sink, countertop, or a refrigerator? If so, these amenities will need protection from the elements. However, some refrigerators designed specifically for outdoor use can withstand harsh weather conditions. These high-end units are vented from the front and can be built-in or freestanding on casters.

Typically, outdoor refrigerators are countertop height (often the same size as standard wine chilling units that mount underneath a kitchen countertop) and have shelving for food trays or drinks and indoor storage for condiments. Outdoor refrigerators intended strictly for cold beer storage come with a tap and can accommodate a half-keg.

More Entertainment Options

Do you entertain frequently? Think about including a custom-designed wet bar and countertop in your plans. Besides a sink, the unit can offer enclosed storage for beverages, ice, and glasses, and the countertop will be handy for serving or buffets. But if you can't handle the expense, consider a prefabricated open-air wet bar. It can be portable or built-in. Some portable wet-bars feature: a sink that you can hook up to the house plumbing or a garden hose (with a filter), ice bins with sliding lids, sectioned compartments for garnishes, a speed rail for bottles, and a beverage-chilling well. Deluxe models may come with extra shelves and side-mounted food warmers.

Practical Advantages

Integrating a cooking center with your deck provides easy access to the kitchen indoors. Remember, elaborate outdoor kitchens require gas, electricity, and plumbing; it is easier and less expensive to run those lines when the cooking area isn't at the other end of the yard. However, you'll have to carefully plan the cooktop so that it isn't too close to the house and so that the heat and smoke are directed away from seating areas.

In general, when arranging any outdoor cooking area, be sure that all accoutrements—including serving platters, insulated mitts, basting brushes, spatulas, forks and knives, and long-handled tongs—are

readily at hand for the cook. And don't forget to plan enough surface room for setting down a tray of spices, condiments, sauces, and marinade, or swiftly unloading a plate of hot grilled meats or vegetables. Because you'll have to juggle both uncooked and cooked foods, a roll-around cart may suffice. For safety's sake, always keep the pathway from the kitchen to the outdoor cooking area clear, and as a precaution, keep a fire extinguisher nearby.

Countertop Options

Any outdoor countertop should be able to withstand varying weather conditions. Rain, snow, and bright sunlight will pit and rot some materials, so choose carefully. Tile, concrete, or natural stone (such as slate) are the best options. Concrete can be tinted and inlaid for decorative effect but, like stone, it is porous and must be sealed. Avoid a surface laminate unless it's for use in a well-protected area because exposure to the weather causes the layers to separate. Solid-surfacing material is more durable, but it's better left to a sheltered location.

Think twice about using teak or other decay-resistant woods for a countertop. Although these woods weather handsomely, they are not sealed against bacteria, so you can't expose them directly to food. If you do select a wooden countertop, insert a tray or plate under any uncooked meats and vegetables. Decay-resistant woods such as redwood, cedar, teak, or mahogany are, however, good choices for outdoor cabinetry. Other types of wood will have to be sealed and stained or painted. Another option is oriented-strand board (OSB) that is weatherproof.

Side burners, opposite, help you prepare an entire meal at the grill.

Small, outdoor refrigerators, far right, save steps when entertaining outdoors.

What to Look for in a Grill

A grill cover should fit snugly. Some covers have adjustable lids, which allow airflow so that food cooks slowly and evenly.

Adjustable controls allow you to control the heat level of burners.

Side burners let you sauté toppings, simmer sauces, or fry side dishes. A side burner can come with a protective cover that also doubles as an extra landing surface for utensils.

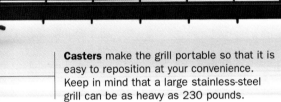

A towel hook is a useful detail on a grill. Check for other extras, such as utility hooks for utensils, condiment compartments on side shelves, or warming racks.

Casters make the grill portable so that it is easy to reposition at your convenience. Keep in mind that a large stainless-steel grill can be as heavy as 230 pounds.

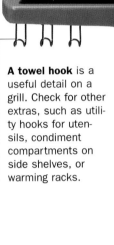

Grill Checklist

Look for these important features:

■ **An electronic push-button ignition.** It starts better because it emits a continuous spark; knob igniters emit two to three sparks per turn.

■ **Insulated handles.** These are convenient because they don't get hot. Otherwise you'll need a grilling mitt to protect yourself from burns when using the controls.

■ **Easy access to the propane tank.** Some gas grills feature tilt-out bins, which make connecting and changing the tank a snap.

Large grills, left, offer multiple, individually controlled burners, warming trays, and storage.

Outdoor Lighting

In terms of lighting and electricity, a deck can be as fully functional as any room inside your house. And if you add outdoor lighting, you will find that you get much more use out of your deck, patio, or outdoor living area. In addition to natural light, a pleasing combination of even, diffused general (also called "ambient") light, as well as accent and task lighting from artificial sources, can illuminate your deck for use after the sun goes down.

Developing an outdoor lighting plan differs from developing an interior lighting scheme. The basics are the same, but exterior lighting relies heavily on low-voltage systems. These operate on 12 volts as opposed to the 120 volts of a standard line system. A good outdoor plan will combine both types of lighting.

Developing a Lighting Plan

First decide how much light you need and where it should go. Besides general overall illumination, locate fixtures near activity zones: the food preparation and cooking area, the wet bar, or wherever you plan to set up drinks, snacks, or a buffet when you entertain. Be sure that there is adequate light near the dining table, conversation areas, and recreational spots, such as the hot tub, if you plan to use them in the evening. You may want separate switches for each one, and you might consider dimmers; you don't need or want the same intensity of light required for barbecuing as you do for relaxing in the hot tub.

What type of fixtures should you choose? That partly depends on the location. Near a wall or under a permanent roof, sconces and ceiling fixtures will provide light while staying out of the way. For uncovered areas, try post or railing lamps.

Lighting the Way

Walkways and staircases need lighting for safety. There are a number of practical options: path lights (if the walkway is ground level), brick lights that can be inserted into your walls near the steps, and railing fixtures that can be tucked under

Selecting a Grill

It's not the size of the grill that counts, it's whether you have the space on the deck to accommodate it. Measure the intended cooking area before shopping, and take those measurements with you to the store or home center. Depending upon your budget, you may also want to consider one of the high-end units that luxury kitchen appliance manufacturers have introduced into the marketplace. They have lots of features and are built to last, but they are expensive and must be professionally installed. Serious cooks like them.

Think about the grill's location in relationship to the traffic, dining, and lounging zones. How far away will the grill be from the house? If your space is limited or if you expect a lot of activity—large crowds or kids underfoot—you may have to relegate the cooking area to someplace close, but not on the deck itself. Also consider how many people you typically cook for. Check out the grill's number of separate heating zones (there should be at least two) before buying it. If you have a large family or entertain frequently, you'll need a grill that can accommodate large quantities or different types of food at the same time.

Grill Features

Because you'll probably be using your new grill more often and with a greater variety of foods, buy one that has some important basic options. Are there any special features that you'd like with your grill? Extra burners, a rotisserie, a warming rack, or a smoker? What do you like to cook? Today, you can prepare more than hamburgers and barbecued chicken on your grill. In fact, tasty, healthy grilled food is popular year-round, and so you may be cooking outdoors from spring through late fall.

Many models now come with two burners, but larger ones have more. The burners should have adjustable temperature controls that will allow you to set the heat at high, medium, or low. Ideally, a unit should sustain an even cooking temperature and provide at least 33,000 Btu (British thermal units, the measurement for heat output) when burners are set on high. Generally, the larger the grill the higher the Btu output. A slow-roasting setting is optional on some models. Another good option is a gauge that records the temperature when the lid is closed. If you enjoy sauces, make sure your grill comes with adjustable side burners, which can accommodate pots.

deck railings or steps. Less-functional but more-decorative lighting such as post lamps can provide illumination for high traffic areas; sconces can be effective on stair landings or near doors. Walk lights also provide a needed measure of safety.

Don't forget about areas that may call for motion-sensitive floodlights, such as entrances into the house and garage, underneath a raised deck, and deep yards are all excellent locations for floodlights. Keep these fixtures on separate switches so that they don't interfere with the atmosphere you want to create while you are using the deck.

Railing- and bench-mounted lights, above, provide a subtle lighting option. They illuminate small areas without casting glare into the eyes of those on the deck.

Step lights, right, are a must for stairs leading down into the yard. Use these lights sparingly as shown. A little outdoor light goes a long way.

Provide a lighted backdrop to your outdoor living area by installing yard and garden lighting, above. Use lights to line walks, accent flower beds, or highlight a fountain or pond.

Adding Accent Light

Are there any noteworthy plantings or objects in your garden that you can highlight? By using in-ground accent lighting or spotlights, you can create dramatic nighttime effects or a focal point. Artful lighting can enhance the ambience of your deck by drawing attention to the shape of a handsome tree, a garden statue, a fountain or pond, or an outdoor pool.

Choosing the Right Fixture

If your home is formal, traditional fixtures in brass or an antique finish will complement the overall scheme nicely. For a modern setting, choose streamlined fixtures with matte or brushed-metal finishes. Landscape lighting is often utilitarian, but it is intended to blend unobtrusively into the landscape; the light, not the fixture, is noticeable. Path and post lighting, however, can be decorative and comes in a variety of styles and finishes, from highly polished metals to antique and matte looks.

Depending on the lighting system you buy, you may be able to install the fixtures yourself. But working with electricity does pose technical, code, and safety concerns. It's probably best to hire a qualified professional for the installation. For complex projects, you may also want to consult a landscape lighting professional. Home centers sometimes provide this type of expertise. If you decide to plot a design yourself, remember not to overlight the deck.

Other Considerations

As you plan to install deck lighting, think about the space's other electrical or wiring needs. If there is an outdoor kitchen, a grill area, or a bar, you may want outlets for a refrigerator or small appliances. You might include additional outlets for a stereo or speakers, or even a TV. Don't overlook a phone jack for the modem on your laptop computer. Some decking systems come prewired and are ready to be hooked up. So with forethought, you can incorporate everything you need into your outdoor living plans.

Water Features

There is nothing like the sight and sound of water to add a refreshing quality to your deck or patio. In fact, water can be a dynamic element in both the deck's design and its function. It can be in the form of one of the ultimate outdoor luxuries—a pool, spa, or hot tub—or in a water feature such as a fountain, waterfall, or pond. In any case, because of the relaxing qualities of water, you should consider integrating some form of it into your plans.

Planning a deck or patio near a pool requires taking the size and shape of the pool into consideration. In most cases, the pool will be a focal point in a landscape, so the design of the surrounding deck, including the flooring patterns, materials, and other details, can either enhance or detract

from its appeal. Aside from looks, think about how a pool deck will function.

Adding a Spa. Another way to enjoy water with your deck is with a soothing spa. Requiring less space than a pool, a spa uses hydrojets to move heated water. One type, a hot tub, is a barrel-like enclosure filled with water. It may or may not have jets and usually features an adjustable but simple bench. It offers a deeper soak—as much as 4 feet—than other types of spas, and many homeowners like the look of an aboveground hot tub's wood exterior. The tub comes with a vinyl or plastic liner.

A built-in spa is set into a deck or the ground (in-ground). It can be acrylic, or it can be constructed of poured concrete, gunite, or shotcrete. A spa can stand alone or be integrated with a large pool.

A portable spa is a completely self-contained unit that features an acrylic shell, a wooden surround, and all of the equipment needed to heat and move the water. A small portable spa costs less than an in-ground unit, and it runs on a standard 120-volt circuit. You can locate a portable spa on a concrete slab. But you can also install one on the deck. Just make sure there is proper structural support underneath the deck to sustain the additional weight of the unit, the water, and bathers.

Small, portable spas, opposite, are self-contained units that run on standard line-voltage electricity. Check weight restrictions if installing a spa on a deck.

Spas complete an outdoor living area, above. This sunken spa is a natural complement to the nearby pool and to the large multilevel deck.

Plan #121047

Dimensions: 67'8" W x 57' D
Levels: 2
Square Footage: 3,072
Main Level Sq. Ft.: 2,116
Upper Level Sq. Ft.: 956
Bedrooms: 4
Bathrooms: 3½
Foundation: Slab
Materials List Available: Yes
Price Category: G

Images provided by designer/architect.

A long porch and a trio of roof dormers give this gracious home a sophisticated country look.

Features:

- Ceiling Height: 8 ft. unless otherwise noted.

- Balcony: This balcony overlooks the entry and the staircase hall.

- Dining Room: Columns and a cased opening lend elegance, making this the perfect venue for stylish dinner parties.

- Family Room: A cathedral ceiling gives this room a light and airy feel. The handsome fireplace framed by windows is sure to become a favorite family gathering place.

- Master Bedroom: This architecturally distinctive bedroom features a bayed sitting area and a tray ceiling.

- Bedrooms: One of the bedrooms enjoys a private bath, making it a perfect guest room. Other bedrooms feature walk-in closets.

Main Level Floor Plan

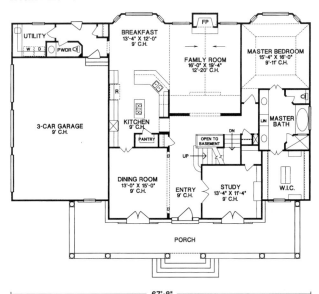

Upper Level Floor Plan

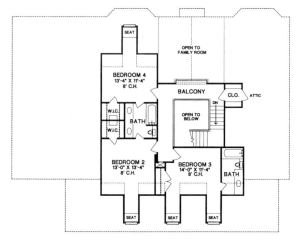

Copyright by designer/architect.

Plan #271096

Dimensions: 66' W x 98' D

Levels: 2

Square footage: 3,190

Main Level Sq. Ft.: 2,152

Upper Level Sq. Ft.: 1,038

Bedrooms: 4

Bathrooms: 3½

Foundation: Crawl space

Materials List Available: No

Price Category: G

Images provided by designer/architect.

This traditional home contains quite possibly everything you're dreaming of, and even more!

Features:

- **Formal Rooms:** These living and dining rooms flank the entry foyer, making a large space for special occasions.

- **Family Room:** A fireplace is the highlight of this spacious area, where the kids will play with their friends and watch TV.

- **Kitchen:** A central island makes cooking a breeze. The adjoining dinette is a sunny spot for casual meals.

- **Master Suite:** A large sleeping area is followed by a deluxe private bath with a whirlpool tub and a walk-in closet. Step through a French door to the backyard, which is big enough to host a deck with an inviting hot tub!

- **Guest Suite:** One bedroom upstairs has its own private bath, making it perfect for guests.

- A future room above the garage awaits your decision on how to use it.

Copyright by designer/architect.

Plan #171010

Dimensions: 76' W x 61' D
Levels: 1
Square Footage: 1,972
Bedrooms: 3
Bathrooms: 2
Foundation: Slab, crawl space
Materials List Available: Yes
Price Category: D

Images provided by designer/architect.

SMARTtip

Testing Grill Hoses for Leaks

Hoses on gas grills can develop leaks. To check the hose on your gas grill, brush soapy water over it. If you see any bubbles, turn off the gas valve and disconnect the tank. Then replace the hose.

Main Level Floor Plan

Plan #241013

Dimensions: 68' W x 46' D
Levels: 2
Square Footage: 2,779
Main Level Sq. Ft.: 1,918
Upper Level Sq. Ft.: 861
Bedrooms: 4
Bathrooms: 3½
Foundation: Slab
Materials List Available: No
Price Category: F

Images provided by designer/architect.

Upper Level Floor Plan

Copyright by designer/architect.

Plan #191033

Dimensions: 68'4" W x 80' D

Levels: 1

Square Footage: 2,214

Bedrooms: 3

Bathrooms: 2

Foundation: Crawl space, slab

Materials List Available: No

Price Category: E

Images provided by designer/architect.

Rear Elevation

Copyright by designer/architect.

Plan #191037

Dimensions: 57'4" W x 65' D

Levels: 1

Square Footage: 1,575

Bedrooms: 3

Bathrooms: 2

Foundation: Crawl space, slab

Materials List Available: No

Price Category: C

Images provided by designer/architect.

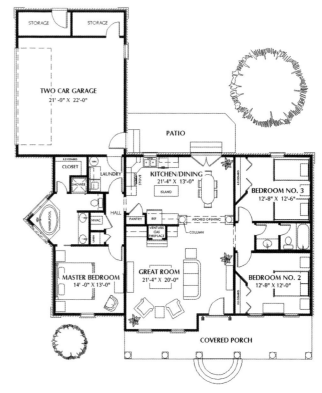

Copyright by designer/architect.

Plan #161017

Dimensions: 61' W x 37'6" D

Levels: 2

Square Footage: 2,653

Main Level Sq. Ft.: 1,365

Upper Level Sq. Ft.: 1,288

Bedrooms: 4

Bathrooms: 2½

Foundation: Basement

Materials List Available: No

Price Category: F

If a traditional look makes you feel comfortable, you'll love this spacious, family-friendly home.

Features:

- Family Room: Accessorize with cozy cushions to make the most of this sunken room. Windows flank the fireplace, adding warm, natural light. Doors leading to the rear deck make this room a family "headquarters."

- Living and Dining Rooms: These formal rooms open to each other, so you'll love hosting gatherings in this home.

- Kitchen: A handy pantry fits well with the traditional feeling of this home, and an island adds contemporary convenience.

- Master Suite: Relax in the whirlpool tub in your bath and enjoy the storage space in the two walk-in closets in the bedroom.

Images provided by designer/architect.

Main Level Floor Plan

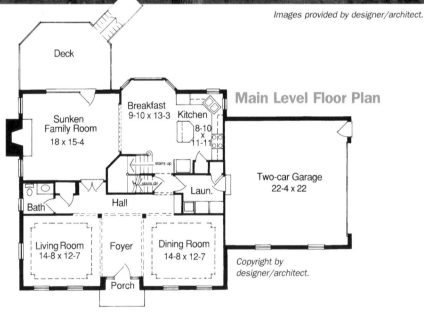

Copyright by designer/architect.

Upper Level Floor Plan

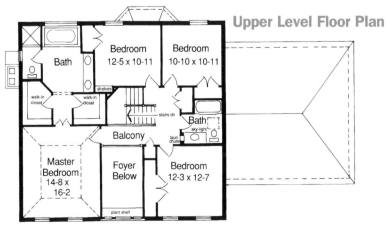

Plan #141012

Dimensions: 44'4" W x 38' D
Levels: 2
Square Footage: 1,870
Main Level Sq. Ft.: 1,159
Upper Level Sq. Ft.: 711
Bedrooms: 3
Bathrooms: 2½
Foundation: Basement
Materials List Available: Yes
Price Category: D

Images provided by designer/architect.

Country charm comes to mind with this classic 1½ story design.

Features:

- Ceiling Height: 8 ft.

- Porch: This full shed porch with dormers creates a look few can resist.

- Living/Dining: This open living/dining area invites you to come in and sit a spell.

- Kitchen: This kitchen allows the host to see their guests from the sink through the opening in the angled walls.

- Breakfast Area: The cathedral ceiling in this breakfast area creates a sunroom effect at the rear of the house.

- Master Suite: This spacious master suite has all the amenities, including a double bowl vanity, corner tub, walk in closet, and 5-ft. shower.

- Bedrooms: Two large bedrooms upstairs share a hall bath.

- Balcony: This upstairs balcony is lit by the center dormer, creating a cozy study alcove.

Copyright by designer/architect.

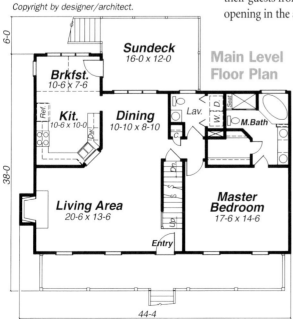

Main Level Floor Plan

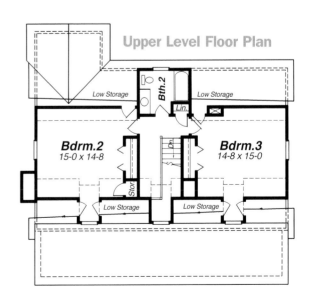

Upper Level Floor Plan

Plan #241007

Dimensions: 58'10" W x 59'1" D

Levels: 1

Square Footage: 2,036

Bedrooms: 3

Bathrooms: 2

Foundation: Slab

Materials List Available: No

Price Category: D

• **Kitchen:** This well-designed kitchen with extensive counter space offers a delightful eating bar, perfect for quick or informal meals.

• **Master Suite:** This luxurious master suite, located on the first floor for privacy, features his and her walk-in closets, separate vanities, a deluxe corner tub, a linen closet, and a walk-in shower.

• **Additional Bedrooms:** Two secondary bedrooms and an optional, large game room —well suited for a growing family—are located on the second floor.

Enjoy summer breezes while relaxing on the large front porch of this charming country cottage.

Features:

• **Great Room:** Whether you enter from the front door or from the kitchen, you will feel welcome in this comfortable great room, which features a corner fireplace.

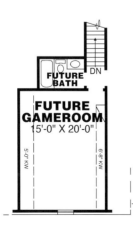

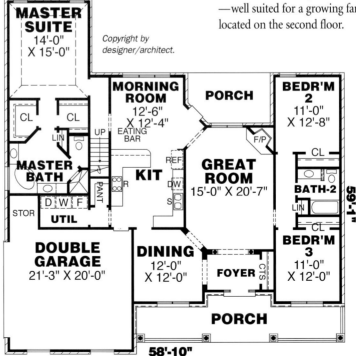

Plan #171013

Dimensions: 74' W x 72' D
Levels: 1
Square Footage: 3,084
Bedrooms: 4
Bathrooms: 3½
Foundation: Slab, crawl space
Materials List Available: Yes
Price Category: G

Impressive porch columns add to the country charm of this amenity-filled family home.

Features:

- Ceiling Height: 10 ft.

- Foyer: The sense of style continues from the front porch into this foyer, which opens to the formal dining room and the living room.

- Dining Room: Two handsome support columns accentuate the elegance of this dining room.

- Living Room: This living room features a cozy corner fireplace and plenty of room for the entire family to gather and relax.

- Kitchen: You'll be inspired to new culinary heights in this kitchen, which offers plenty of counter space, a snack bar, a built-in pantry, and a china closet.

- Master Suite: The bedroom of this master suite has a fireplace and overlooks a rear courtyard. The bath has two vanities a large walk-in closet, a deluxe tub, a walk-in shower, and a skylight.

Images provided by designer/architect.

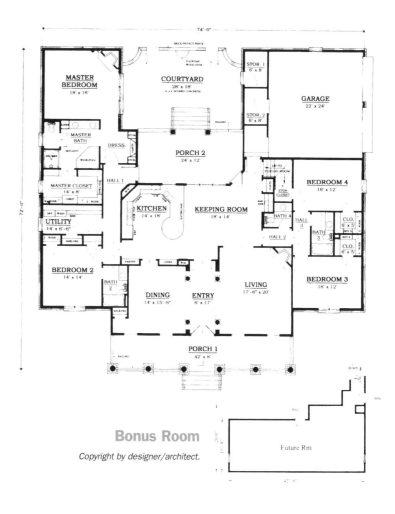

Bonus Room

Copyright by designer/architect.

Plan #311025

Dimensions: 76'8" W x 62' D

Levels: 1

Square Footage: 2,561

Main Level Sq. Ft.: 2,561

Opt. Bonus Sq. Ft. 1,494

Bedrooms: 3

Bathrooms: 2½

Foundation: Basement, crawl space, or slab

Materials List Available: Yes

Price Category: E

Images provided by designer/architect.

Rear View

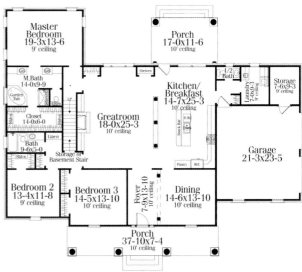

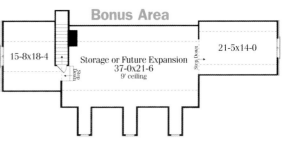

Bonus Area

Plan #311030

Dimensions: 76'10" W x 55'6" D

Levels: 1

Square Footage: 2,286

Main Level Sq. Ft.: 2,286

Opt. Bonus Sq. Ft.: 443

Bedrooms: 3

Bathrooms: 2½

Foundation: Basement, crawl space, or slab

Materials List Available: No

Price Category: E

Images provided by designer/architect.

Rear View

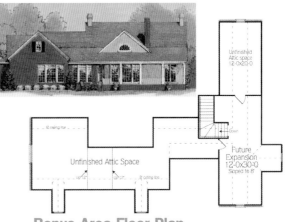

Bonus Area Floor Plan

Plan #241030

Dimensions: 63'6" W x 65'4" D
Levels: 1
Square Footage: 2,185
Bedrooms: 3
Bathrooms: 2
Foundation: Slab
Materials List Available: No
Price Category: D

Images provided by designer/architect.

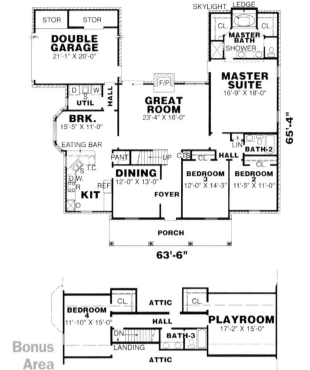

Copyright by designer/architect.

Plan #311022

Dimensions: 73'1" W x 58'6" D
Levels: 1
Square Footage: 2,373
Main Level Sq. Ft.: 2,373
Opt. Bonus Sq. Ft. 1,178
Bedrooms: 3
Bathrooms: 2½
Foundation: Basement, crawl space, or slab
Materials List Available: Yes
Price Category: E

Images provided by designer/architect.

Rear View

Stair Location

Copyright by designer/architect.

Plan #151018

Dimensions: 69' W x 69'10" D

Levels: 2

Square Footage: 2,755

Main Level Sq. Ft.: 2,406

Upper Level Sq. Ft.: 349

Bedrooms: 3

Bathrooms: 4½

Foundation: Basement, slab, or crawl space

Materials List Available: Yes

Price Category: F

Images provided by designer/architect.

Treasure the countless amenities that make this home ideal for a family and welcoming to guests.

Features:

- **Great Room:** A gas fireplace and built-in shelving beg for a warm, comfortable decorating scheme.

- **Kitchen:** An island counter here opens to the breakfast room, and a swinging door leads to the dining room with its formal entry columns.

- **Laundry Room:** You'll wonder how you ever kept the laundry organized without this room and its built-in ironing board and broom closet.

- **Master Suite:** Atrium doors to the porch are a highlight of the bedroom, with its two walk-in closets, a corner whirlpool tub with glass blocks, and a separate shower.

- **Bedrooms:** These large rooms will surely promote peaceful school-day mornings for the children because each room has both a private bath and a walk-in closet.

Main Level Floor Plan

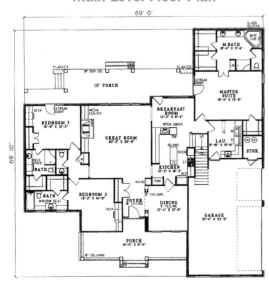

Upper Level Floor Plan

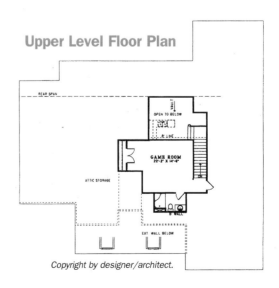

Copyright by designer/architect.

Plan #121063

Dimensions: 84' W x 52' D
Levels: 2
Square Footage: 3,473
Main Level Sq. Ft.: 2,500
Upper Level Sq. Ft.: 973
Bedrooms: 4
Bathrooms: 3½
Foundation: Basement
Materials List Available: Yes
Price Category: G

Images provided by designer/architect.

Enjoy the many amenities in this well-designed and gracious home.

Features:

- Entry: A large sparkling window and a tapering split staircase distinguish this lovely entryway.

- Great Room: This spacious great room will be the heart of your new home. It has a 14-ft. spider-beamed window that serves to highlight its built-in bookcase, built-in entertainment center, raised hearth fireplace,

wet bar, and lovely arched windows topped with transoms.

- Kitchen: Anyone who walks into this kitchen will realize that it's designed for both convenience and efficiency.

- Master Suite: The tiered ceiling in the bedroom gives an elegant touch, and the bay window adds to it. The two large walk-in closets and the spacious bath, with columns setting off the whirlpool tub and two vanities, complete this dream of a suite.

Main Level Floor Plan

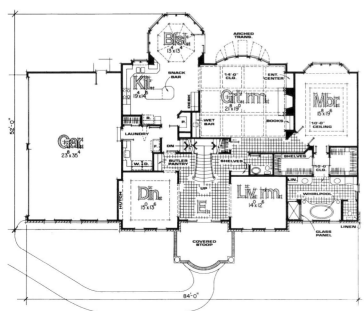

Upper Level Floor Plan

Copyright by designer/architect.

Plan #151014

Dimensions: 70'2" W x 51'4" D
Levels: 2
Square Footage: 2,698
Main Level Sq. Ft.: 1,813
Upper Level Sq. Ft.: 885
Bedrooms: 5
Bathrooms: 3
Foundation: Crawl space, slab, optional basement for fee
Price Category: D

Images provided by designer/architect.

A comfortable front porch welcomes you into this home that features a balcony over the great room, a study, and a kitchen designed for gourmet cooks.

Features:

• Ceiling Height: 9 ft.

• Front Porch: Stately 12-in.-wide pillars form the entryway.

• Foyer: Open to upper story.

• Great Room: A fireplace, vaulted 9-ft. ceiling, and balcony from the second floor add character to this lovely room.

• Dining Room: Open to the kitchen for convenience.

• Kitchen: A large walk-in pantry, well-designed work areas, and eat-in bar make this room a treasure.

• Breakfast Room: Enjoy this spot that opens to both the kitchen and a large covered porch at the rear of the house.

• Study: This quiet room has French doors leading to the yard.

• Master Suite: This spacious area has cozy window seats as well as his and her walk-in closets. The master bathroom is fitted with a whirlpool tub, a glass shower, and his and her sinks.

Copyright by designer/architect.

Plan #211005

Dimensions: 68' W x 64' D
Levels: 1
Square Footage: 2,000
Bedrooms: 3
Bathrooms: 2
Foundation: Slab
Materials List Available: Yes
Price Category: D

Images provided by designer/architect.

A brick veneer exterior complements the columned porch to make this a striking home.

SMARTtip

Do-It-Yourself Ponds

To avoid disturbing utility lines, contact your utility companies before doing any digging. Locate a freestanding container pond on your deck near an existing (GFCI) outlet. For an in-ground pond, have an electrician run a buried line and install a GFCI outlet near the pond so you can plug in a pump or fountain.

Features:

- Ceiling Height: 9 ft. unless otherwise noted.

- Living Room: From the front porch, the foyer unfolds into this expansive living room. Family and friends will be drawn to the warmth of the living room's cozy fireplace.

- Formal Dining Room: This elegant room is designed for dinner parties of any size.

- Kitchen: Located between the formal dining room and the dinette, the kitchen can serve formal meals as easily as quick family repasts.

- Master Suite: There's plenty of room to unwind at the end of a long day in the huge master bedroom. Luxuriate in the private bath, with its spa tub, separate shower, dual sinks, and two walk-in closets.

- Home Office: The home office, accessible from the master bedroom, is the perfect quiet spot to work, study, or pay the bills.

Copyright by designer/architect.

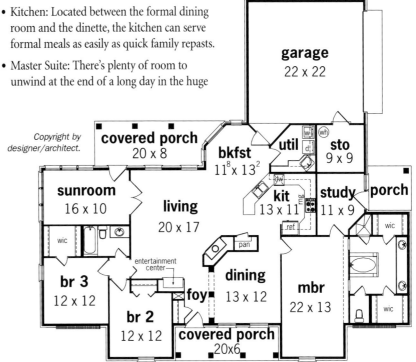

Plan #141016

Dimensions: 64' W x 52' D
Levels: 2
Square Footage: 2,416
Main Level Sq. Ft.: 1,250
Upper Level Sq. Ft.: 1,166
Bedrooms: 4
Bathrooms: 2½
Foundation: Basement
Materials List Available: Yes
Price Category: E

Images provided by designer/architect.

Here is a classic American home with a generous wraparound front porch.

Features:

• Ceiling Height: 9 ft. unless otherwise noted.

• Formal Dining Room: Located just off the foyer you'll find this inviting dining room, which is perfect for dinner parties of all sizes.

• Formal Living Room: This room is located in close proximity to the dining room, making it easy to usher guests in to dine.

• Family Room: The whole family will want to gather in this spacious area. Columns separate it from the breakfast area while keeping an open feeling across the entire rear of the house.

• Kitchen: This warm and inviting kitchen features corner windows that look into the side yard and a rear screen porch.

• Master Bedroom: This bedroom has a modified cathedral ceiling that highlights a large Palladian window on the rear wall. Access to a second-floor deck creates the perfect master retreat.

Main Level Floor Plan

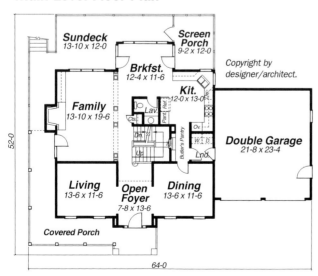

Copyright by designer/architect.

Upper Level Floor Plan

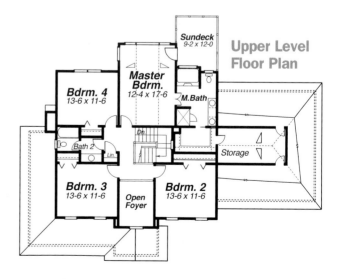

Plan #111003

Dimensions: 48' W x 66' D

Levels: 2

Square Footage: 3,319

Main Level Sq. Ft.: 2,331

Upper Level Sq. Ft.: 988

Bedrooms: 3

Bathrooms: 3½

Foundation: Pier

Materials List Available: No

Price Category: G

Images provided by designer/architect.

Main Level Floor Plan

Copyright by designer/architect.

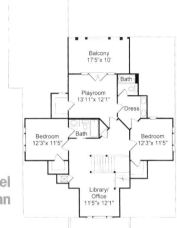

Upper Level Floor Plan

Plan #141020

Dimensions: 58' W x 40'4" D

Levels: 2

Square Footage: 3,140

Main Level Sq. Ft.: 1,553

Upper Level Sq. Ft.: 1,587

Bedrooms: 5

Bathrooms: 4

Foundation: Basement

Materials List Available: No

Price Category: G

Images provided by designer/architect.

Main Level Floor Plan

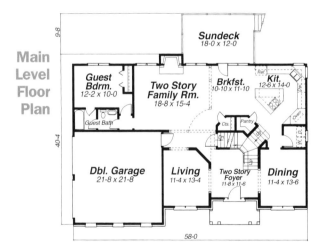

Upper Level Floor Plan

Copyright by designer/architect.

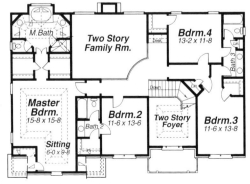

The Right Light

Lighting is one of the most important design elements in any home. Coordinating all of your artificial lighting sources—lamps, recessed or track lighting, sconces, ceiling-mounted fixtures, even pendants—can make the difference between a place that is warm and welcoming or one that is dark and depressing. In addition, light can be used in more focused ways—whether that be illuminating your desk in a home office or minimizing reflection as you watch a DVD on your big-screen television.

Light even has the power to visually reconfigure space, making rooms seem larger or smaller than they are. Lastly, the smart use of lighting can shine attention on architectural high points while obscuring less desirable details.

Lighting Plans

The rooms in your new home will combine the three types of lighting: ambient, task, and accent light. How you plan to use the room will determine the amount and type of lighting you will need. Although there are some general rules and an actual formula to determine how many watts of light to use for every square foot of space in your house, you must be the ultimate judge of your lighting needs.

General Lighting

Ambient Light. Because this is the soft diffused overall light that fills a room, ambient lighting is also called general lighting. Obviously, it is critical to the mood of a room. Aside from natural light, there are numerous artificial sources of ambient light. You can use all or some of them for your home.

Ceiling Fixtures. Standard ceiling-mounted fixtures, such as pendants and chandeliers, and recessed canisters are good sources of general lighting.

Sconces and Torcheres. Wall fixtures usually direct light upward, where it washes the wall and is reflected back into the room. Other possible sources of good general lighting are lamps with opaque shades. But the important thing to remember is that ambient light is inconspicuous. Although you know the source of the light, the glow is diffused. Of course, never use an exposed bulb, which is much too harsh.

How bright you should make the rooms in your new home depends on the way and the time of day the room will be used. To create the precise level of light, wire ambient light sources to dimmer switches. This puts you in control and allows you to easily

Recessed accent lighting highlights the painting and the shelves of collectibles.

adjust the light level. For example, in a family room you may want subdued lighting for watching a movie, and stronger, more cheerful lighting when you're hosting a kid's birthday party.

Task Lighting

Task lighting focuses on a specific area. It illuminates the work surface—whether it be the kitchen counter or the top of your desk in a home office. Metal architects' lamps, under-cabinet lights, reading lamps, and desk lamps are all excellent examples

Wall sconces, above left, placed on both sides of a bathroom mirror are good sources of light for applying makeup and general grooming.

Track-mounted spotlights, above right, serve a number of lighting needs. Here some provide general lighting while others accentuate the wall of art.

Use light to set off a collection, right, of personal objects. Here the items alone draw attention, but the lighting makes this area a focal point of the room.

of task lighting. Optimally, task lights should be angled between you and the work. A reading lamp functions best, after all, when it is positioned behind you and over your shoulder. Aiming light directly on a surface creates glare, which causes eye strain.

In bathrooms, include task lights for grooming. Sconces on either side of the mirror are preferable to a strip of light above the mirror because the latter will cast shadows. If the room is small, the sconces may serve as general lighting as well.

Accent Lighting

Designers like to use accent lighting because it is decorative and often dramatic. Accent lighting draws attention to a favorite work of art, a recessed niche on a stairway landing, or a tall plant at the end of a long room, for example. Designers agree that when you want to highlight something special, be sure the light source is concealed in order not to detract from the object you are spotlighting.

Room-by-Room Guide to Lighting

With lighting, one size doesn't fit all. Each room presents its own lighting challenges and solutions. Think outside of the box. Recessed lighting, for example, can be tucked away under bookshelves, not just in the ceiling; track lighting can be installed in a circular pattern to mirror a room with sweeping curves rather than in straight strips. Here are some other strategies for lighting each of your new rooms.

Family/Play Room. Pendants or chandeliers are obvious choices here if headroom is not an issue. Add recessed lighting in the corners or near doors and windows. Or if the room is designed for active play, install recessed lighting throughout. Use lamps or track lighting for areas that will be used for reading or hobbies. And don't forget about accent lighting to highlight wall-hung photographs or paintings.

Media/TV Room. No light should be brighter than the TV screen. Instead of one bright light source, try several low-level lights—recessed lighting, lamps, and lighting under shelves. Three-way bulbs or dimmers are often the best solution. Remember: light should be behind you, not between you and the screen.

Home Office. A good lighting arrangement combines indirect overhead illumination with table lamps. Indirect light means that the light is softy diffused throughout the home office, not shining down on you. Use a desktop lamp, preferably an adjustable fixture, to focus light on the task at hand and to deflect glare from the computer screen. Install unobtrusive light fixtures in a hutch above the work surface or create a light bridge, a horizontal strip of wood with a light built into it, fastened to the underside of two upper cabinets.

In media room, try to keep the lighting levels below that of the TV.

Bedrooms. Any number of lighting combinations could work in this room, but generally an overhead fixture that you flip on when you first enter the room is practical and, depending on your choice of fixture, stylish. For a more intimate mood, wiring bedside lamps to a light switch will also work. A must-have is a swing-arm reading lamp with a narrow beam of light that enables you to finish your novel while your spouse gets some shuteye. These types of reading lamps are responsible for saving more than one marriage.

Bathrooms. As with a home office, you need ambient (general) light (to help you find your way to the toilet or shower without tripping) and task lighting (for personal grooming). The ideal task lighting should come from both sides of the mirror at eye level.

Kitchens. Team up general illumination—recessed or ceiling-mounted fixtures installed about 12 to 15 inches from the front of the upper cabinets is a good choice and a fixture or two over the sink—with under-the-cabinet task lighting for food preparation. Install decorative wood trim to hide the light strips.

Home Workshop. A workable solution that has stood the test of time is fluorescent fixtures at regular intervals along the ceiling and work lights for specific tasks. Installing a strip of outlets along the length of a worktable and plugging in lights, either portable ones or those attached to the underside of the cabinet, provides illumination on demand.

Staircase. Sufficient light is critical around staircases, where one false step can lead to injury. As a rule, figure you will need at least one 60-watt fixture per 10 feet of running stairs. Try recessed lighting in the ceiling, or for a more dramatic look, install lighting in several recessed niches along the staircase wall that won't invade the stair area.

Light home offices, right, using indirect general lighting combined with desk-mounted task lighting.

Kitchens, below, require overhead ambient lighting and concentrated task lighting over work surfaces.

For workshops, bottom, install overhead lights that won't cast shadows on the work.

207

Plan #101023

Dimensions: 52' W x 42' D

Levels: 1

Square Footage: 1,197

Bedrooms: 3

Bathrooms: 2

Foundation: Crawl space, slab

Materials List Available: No

Price Category: B

Images provided by designer/architect.

The open floor plan in this well-designed home makes everyone feel welcome in the public spaces but still allows privacy in the bedrooms.

Features:

- Family Room: A large fireplace flanked by windows and the vaulted ceiling are the focal points in this spacious room.

- Dining Area: Build the optional bay for an added design feature, or install sliding glass doors (and a back deck) to gain the maximum amount of natural light.

- Kitchen: A door to the garage and one to the adjacent laundry room both add convenience to this step-saving design.

- Master Suite: You'll love the walk-in closet and large corner windows here, as well as the bath with vaulted ceiling, tub, separate shower, and dual vanity.

- Additional Bedrooms: Both bedrooms have large closets and easy access to a nearby bath.

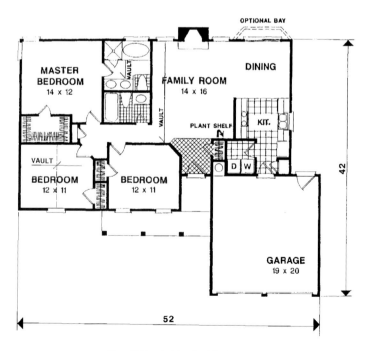

Copyright by designer/architect.

Plan #151169

Dimensions: 51'6" W x 49'10" D
Levels: 1
Square Footage: 1,525
Bedrooms: 3
Bathrooms: 2
Foundation: Basement, daylight basement, crawl space, or slab
Materials List Available: Yes
Price Category: C

This comfortable home is filled with amenities that will thrill both friends and family.

Features:

- Great Room: This spacious room has a gas fireplace in the corner, 9-ft. boxed ceiling, and convenient door to the rear covered porch.

- Dining Room: Bay windows look out to the rear porch and let light flood into this room.

- Kitchen: An angled work and snack bar and large pantry are highlights in this well-planned room.

- Breakfast Room: A door to the rear porch, wide windows, and computer desk are highlights here.

- Master Suite: You'll feel pampered by the 9-ft. boxed ceiling and bath with two huge closets, whirlpool tub, separate shower, and dual vanity.

- Additional Bedrooms: Transform bedroom 3 into a study or home office if you can, and add the optional door to the foyer for total convenience.

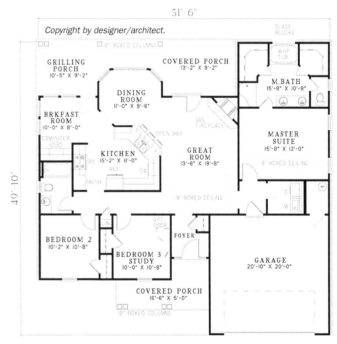

Rear View

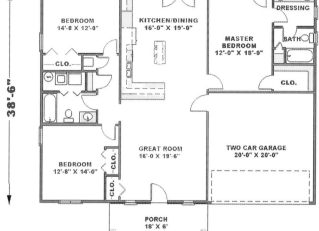

Plan #191035

Dimensions: 50'8" W x 38'6" D

Levels: 1

Square Footage: 1,551

Bedrooms: 3

Bathrooms: 2

Foundation: Slab

Materials List Available: No

Price Category: C

Images provided by designer/architect.

PATIO
20' X 10'

BEDROOM
14'-8 X 12'-0"

KITCHEN/DINING
16'-0" X 19'-0"

DRESSING

MASTER BEDROOM
12'-0" X 18'-0"

BATH

CLO.

CLO.

38'-6"

BEDROOM
12'-8 X 14'-0"

CLO.

GREAT ROOM
16'-0 X 19'-6"

TWO CAR GARAGE
20'-0" X 20'-0"

PORCH
18' X 6'

50'-8"

Copyright by designer/architect.

Plan #191036

Dimensions: 45'6" W x 51' D

Levels: 1

Square Footage: 1,438

Bedrooms: 3

Bathrooms: 1

Foundation: Crawl space, slab

Materials List Available: No

Price Category: B

Images provided by designer/architect.

PORCH NO. 2

LAUNDRY
12'-6" X 6'-8"

SCREENED PORCH
14'-0" X 13'-8"

KITCHEN/DINING
15'-6" X 19'-4"

BEDROOM 2
12'-0" X 12'-6"

MASTER BEDROOM
13'-10" X 13'-6"

PANTRY

LINEN

LINEN

GREAT ROOM
17'-10" X 18'-6"

STOVE

WIDTH AND DEPTH
45'-6" X 51'-0"

BEDROOM 3
12'-6" X 11'-0"

GAS FIREPLACE

PORCH NO. 1

Copyright by designer/architect.

Plan #191034

Dimensions: 50'8" W x 38'6" D

Levels: 1

Square Footage: 1,551

Bedrooms: 3

Bathrooms: 2

Foundation: Slab

Materials List Available: No

Price Category: C

Images provided by designer/architect.

Copyright by designer/architect.

Plan #351004

Dimensions: 78' W x 49'6" D

Levels: 1

Square Footage: 1,852

Bedrooms: 3

Bathrooms: 2½

Foundation: Crawl space, slab, or basement

Materials List Available: Yes

Price Category: D

Images provided by designer/architect.

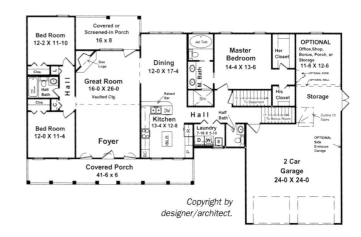

Copyright by designer/architect.

Rear View

Bonus Room

Plan #151193

Dimensions: 43' W x 62' D
Levels: 1
Square Footage: 1,361
Bedrooms: 3
Bathrooms: 2
Foundation: Crawl space, slab
(basement or walk-out basement
option for fee)
Materials List Available: Yes
Price Category: B

Images provided by designer/architect.

Copyright by designer/architect.

Plan #211146

Dimensions: 90' W x 47' D
Levels: 1
Square Footage: 2,203
Bedrooms: 4
Bathrooms: 2½
Foundation: Crawl space, slab
Materials List Available: Yes
Price Category: E

Images provided by designer/architect.

Copyright by designer/architect.

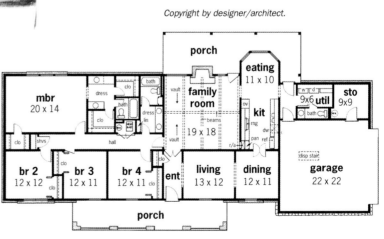

Plan #151196

Dimensions: 89' W x 49'4" D
Levels: 1
Square Footage: 1,800
Bedrooms: 3
Bathrooms: 2
Foundation: Crawl space, slab
Materials List Available: Yes
Price Category: D

Images provided by designer/architect.

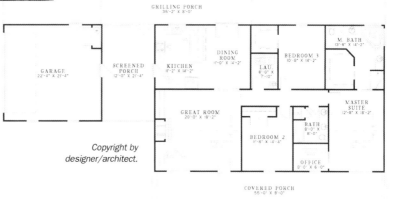

Copyright by designer/architect.

Plan #161065

Dimensions: 69'2" W x 53' D
Levels: 1
Square Footage: 2,341
Opt. Finished Basement Sq. Ft.: 1,964
Bedrooms: 3
Bathrooms: 2
Foundation: Basement, walk-out basement
Materials List Available: Yes
Price Category: E

Images provided by designer/architect.

Copyright by designer/architect.

Rear Elevation

Optional Basement Level Floor Plan

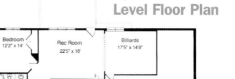

Plan #151194

Dimensions: 48' W x 50' D
Levels: 1
Square Footage: 1,407
Bedrooms: 3
Bathrooms: 2
Foundation: Crawl space, slab (basement or walk-out basement option for fee)
Materials List Available: Yes
Price Category: B

Images provided by designer/architect.

Copyright by designer/architect.

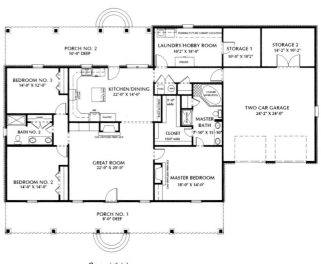

Plan #191032

Dimensions: 80'4" W x 52' D
Levels: 1
Square Footage: 2,091
Bedrooms: 3
Bathrooms: 2
Foundation: Slab
Materials List Available: No
Price Category: D

Images provided by designer/architect.

Copyright by designer/architect.

Plan #151200

Dimensions: 48' W x 59' D

Levels: 1

Square Footage: 1,224

Bedrooms: 3

Bathrooms: 2

Foundation: Crawl space, slab
(basement or walk-out basement
option for fee)

Materials List Available: Y

Price Category: B

*Images provided by
designer/architect.*

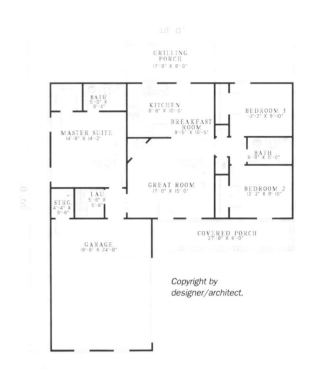

*Copyright by
designer/architect.*

Plan #371002

Dimensions: 67'2" W x 40'6" D

Levels: 1

Square Footage: 1,590

Bedrooms: 3

Bathrooms: 2

Foundation: Slab
(crawl space option for fee)

Materials List Available: No

Price Category: C

*Images provided by
designer/architect.*

Copyright by designer/architect.

Plan #151175

Dimensions: 52'4" W x 52'2" D
Levels: 1
Square Footage: 1,499
Bedrooms: 3
Bathrooms: 2
Foundation: Crawl space, slab
Materials List Available: Yes
Price Category: B

This home is as comfortable on the inside as it is substantial on the outside.

Features:

- **Great Room:** A corner fireplace makes a cozy area, and a handy door opens to the rear grilling porch, making this an ideal spot for entertaining.

- **Dining Room:** Columns define the perimeter of this elegant room with a high pan ceiling.

- **Kitchen:** The U-shaped counters make it efficient to work in this well-designed room.

- **Breakfast Room:** Set the table under the large windows to let sunlight give morning cheer.

- **Master Suite:** Set off for privacy, this lovely suite has a 9-ft. boxed ceiling in the bedroom, a large walk-in closet, and bath with whirlpool, separate shower, and two vanities for total pampering.

- **Additional Bedrooms:** Both bedrooms have large closets and easy access to a nearby bathroom.

Images provided by designer/architect.

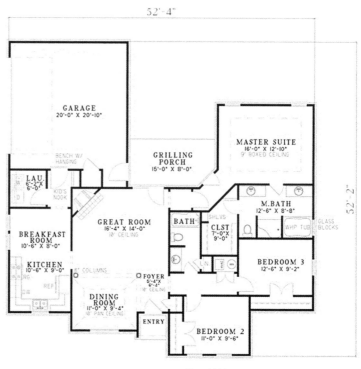

Copyright by designer/architect.

Plan #151197

Dimensions: 60' W x 62' D
Levels: 1
Square Footage: 1,800
Bedrooms: 3
Bathrooms: 2
Foundation: Crawl space, slab
(basement or walk-out basement
option for fee)
Materials List Available: Yes
Price Category: D

*Images provided by
designer/architect.*

*Copyright by
designer/architect.*

Plan #151203

Dimensions: 46' W x 38'10" D
Levels: 1
Square Footage: 1,214
Bedrooms: 3
Bathrooms: 2
Foundation: Crawl space, slab
(basement or walk-out basement
option for fee)
Materials List Available: Yes
Price Category: B

*Images provided by
designer/architect.*

Copyright by designer/architect.

Plan #151192

Dimensions: 51' W x 56'2" D

Levels: 1

Square Footage: 1,288

Bedrooms: 3

Bathrooms: 2

Foundation: Crawl space, slab (basement or walk-out basement option for fee)

Materials List Available: Yes

Price Category: B

Images provided by designer/architect.

Copyright by designer/architect.

Plan #161064

Dimensions: 62'8" W x 42'2" D

Levels: 1

Square Footage: 1,751

Bedrooms: 3

Bathrooms: 2

Foundation: Basement, walk-out basement

Materials List Available: Yes

Price Category: C

Images provided by designer/architect.

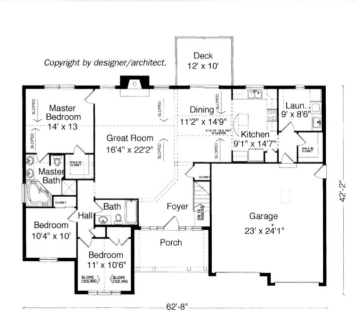

Copyright by designer/architect.

Rear Elevation

Rear
Elevation

Plan #161066

Dimensions: 62'8" W x 57'11" D

Levels: 1

Square Footage: 2,078

Bedrooms: 3

Bathrooms: 2

Foundation: Basement,
walk-out basement

Materials List Available: Yes

Price Category: D

*Images provided by
designer/architect.*

Copyright by designer/architect.

Plan #371001

Dimensions: 52' W x 45' D

Levels: 1

Square Footage: 1,418

Bedrooms: 3

Bathrooms: 2

Foundation: Slab
(crawl space option for fee)

Materials List Available: No

Price Category: B

*Images provided by
designer/architect.*

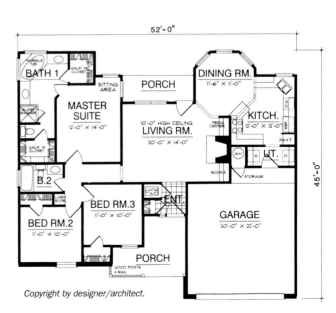

Copyright by designer/architect.

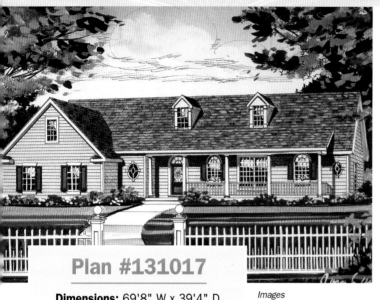

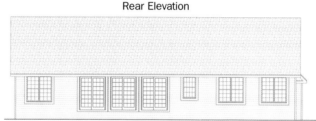

Plan #131017

Dimensions: 69'8" W x 39'4" D

Levels: 1

Square Footage: 1,480

Bedrooms: 3

Bathrooms: 2

Foundation: Basement, crawl space, or slab

Materials List Available: Yes

Price Category: C

Images provided by designer/architect.

Alternate Floor Plan

Part Plan with Optional Basement

Copyright by designer/architect.

Rear Elevation

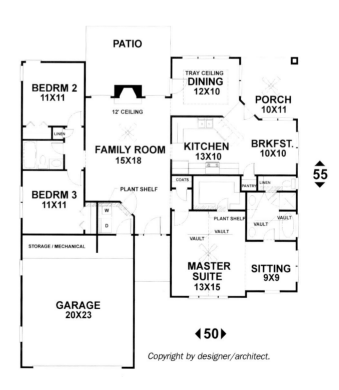

Plan #101003

Dimensions: 50' W x 55' D

Levels: 1

Square Footage: 1,593

Bedrooms: 3

Bathrooms: 2

Foundation: Slab, crawl space, or basement

Materials List Available: Yes

Price Category: C

Images provided by designer/architect.

Copyright by designer/architect.

Plan #221011

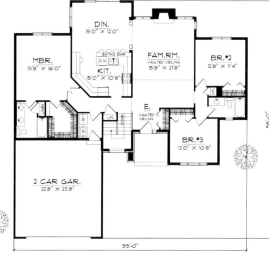

Images provided by designer/architect.

Copyright by designer/architect.

Dimensions: 59' W x 58' D

Levels: 1

Square Footage: 1,756

Bedrooms: 3

Bathrooms: 2

Foundation: Basement

Materials List Available: No

Price Category: C

Rear Elevation

Plan #161007

Dimensions: 66'4" W x 43'10" D

Levels: 1

Square Footage: 1,611

Bedrooms: 3

Bathrooms: 2

Foundation: Basement

Materials List Available: Yes

Price Category: C

Images provided by designer/architect.

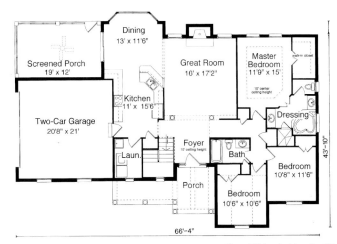

Copyright by designer/architect.

Rear Elevation

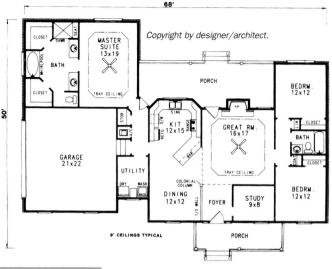

Plan #171009

Images provided by designer/architect.

Dimensions: 68' W x 50' D
Levels: 1
Square Footage: 1,771
Bedrooms: 3
Bathrooms: 2
Foundation: Slab, crawl space
Materials List Available: Yes
Price Category: C

SMARTtip

Deck Awnings

Awnings come in bright colors. As light filters through, it will cast a hue to anything under the deck. Warm colors, such as red or pink, will create a rosy glow; cool colors, such blues or greens, will enhance the shade.

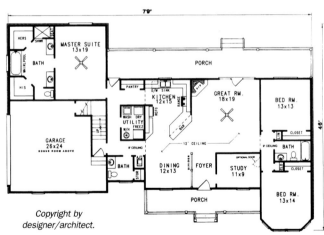

Plan #171015

Images provided by designer/architect.

Dimensions: 79' W x 46' D
Levels: 1
Square Footage: 2,089
Bedrooms: 3
Bathrooms: 2½
Foundation: Slab, crawl space
Materials List Available: Yes
Price Category: D

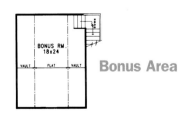

Bonus Area

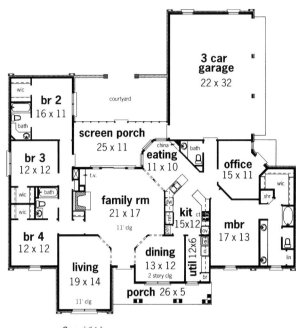

Plan #211062

Dimensions: 74'6" W x 75' D

Levels: 1

Square Footage: 2,682

Bedrooms: 4

Bathrooms: 3½

Foundation: Slab, optional crawl space

Materials List Available: Yes

Price Category: F

Images provided by designer/architect.

Copyright by designer/architect.

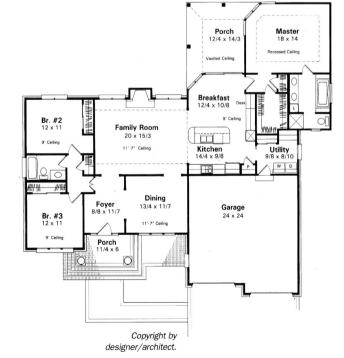

Plan #251006

Dimensions: 65'5" W x 59'11" D

Levels: 1

Square Footage: 1,849

Bedrooms: 3

Bathrooms: 2

Foundation: Crawl space

Materials List Available: Yes

Price Category: D

Images provided by designer/architect.

Copyright by designer/architect.

Images provided by designer/architect.

Plan #211004

Dimensions: 64' W x 62' D

Levels: 1

Square Footage: 1,828

Bedrooms: 4

Bathrooms: 2

Foundation: Slab, crawl space, basement

Materials List Available: Yes

Price Category: D

This super-energy-efficient home has the curb appeal of a much larger house.

Features:

- Ceiling Height: 9 ft.

- Kitchen: You will love cooking in this bright, airy, and efficient kitchen. It features an angled layout that allows a great view to the outside through a window wall in the breakfast area.

- Breakfast Area: With morning sunlight streaming through the wall of windows in

this area, you won't be able to resist lingering over a cup of coffee.

- Rear Porch: This breezy rear porch is designed to accommodate the pleasure of old-fashioned rockers or swings.

- Master Bedroom: Retreat at the end of a long day to this bedroom, which is isolated for privacy yet conveniently located a few steps from the kitchen and utility area.

- Attic Storage: No need to fuss with creaky pull-down stairs. This attic has a permanent stairwell to provide easy access to its abundant storage.

SMARTtip

Resin Furniture

Resin furniture is made of molded plastic. Most resin pieces are quite affordable, but lacquered resin with brass fittings is a high-end item. Resin doesn't corrode and cleans easily, but a scratched finish cannot be repaired. However, lacquered resin can be touched up.

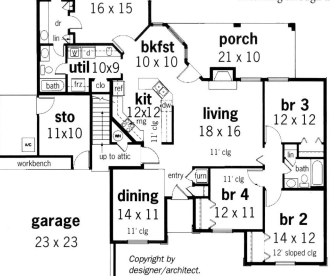

Copyright by designer/architect.

Plan #211009

Dimensions: 72' W x 60' D
Levels: 1
Square Footage: 2,396
Bedrooms: 4
Bathrooms: 2
Foundation: Slab
Materials List Available: Yes
Price Category: E

Beautiful arched windows lend a luxurious feeling to the exterior of this one-story home.

Features:

- **Ceiling Height:** 9 ft. unless otherwise noted.

- **Entry:** Guests will be greeted by a dramatic 12-ft. ceiling in this elegant foyer.

- **Living Room:** The 12-ft. ceiling continues through the foyer into this inviting living room. Everyone will feel welcomed by the crackling fire in the handsome fireplace.

- **Covered Porch:** When the weather is warm, invite guests to step out of the living room directly into this covered porch.

- **Kitchen:** This bright and cheery kitchen is designed for the way we live today. It includes a pantry and an angled eating bar that will see plenty of impromptu family meals.

- **Energy-Efficient Walls:** All the outside walls are framed with 2x6 lumber instead of 2x4. The extra thickness makes room for more insulation to lower your heating and cooling bills.

Images provided by designer/architect.

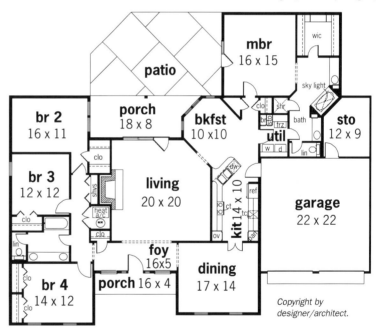

Copyright by designer/architect.

SMARTtip

Ornaments in a Garden

Placement is everything with ornaments in a garden. Some elements are best sitting by themselves. Others are better when they are part of a cohesive whole, perhaps placed in the greenery at a corner or flanking a structure.

Plan #211077

Dimensions: 94' W x 68' D

Levels: 2

Square Footage: 5,560

Main Level Sq. Ft.: 4,208

Upper Level Sq. Ft.: 1,352

Bedrooms: 4

Bathrooms: 4 full, 2 half

Foundation: Slab, or crawl space

Materials List Available: No

Price Category: I

This palatial home has a two-story veranda and offers room and amenities for a large family.

Features:

- Ceiling Height: 10 ft.

- Library: Teach your children the importance of quiet reflection in this library, which boasts a full wall of built-in bookshelves.

- Master Suite: Escape the pressures of a busy day in this truly royal master suite. Curl up in front of your own fireplace. Or take a long, soothing soak in the private bath, with his and her sinks and closets.

- Kitchen: This room offers many modern comforts and amenities, and free-flowing traffic patterns.

Images provided by designer/architect.

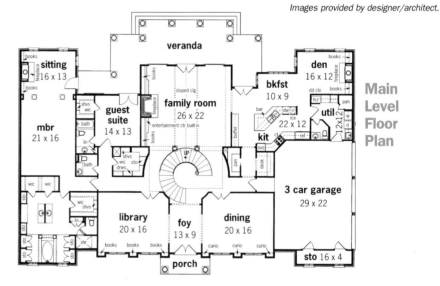

Main Level Floor Plan

Copyright by designer/architect.

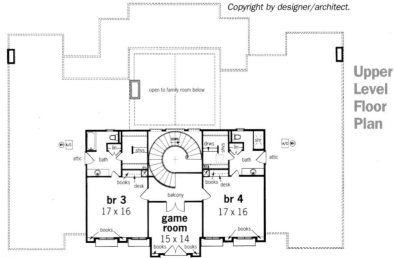

Upper Level Floor Plan

Plan #161025

Dimensions: 63'4" W x 48' D

Levels: 2

Square Footage: 2,738

Main Level Sq. Ft.: 1,915

Upper Level Sq. Ft.: 823

Bedrooms: 4

Bathrooms: 3½

Foundation: Basement

Materials List Available: No

Price Category: F

One look at the octagonal tower, boxed window, and wood-and-stone trim, and you'll know how much your family will love this home.

Features:

- Foyer: View the high windows across the rear wall, a fireplace, and open stairs as you come in.

- Great Room: Gather in this two-story-high area.

- Hearth Room: Open to the breakfast room, it's close to both the kitchen and dining room.

- Kitchen: A snack bar and an island make the kitchen ideal for family living.

- Master Suite: You'll love the 9-ft. ceiling in the bedroom and 11-ft. ceiling in the sitting area. The bath has a whirlpool tub, double-bowl vanity, and walk-in closet.

- Upper Level: A balcony leads to a bedroom with a private bath and 2 other rooms with private access to a shared bath.

Main Level Floor Plan

Upper Level Floor Plan

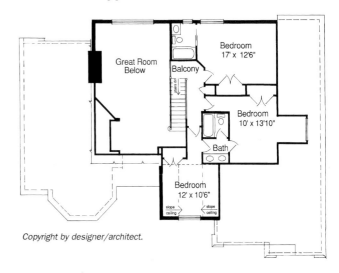

Plan #331005

Dimensions: 85'11" W x 55'7" D

Levels: 2

Square Footage: 3,585

Main Level Sq. Ft.: 2,691

Upper Level Sq. Ft.: 894

Bedrooms: 4

Bathrooms: 3½

Foundation: Basement, crawl space, or slab

Materials List Available: No

Price Category: H

Images provided by designer/architect.

Features:

- Foyer: The highlight of this spacious area is the curved stairway to the balcony over head.

- Family Room: The two-story ceiling and second-floor balcony overlooking this room add to its spacious feeling, but you can decorate around the fireplace to create a cozy, intimate area.

- Study: Use this versatile room as a guest room, home office or media room.

- Kitchen: Designed for the modern cook, this kitchen features a step-saving design, an island for added work space, and ample storage space.

- Master Suite: Step out to the rear deck from the bedroom to admire the moonlit scenery or bask in the morning sun. The luxurious bath makes an ideal place to relax in privacy.

You'll love the stately, traditional exterior design and the contemporary, casual interior layout as they are combined in this elegant home.

Main Level Floor Plan

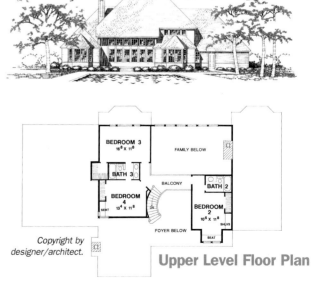

Rear View

Copyright by designer/architect.

Upper Level Floor Plan

Plan #161028

Dimensions: 84'6" W x 69'4" D

Levels: 1

Square Footage: 3,570

Optional Finished Basement Sq. Ft.: 2,367

Bedrooms: 3

Bathrooms: 3½

Foundation: Basement

Materials List Available: Yes

Price Category: H

From the gabled stone-and-brick exterior to the wide-open view from the foyer, this home will meet your greatest expectations.

Images provided by designer/architect.

Features:

- Great Room/Dining Room: Columns and 13-ft. ceilings add exquisite detailing to the dining room and great room.

- Kitchen: The gourmet-equipped kitchen with an island and a snack bar merges with the cozy breakfast and hearth rooms.

- Master Bedroom: The luxurious master bed room pampers with a separate sitting room with a fireplace and a dressing room boasting a whirlpool tub and two vanities.

- Additional: Two bedrooms upstairs include a private bath and walk-in closet. The optional finished basement solves all your recreational needs: bar, media room, billiards room, exercise room, game room, as well as an office and fourth bedroom.

Rear Elevation

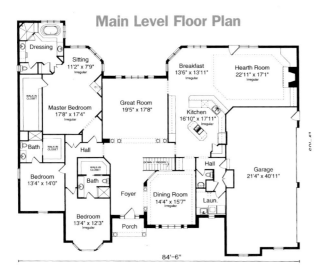

Copyright by designer/architect.

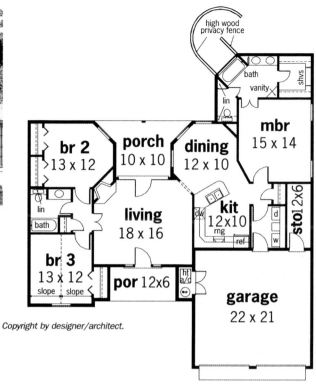

Plan #211145

Dimensions: 52' W x 56' D

Levels: 1

Square Footage: 1,420

Bedrooms: 3

Bathrooms: 2

Foundation: Crawl space, slab

Materials List Available: Yes

Price Category: B

Images provided by designer/architect.

Copyright by designer/architect.

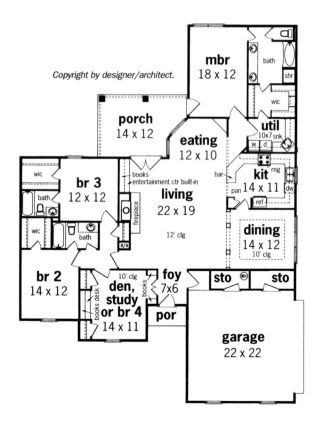

Plan #211147

Dimensions: 56' W x 74' D

Levels: 1

Square Footage: 2,200

Bedrooms: 4

Bathrooms: 3

Foundation: Crawl space, slab

Materials List Available: Yes

Price Category: E

Images provided by designer/architect.

Copyright by designer/architect.

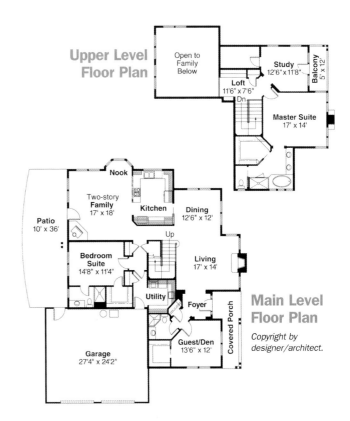

Upper Level Floor Plan

Open to Family Below

Loft 11'6" x 7'6"

Study 12'6" x 11'8"

Balcony 5' x 12'

Master Suite 17' x 14'

Main Level Floor Plan

Nook

Two-story Family 17' x 18'

Kitchen

Dining 12'6" x 12'

Patio 10' x 36'

Bedroom Suite 14'8" x 11'4"

Utility

Living 17' x 14'

Foyer

Guest/Den 13'6" x 12'

Covered Porch

Garage 27'4" x 24'2"

Copyright by designer/architect.

Plan #361012

Dimensions: 54'8" W x 63'8" D

Levels: 2

Square Footage: 2,602

Main Level Sq. Ft.: 1,867

Upper Level Sq. Ft.: 735

Bedrooms: 4

Bathrooms: 3

Foundation: Crawl space

Materials List Available: No

Price Category: F

Images provided by designer/architect.

Main Level Floor Plan

Patio

Patio

Master Suite 14'8" x 15'4"

Vaulted Great Room 17'6" x 19'4"

Country Kitchen 13' x 22'8"

Garage 23'2" x 23'8"

Utility

Vaulted Entry

Coffered Ceiling Dining 13' x 13'

Storage 6'2" x 9'8"

Porch

Upper Level Floor Plan

Bedroom 11'8" x 11'

Bedroom 11' x 10'6"

Dn

Bonus Room 14'4" x 19'6"

Copyright by designer/architect.

Plan #361017

Dimensions: 56' W x 46' D

Levels: 2

Square Footage: 2,116

Main Level Sq. Ft.: 1,643

Upper Level Sq. Ft.: 473

Bedrooms: 3

Bathrooms: 2½

Foundation: Crawl space

Materials List Available: No

Price Category: D

Images provided by designer/architect.

Plan #161032

Dimensions: 75'8" W x 70'6" D
Levels: 2
Square Footage: 4,517
Main Level Sq. Ft.: 2,562
Finished Lower Level Sq. Ft.: 1,955
Bedrooms: 3
Full Baths: 2
Half Baths: 3
Foundation: Basement
Materials List Available: Yes
Price Category: I

Images provided by designer/architect.

The brick-and-stone exterior, a recessed entry, and a tower containing a large library combine to convey the strength and character of this enchanting house.

Features:

• Hearth Room: Your family or guests will enjoy this large, comfortable hearth room, which has a gas fireplace and access to the rear deck, perfect for friendly gatherings.

• Kitchen: This spacious kitchen features a walk-in pantry and a center island.

• Master Suite: Designed for privacy, this master suite includes a sloped ceiling and opens to the rear deck. It also features a deluxe whirlpool bath, walk-in shower, separate his and her vanities, and a walk-in closet.

• Lower Level: This lower level includes a separate wine room, exercise room, sauna, two bedrooms, and enough space for a huge recreation room.

SMARTtip

Art Underfoot

Make a simple geometric pattern with your flooring materials. Create a focal point in a courtyard or a small area of a patio by fashioning an intricate mosaic with tile, stone, or colored concrete. By combining elements and colors, a simple garden room floor becomes a wonderful work of art. Whether you commission a craftsman or do it yourself, you'll have a permanent art installation right in your own backyard.

Rear View

Main Level Floor Plan

- Deck
- Deck
- Hearth Room 19'10" x 17'7"
- Master Bedroom 15'4" x 18'9"
- Great Room 17'9" x 17'10"
- Breakfast 11'7" x 9'6" irregular
- Kitchen 15'5" x 13'10" irregular
- Garage 13'8" x 20'
- Dressing
- Bath
- Laun.
- walk-in closet
- Foyer
- Dining Room 12' x 15'
- Library 13' x 14'7"
- Porch
- Two Car Garage 23' x 30'6"

Basement Level Floor Plan

- Rec. Room 15' x 17'2"
- Bedroom 15' x 12'
- Rec. Room 34'5" x 19'6"
- Bath
- walk-in closet
- cabinets
- Exercise Room 9'7" x 15'3"
- Unexcavated
- Bedroom 16'6" x 13'
- Bath
- Wine Room
- Sauna
- Basement
- walk-in closet
- Unexcavated

Copyright by designer/architect.

Rear Elevation

Kitchen

Kitchen

Living Room

Accessorizing Your Landscape

Your new cottage home won't be complete until the lawns and plants in the landscape are established. That takes time, but one way to move the design along and to provide some design punch in the established garden is to include landscape accessories, such as trellises, arbors, distinctive planters, and landscape lighting.

Trellises

Trellises were a key element in Renaissance gardens and continued in popularity through the eighteenth century. Trellises enjoyed a resurgence of popularity in the late-nineteenth century, but never to the extent of earlier times.

Trellises lend an air of mystery to a cottage garden. Generally we think of trellises in terms of the prefabricated sheets of diamond- or square-grid lattice and the fan-shaped supports for training climbers, both of which are readily available at home and garden centers in both wood and plastic. Lacking a pattern book, most gardeners are unaware of the incredible variety of designs, patterns, and optical illusions that can be created with trellises.

Uses for Trellises

A trellis screen is a wonderfully airy way to achieve privacy or to partition off a space.

The lath slats of lattice interrupt the view without totally obscuring it, creating the effect of a transparent curtain. Left bare, the pretty design of diamonds or squares makes an attractive effect. Covered in vines a trellis screen is enchanting.

Cover a Wall with a Trellis. The art of treillage, as the French call it, is not limited to screens. You can cover a bare wall or unattractive fence with a trellis pattern. Arrange the trellis pieces to create an optical illusion of an archway in the wall. Use a trellis for the walls of a gazebo to provide enclosure without being claustrophobic. Put a trellis screen with a pleasing, intricate pattern at the end of a walkway.

A metal trellis adorns a blank brick wall.

This stand-alone trellis provides interest even without plants.

Installing a ready-made trellis is a good way to jump-start your cottage landscape design.

Arbors and Pergolas

Arbors and pergolas can play a vital role in elevating the design and use of space from the ordinary to something special. The differences between an arbor and a pergola are somewhat technical, and you'll find people using the terms interchangeably. An arbor is a sheltered spot in which to sit. A pergola is generally a tunnel-like walkway or seating area created with columns or posts that support an open "roof" of beams or trelliswork. An arch (whether or not it has a curved top) is a structure through which you can walk. Usually all three structures are covered with vines.

Designing with Arbors and Pergolas

Because they stand tall, they add drama and importance to the scenery, especially if the rest of the garden features are predominantly horizontal. Take advantage of the upright supports to indulge in vertical gardening, growing climbing vines—preferably ones that flower profusely—up and over the structure. In addition, an arbor or pergola creates a shady, private retreat.

Create Transitions. Arches, arbors, and pergolas are stylish ways to mark the transition from one part of the cottage garden to another. Place an arch or arbor around the gate into the garden, or to mark the entrance from one garden room to another. Design the garden with reference to the arch or arbor so that it works like a picture window, framing a vista or a pretty vignette. Another idea is to nestle an arbor on the edge of the property to give the illusion that there is a passageway to another section. Place a bench beneath the arch for a protected, private place to sit. Design it so there is an appealing view from the arbor seat into the rest of the garden.

The English language is rich with synonyms for garden structures. Pergolas are also known as colonnades, galleries, piazzas, or porticos. Whatever you call them, these structures play a valuable role in the landscape design. In addition to being a walkway leading from one place to another, a pergola or gallery also can function as a garden wall, dividing two spaces. Instead of using a pergola as a walkway, you might place one across the far side of a patio so it serves as a partition, dividing the paved space from the planted area beyond. In addition to being a handsome architectural feature, the vine-covered structure will provide a shady retreat where people can comfortably sit, and if the central support posts are spaced properly, they can frame the view into the rest of the garden.

Integrate Arbors into the Cottage Landscape

Proper siting of an arbor or pergola is essential to its success in the design. All too often people plunk down an arbor in the middle of a lawn or garden space with no reference to the rest of the environment. Instead of being a beautiful feature, such an oddly placed structure is a curious anomaly, looking uncomfortably out of place.

Arches, arbors, and pergolas must be

An arbor or pergola placed along a path anchors the path and creates a destination for someone walking in the garden. It allows you to engage in vertical gardening.

connected to the overall design. For example, a path should lead to an arch or arbor. Place an arbor on the edge of the property, and then enhance the illusion that it is leading to additional grounds by camouflaging the property boundary with shrubs. Be sure to have a path leading to the arbor to anchor its position and to encourage people to stroll over and enjoy it.

Position Pergolas Over Paths. The best location for a pergola is over an important path. Ideally a pergola should not lead to a dead end. Even a small garden can have room for a pergola. Instead of running it down the center of the property, set it along the property line. Plant shade-loving plants under its protected canopy, and place a bench underneath to create a shady retreat. A vine-covered pergola gives much-valued privacy from the upper stories of adjacent houses.

Although a pergola often covers a straight walkway, there is no rule that says a pergola cannot cover a curving path. In such a case, the curve prompts curiosity.

The curving top of an arbor is a good shape to copy for other structures, such as the fence above, in a cottage garden.

A pergola and trellis combine to provide shade and a certain level of privacy to the patio shown below.

A pergola-like structure, right, supported by a deck railing provides dappled shade for the benches below it.

Near the house it is wise to choose a design for your arbor or pergola that complements the design of the building. For a traditional-style house like a cottage you may want to support your arbor or pergola with classical columns made of concrete, fiberglass, or stone. Augment a brick house with brick support posts. Cast-iron or aluminum posts could echo other wrought-iron features, such as a balcony, railing, or gate. Farther from the house, you can have more leeway.

Scale Pergolas to Garden Size. In a small cottage garden, make a pergola less architecturally domineering by building the support posts and rafters out of thinner material such as metal or finer-cut lumber. In a large garden where you need the extra mass, opt for columns built of brick, stone, or substantial pieces of lumber.

Place arbors and pergolas so that they become a destination in the yard, left.

An unusual shape draws attention to this arbor and the property beyond, above.

Plants for Arches, Arbors, and Pergolas

BOTANICAL NAME	COMMON NAME	ZONE
Aristolochia macrophylla	Dutchman's pipe	4–8
Bignonia capreolata	cross vine	6–9
Bougainvillea cultivars		10
Campsis radians	trumpet creeper	4–9
Clematis species and cultivars		
	'Comtesse de Bouchard'	4–9
	'Duchess of Albany'	4–9
	'Ernest Markham'	4–9
	'Gypsy Queen'	4–9
	'Gravetye Beauty'	4–9
	'Hagley Hybrid'	4–9
	'Henryi'	4–9
	'Horn of Plenty',	4–9
	C. x jackmanii 'Superba'	3–9
	C. montana	6–9
	C. tangutica 'Bill MacKenzie'	5–7
	C. terniflora sweet autumn clematis	5–9
Hydrangea petiolaris	climbing hydrangea	4–9, 4–10 in west
Lonicera species	honeysuckle	zones vary with species
Parthenocissus tricuspidata	Boston ivy	4–9
Rosa cultivars	climbing rose	
	'Alberic Barbier'	4–10
	'Albertine'	4–10
	'Blaze'	4–10
	'Chaplin's Pink Companion'	4–10
	'Felicite Perpetue'	4–10
	R. filipes 'Kiftsgate'	5–10
	'Mme. Gregoire Staechelin'	4–10
	'New Dawn'	4–10
	'Veilchenblau'	4–10
Schizophragma hydrangeoides	Japanese hydrangea vine	5–9
Trachelospermum jasminoides	star jasmine	8–10
Vitis coignetiae	crimson glory vine	6–9
Vitis vinifera 'Purpurea'	purpleleaf grape	6–9
Wisteria species	wisteria	5–10

Pergolas should always be somewhat higher than they are wide. A minimum width of about 5 feet allows two people to walk through the pergola abreast. The structure should be high enough to allow a tall adult to walk underneath comfortably. The upright support posts also need to be in proportion to the roof. If the supports are hefty, the overhead beams also should be substantial. How far apart you space the roof beams depends on the final effect you want. Wide spacing creates a skylight. Close spacing of the beams makes the pergola more tunnel-like.

Bear in mind that an arbor or pergola covered in vines must bear a lot of weight. The upright posts should be strong and properly rooted in a solid foundation, and the roof structure should be well built.

You can build your own or purchase ready-made units from a home center or garden-supply outlet. In most cases, large trellises, arbors, and pergolas come unassembled. Check with the local building department (or your house builder may know) for code requirements for foundations and construction.

Tips for Containers and Hanging Baskets

- To keep down the weight of containers filled with soil, fill the lower half of large pots with foam peanuts, perlite, or any other lightweight material that will not compact over time. Put potting mix in the remaining space, and plant as usual.

- To keep up with the heavy feeding most container-grown plants need, add compost to the planting mix or add liquid seaweed or a fish emulsion/liquid seaweed combination to the water every few weeks to ensure a well-balanced supply of all essential micronutrients.

- To remoisten peat moss if it becomes dry, fill a tub with water and add a drop of liquid detergent to help the water stick to the peat moss. Set the basket in the water, and leave it for several hours until the potting soil and peat moss mix is saturated with water.

- Pinch off dead blossoms regularly to keep container plants bushy and full of flowers.

- Cluster your pots together in a sheltered spot if you will be away for several days. The plants will need watering less frequently, and it will be easier to water if the containers are all in one place.

- To automatically water containers, bury one end of a long wick (such as those sold with oil-fueled lanterns) near the plant's roots. Insert the other end in a bucket of water. The wick will gradually soak up the water and provide a slow, continuous source of water for the plant.

- If a plant is root-bound, prune the roots by cutting back the outer edges of the root ball instead of transplanting it to a larger container. Then repot it in the same container with fresh soil.

- Consider watering many containers with an automatic drip irrigation system; install a line to each container.

- To reduce moisture loss, top the soil in your containers with mulch.

Containers for Plants

People have been gardening in containers at least since King Nebuchadnezzar built the Hanging Gardens of Babylon in 600 BC. While most people do not attempt container gardening on the massive scale achieved by Nebuchadnezzar, containers still play an important role in enhancing a garden. There are many advantages to container gardening.

Container Gardens are Versatile.
Container gardens can be moved when they are past their prime. You can grow tropical plants in containers by keeping them outside in the summer and moving them indoors to overwinter where winters are harsh. If your soil is alkaline, you can grow acid-loving plants in pots. Containers add color and excitement to patios. Cluster a group of containers to create a pleasing composition of shapes, sizes, and colors.

Attach baskets of cascading plants to pergolas, arbors, and eaves to bring color up high.

Designing with Containers
Choose your containers with the same care as you would a sculpture or any other garden ornament. In addition to finding pots that complement your garden style, think about which plants to put in them.

Match Plants to Containers. Showy plants such as palms, Dracaena, and shrubs pruned as standards look best in traditionally designed planters such as classic urns or white planter boxes. Rustic barrels or half barrels are inexpensive and unpretentious containers in an informal setting.

Try Unusual Containers. Fill an old wheelbarrow with potted plants, or give new life to a leaky metal watering can by turning it into a planter. Or plant an old shoe with shallow-rooted succulents.

Use your imagination and have fun. Whatever container you use, however, make sure it has drainage holes in the bottom. Unless you're growing bog plants, they'll be short-lived if their roots are sitting permanently in water.

Plant containers can be as distinctive or as simple as you like. The decorative planters shown top left look good on a porch or patio. The tall white bucket above add height to an arrangement of planters. A copper-finish planter on a table, left, decorates an entrance.

Maintaining Container Plants

Plants growing in containers need special care. Small containers dry out quickly and need frequent watering. In dry climates or on windy days, some containers should be watered at least once, if not twice, daily. However, frequent watering leaches out soil nutrients, so container-grown plants should be fertilized regularly.

Use Light, Well-Draining Soil. The soil in containers should be light and nutritious. Soil collected from the garden is too heavy. But soilless container mixes are often so light they dry out quickly. As a compromise, combine 2 parts potting mix with 1 part compost. The compost will give more body to the mix, as well as provide important nutrients.

Choice of Fertilizer Depends on What's Growing. The type and frequency of fertilizing depends on what's growing in the container. Some experts recommend fertilizing with half-strength fish emulsion every time you water. This makes it easier to remember when you last fed the plants. Or fertilize your plants with organic slow-release fertilizer pellets every 4 to 6 weeks. Mix the pellets with the potting mix at planting time; a good dose should feed annuals for the entire season.

Create a theme, such as the frogs shown left, if you are looking for an easy way to add some whimsy to a cottage garden.

Hide small sculptures or other items throughout the garden. The frog above would be at home near a water feature.

To highlight an arbor, string small lights over it. The arbor shown opposite left is covered with blanket lights.

A candle in a lantern, opposite right, isn't for everyday lighting, but it does make an interesting accent for special occasions.

Humor in the Landscape

A touch of levity adds to the pleasure of a cottage garden. Even in a formal landscape, there is room for a subtle, sophisticated joke—or some broad humor.

A childlike enthusiasm is often a factor in successful whimsy. Treehouses, in addition to being wonderful places for children to play, suggest a gardener who remembers the wonders of climbing trees for a bird's-eye view of the territory. Garden animal sculptures can be elevated to whimsy with careful placement. For example, concrete stalking cat sculptures with marble eyes are readily available and inexpensive. Stuck in plain view, these cats lack subtlety. But try placing one where it is partially hidden by arching shrubbery or cascading plants. Now you have a creature of the jungle on the prowl, glimpsed but not completely seen.

Be True to Yourself. Don't be daunted by the views of others. Be true to yourself, and express your own personality and sense of humor. With some thought and creativity, you can create a whimsical vignette or two in your garden that will lift your heart and tickle your funny bone.

Outdoor Lighting

First decide how much light you need and where it should go. Besides general overall illumination, locate fixtures near activity zones: the food preparation and cooking area, the wet bar, or wherever you plan to set up drinks, snacks, or a buffet when you entertain. Be sure that there is adequate light near the dining table, conversation areas, and recreational spots, such as the hot tub, if you plan to use them in the evening. You may want separate switches for each one, and you might consider dim-mers; you don't need or want the same intensity of light required for barbecuing as you do for relaxing in the hot tub.

Lighting the Way

Walkways and staircases need lighting for safety. There are a number of practical options: path lights (if the walkway is ground level), brick lights that can be inserted into your walls near the steps, and railing fixtures that can be tucked under deck railings or steps. Less-functional but more-decorative lighting such as post lamps can provide illumination for high traffic areas; sconces can be effective on stair landings or near doors. Walk lights also provide a needed measure of safety. Be sure to pick fixtures that look as good during the day as they do at night.

Don't forget about areas that may call for motion-sensitive floodlights, such as entrances into the house and garage, underneath a raised deck, and deep yards are all excellent locations for floodlights. Keep these fixtures on separate switches so that they don't interfere with the atmosphere you want to create while you are using the deck.

Adding Accent Light

Are there any noteworthy plantings or objects in your garden that you can highlight? By using in-ground accent lighting or spotlights, you can create dramatic nighttime effects or a focal point. Artful lighting can enhance the ambiance of your deck by drawing attention to the shape of a handsome tree, a garden statue, a fountain or pond, or an outdoor pool.

Depending on the lighting system you buy, you may be able to install the fixtures yourself. But working with electricity poses technical, code, and safety concerns. It's probably best to hire a qualified professional for the installation. For complex projects, you may also want to consult a landscape lighting professional. Home centers sometimes provide this type of expertise. If you decide to plot a design yourself, remember not to overlight the deck.

Other Considerations

As you plan to install deck lighting, think about the space's other electrical or wiring needs. If there is an outdoor kitchen, a grill area, or a bar, you may want outlets for a refrigerator or small appliances. You might include additional outlets for a stereo or speakers, or even a TV. Don't overlook a

phone jack for the modem on your laptop computer. Some decking systems come prewired and are ready to be hooked up.

So with forethought, you can incorporate everything you need into your outdoor living plans.

Decorative Lighting

Add another dimension to your yard or garden, and get more use out of it as well, by installing decorative lighting. Start by covering a garden arch with small decorative lights. You can use multicolor lights, or for a more sophisticated look, use single-color strands or blankets. Supplement the arch lights with lanterns and torches. When selecting lights, pick those that look as good during the day as they do at night.

Stairs and walkways, opposite, require lighting for safety.

Create drama by uplighting arbors, pergolas, and plantings on your property, right.

Outdoor lighting, below, consists of standard line-voltage or low-voltage lights. A low-voltage system is easier to install.

Plan #151188

Dimensions: 63'4" W x 59'10" D

Levels: 1

Square Footage: 2,525

Bedrooms: 3

Bathrooms: 2

Foundation: Basement, walk-out basement, crawl space, or slab

Materials List Available: Y

Price Category: E

Images provided by designer/architect.

Copyright by designer/architect.

Plan #211001

Dimensions: 52' W x 66' D

Levels: 1

Square Footage: 1,655

Bedrooms: 3

Bathrooms: 2

Foundation: Slab

Materials List Available: Yes

Price Category: C

Images provided by designer/architect.

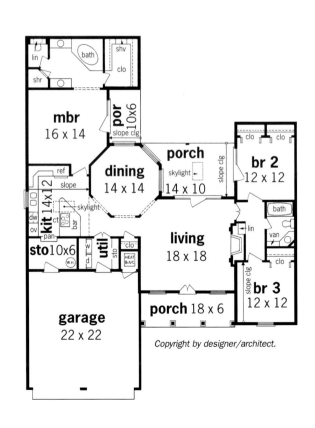

Copyright by designer/architect.

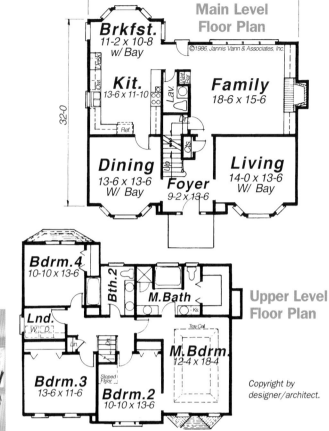

Main Level Floor Plan

©1986, Jannis Vann & Associates, Inc.

38-0

32-0

Brkfst. 11-2 x 10-8 w/ Bay

Kit. 13-6 x 11-10

Family 18-6 x 15-6

Dining 13-6 x 13-6 W/ Bay

Foyer 9-2 x 13-6

Living 14-0 x 13-6 W/ Bay

Plan #141030

Dimensions: 38' W x 32' D

Levels: 2

Square Footage: 2,323

Main Level Sq. Ft.: 1,179

Upper Level Sq. Ft.: 1,144

Bedrooms: 4

Bathrooms: 2½

Foundation: Basement

Materials List Available: Yes

Price Category: E

Images provided by designer/architect.

Upper Level Floor Plan

Bdrm.4 10-10 x 13-6

Bth.2

M.Bath

Lnd. W D

M.Bdrm. 12-4 x 18-4

Bdrm.3 13-6 x 11-6

Bdrm.2 10-10 x 13-6

Copyright by designer/architect.

Plan #141034

Dimensions: 77' W x 66' D

Levels: 2

Square Footage: 3,588

Main Level Sq. Ft.: 2,329

Upper Level Sq. Ft.: 1,259

Bedrooms: 4

Bathrooms: 3½

Foundation: Basement

Materials List Available: Yes

Price Category: H

Images provided by designer/architect.

Upper Level Floor Plan

Copyright by designer/architect.

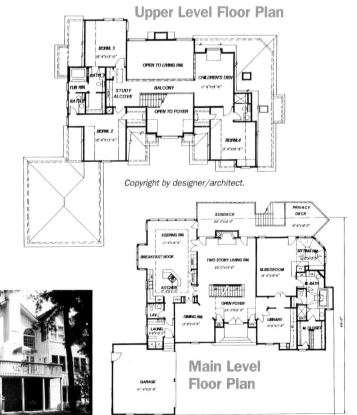

Main Level Floor Plan

Plan #211006

Dimensions: 61' W x 77' D
Levels: 1
Square Footage: 2,177
Bedrooms: 3
Bathrooms: 2
Foundation: Slab, optional basement
Materials List Available: Yes
Price Category: D

This traditional home with a stucco exterior is distinguished by its 9-ft. ceilings throughout and its sleek, contemporary interior.

Features:

- Living Room: A series of arched openings that surround this room adds strong visual interest. Settle down by the fireplace on cold winter nights.

- Dining Room: Step up to enter this room with a raised floor that sets it apart from other areas.

- Kitchen: Ideal for cooking as well as casual socializing, this kitchen has a stovetop island and a breakfast bar.

- Master Suite: The sitting area in this suite is so big that you might want to watch TV here or make it a study. In the bath, you'll find a skylight above the angled tub with a mirror surround and well-placed plant ledge.

- Rear Porch: This 200-sq.-ft. covered porch gives you plenty of space for entertaining.

SMARTtip

DECK Furniture Style

Mix-and-match tabletops, frames, and legs are stylish. Combine materials such as glass, metal, wood, and mosaic tiles.

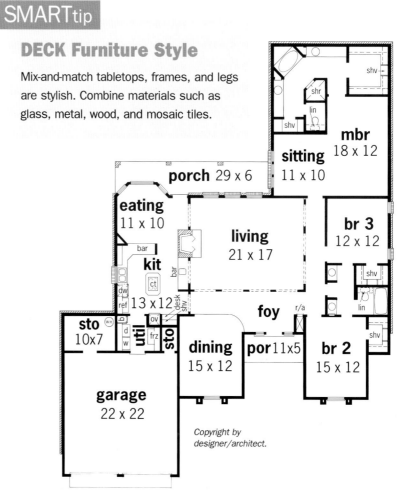

Copyright by designer/architect.

Plan #121019

Dimensions: 70' W x 60' D
Levels: 2
Square Footage: 3,775
Main Level Sq. Ft.: 1,923
Upper Level Sq. Ft.: 1,852
Bedrooms: 4
Bathrooms: 3
Foundation: Basement
Materials List Available: Yes
Price Category: H

Images provided by designer/architect.

The grand exterior presence is carried inside, beginning with the dramatic curved staircase.

Features:

- Ceiling Height: 8 ft.

- Den: French doors lead to the sophisticated den, with its bayed windows and wall of bookcases.

- Living Room: A curved wall and a series of arched windows highlight this large space.

- Formal Dining Room: The living room shares the curved wall and arched windows found in the living room.

- Screened Porch: This huge space features skylights and is accessible by another French door from the dining room.

- Family Room: Family and guests alike will be drawn to this room, with its trio of arched windows and fireplace flanked by bookcases.

- Kitchen: An island adds convenience and distinction to this large, functional kitchen.

- Garage: This spacious three-bay garage provides plenty of space for cars and storage.

Main Level Floor Plan

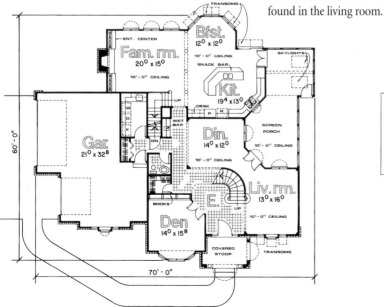

Upper Level Floor Plan

Copyright by designer/architect.

Plan #211002

Dimensions: 68' W x 62' D
Levels: 1
Square Footage: 1,792
Bedrooms: 3
Bathrooms: 2
Foundation: Crawl space
Materials List Available: Yes
Price Category: C

Arched windows on the front of this home give it a European style that you're sure to love.

SMARTtip

Water Features

Water features create the ambiance of a soothing oasis on a deck. A water-filled urn becomes a mirror that reflects the sky— making a small deck look larger. Fish flashing in an ornamental pool add color and act as a focal point for a deck with no view.

A water fountain introduces a pleasant rhythmical sound that helps drown out the background noises of traffic and nearby neighbors.

Images provided by designer/architect.

Features:

- **Living Room:** The 12-ft. ceiling in this large, open room enhances its spacious feeling. A fireplace adds warmth on chilly days and cool evenings.

- **Dining Room:** Decorate to accentuate the 12-ft. ceiling and formal feeling of this room.

- **Kitchen:** Designed for comfort and efficiency, this room also has a 12-ft. ceiling. The cozy breakfast bar is a natural gathering spot for friends and family.

- **Master Suite:** A split design guarantees privacy here. A sloped cathedral ceiling adds elegance, and a walk-in closet makes it practical. The bath has two vanities, a tub, and a walk-in shower.

- **Garage:** Park two cars here, and use the balance of this 520 sq. ft. area as a handy storage area.

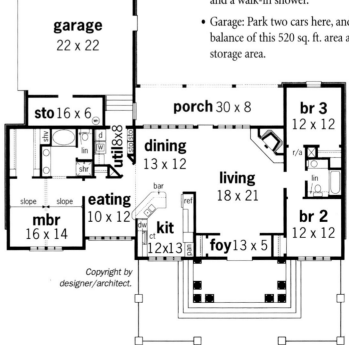

Copyright by designer/architect.

Plan #151011

Dimensions: 59'6" W x 74'4" D
Levels: 2
Square Footage: 3,437
Main Level Sq. Ft.: 2,184
Upper Level Sq. Ft.: 1,253
Bedrooms: 5
Bathrooms: 4
Foundation: Crawl space, slab; optional basement or daylight basement
Price Category: G

Beauty, comfort, and convenience are yours in this luxurious, split-level home.

Main Level Features:

- Ceiling Height: 10 ft. unless otherwise noted.

- Master Suite: The 11-ft. pan ceiling sets the tone for this secluded area, with a lovely bay window that opens onto a rear porch, a pass-through fireplace to the great room, and a sitting room.

- Great Room: The pass-through fireplace makes this spacious room a cozy spot, while the French doors leading to a rear porch make it a perfect spot for entertaining.

- Dining Room: Gracious 8-in. columns set off the entrance to this room.

- Kitchen: An island bar provides an efficient work area that's fitted with a sink.

- Breakfast Room: Open to the kitchen, this room is defined by a bay window and a spiral staircase to the second floor.

- Laundry Room: Large enough to accommodate a folding table, this room can also be fitted with a swinging pet door.

Upper Level Features:

- Play Room: French doors in the children's playroom open onto a balcony where they can continue their games.

- Bedrooms: The 9-ft. ceilings on the second story make the rooms feel bright and airy.

Optional basement foundation or optional daylight basement foundation available for an additional $250.

**Main Level
Floor Plan**

**Upper Level
Floor Plan**

Plan #241005

Dimensions: 53' W x 55'9" D
Levels: 1
Square Footage: 1,670
Bedrooms: 3
Bathrooms: 2
Foundation: Slab
Materials List Available: No
Price Category: C

This charming starter home, in split-bedroom format, combines big-house features in a compact design.

Features:

- **Great Room:** With easy access to the formal dining room, kitchen, and breakfast area, this great room features a cozy fireplace.

- **Kitchen:** This big kitchen, with easy access to a walk-in pantry, features an island for added work space and a lovely plant shelf that separates it from the great room.

- **Master Suite:** Separated for privacy, this master suite offers a roomy bath with whirlpool tub, dual vanities, a separate shower, and a large walk-in closet.

- **Additional Rooms:** Additional rooms include a laundry/utility room—with space for a washer, dryer, and freezer—a large area above the garage, well-suited for a media or game room, and two secondary bedrooms.

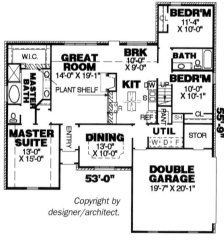

Copyright by designer/architect.

SMARTtip

Window Scarf

The best way to wrap a window scarf around a pole is as follows:

- Lay out the material on a large, clean surface. Gather the fabric at the top of each jabot, and use elastic to hold it together.

- Swing one jabot into place over the pole and, starting from there, wind the swag portion as many times as you need around the pole until you reach the elastic at the second jabot, which should have landed at the opposite pole end.

- Readjust wraps along the pole. Generally, wrapped swags just touch or slightly overlap.

- For a dramatic effect, stuff the wrapped swags with tissue paper or thin foam, depending on the translucence and weight of fabric.

- Release elastics at tops of jabots.

Plan #321008

Dimensions: 57' W x 52'2" D
Levels: 1
Square Footage: 1,761
Bedrooms: 4
Bathrooms: 2
Foundation: Basement
Materials List Available: Yes
Price Category: C

One look at the roof dormers and planter boxes that grace the outside of this ranch, and you'll know that the interior is planned for comfortable family living.

Features:

• Great Room: A vaulted ceiling in this room points up its generous dimensions. Put a grouping of chairs near the fireplace to take advantage of the cozy spot it creates in chilly weather.

• Kitchen: Open to the great room, this kitchen has been planned for convenience. It features a pass-through to the dining area for easy serving when you've got a crowd to feed.

• Master Bedroom: A vaulted ceiling here makes you feel especially pampered, and the walk-in closet and amenity-filled bath add to that feeling.

• Additional Bedrooms: Great closet space characterizes all the rooms in this home, making it easy for children of any age to keep it organized and tidy.

Images provided by designer/architect.

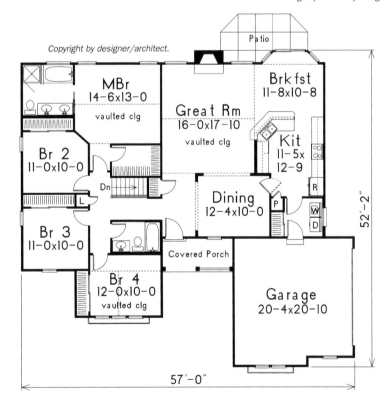

Copyright by designer/architect.

SMARTtip

Hanging Wallpaper

Use liner paper to smooth out a damaged wall and to provide uniform support for expensive paper.

Plan #271030

Dimensions: 56' W x 45' D
Levels: 2
Square Footage: 1,926
Main Level Sq. Ft.: 1,490
Upper Level Sq. Ft.: 436
Bedrooms: 3
Bathrooms: 2½
Foundation: Basement
Materials List Available: Yes
Price Category: D

Images provided by designer/architect.

This traditional home's main-floor master suite is hard to resist, with its inviting window seat and delightful bath.

Features:

- Master Suite: Just off from the entry foyer, this luxurious oasis is entered through double doors, and offers an airy vaulted ceiling, plus a private bath that includes a separate tub and shower, dual-sink vanity, and walk-in closet.

- Great Room: This space does it all in style, with a breathtaking wall of windows and a charming fireplace.

- Kitchen: A cooktop island makes dinnertime tasks a breeze. You'll also love the roomy pantry. The adjoining breakfast room, with its deck access and built-in desk, is sure to be a popular hangout for the teens.

- Secondary Bedrooms: Two additional bedrooms reside on the upper floor and allow the younger family members a measure of desired—and necessary—privacy.

Main Level Floor Plan

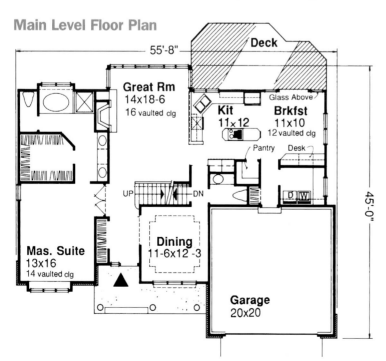

Upper Level Floor Plan

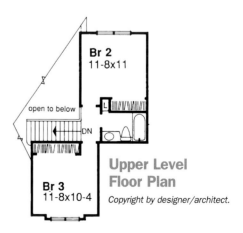

Copyright by designer/architect.

Plan #121020

Dimensions: 64' W x 46' D
Levels: 2
Square Footage: 2,480
Main Level Sq. Ft.: 1,369
Upper Level Sq. Ft.: 1,111
Bedrooms: 4
Bathrooms: 3
Foundation: Basement
Materials List Available: Yes
Price Category: E

Tapered columns and an angled stairway give this home a classical style.

Features:

- Ceiling Height: 8 ft.

- Living Room: Just off the dramatic two-story entry is this distinctive living room, with its tapered columns, transom-topped windows, and boxed ceiling.

- Formal Dining Room: The tapered columns, transom-topped windows, and boxed ceiling found in the living room continue into this gracious dining space.

- Family Room: Located on the opposite side of the house from the living room and dining room, the family room features a beamed ceiling and fireplace framed by windows.

- Kitchen: An island is the centerpiece of this convenient kitchen.

- Master Suite: Upstairs, a tiered ceiling and corner windows enhance the master bedroom, which is served by a pampering bath.

Main Level Floor Plan

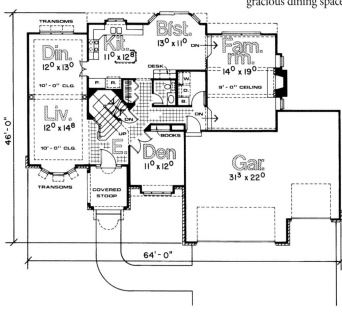

Upper Level Floor Plan

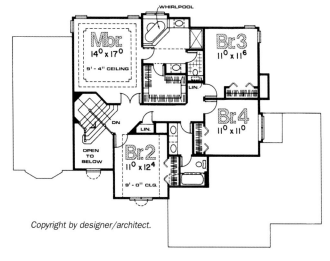

Plan #121076

Dimensions: 64' W x 60'8" D
Levels: 2
Square Footage: 3,067
Main Level Sq. Ft.: 2,169
Upper Level Sq. Ft.: 898
Bedrooms: 4
Bathrooms: 3½
Foundation: Basement
Materials List Available: Yes
Price Category: G

Images provided by designer/architect.

You'll love the combination of formal features and casual, family-friendly areas in this spacious home with an elegant exterior.

Features:

• Entry: The elegant windows in this two-story area are complemented by the unusual staircase.

• Family Room: This family room features an 11-ft. ceiling, wet bar, fireplace, and trio of windows that look out to the covered porch.

• Living Room: Columns set off both this room and the dining room. Decorate to accentuate their formality, or make them blend into a more casual atmosphere.

• Master Suite: Columns in this suite highlight a bayed sitting room where you'll be happy to relax at the end of the day or on weekend mornings.

• Bedrooms: Bedroom 2 has a private bath, making it an ideal guest room, and you'll find private vanities in bedrooms 3 and 4.

Main Level Floor Plan

Upper Level Floor Plan

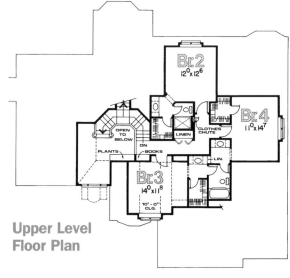

Copyright by designer/architect.

Plan #271012

Dimensions: 48' W x 30' D
Levels: 2
Square Footage: 1,359
Main Level Sq. Ft.: 668
Upper Level Sq. Ft.: 691
Bedrooms: 3
Bathrooms: 2½
Foundation: Basement
Materials List Available: Yes
Price Category: B

This traditional home blends an updated exterior with a thoroughly modern interior.

Features:

- **Living Room:** This sunny, vaulted gathering room offers a handsome fireplace and open access to the adjoining dining room.

- **Dining Room:** Equally suited to intimate family gatherings and larger dinner parties, this space includes access to a spacious backyard deck.

- **Kitchen/Breakfast Nook:** Smartly joined, these two rooms are just perfect for speedy weekday mornings and lazy weekend breakfasts.

- **Master Suite:** A skylighted staircase leads to this upper-floor masterpiece, which includes a private bath, a walk-in closet, and bright, boxed-out window arrangement.

- **Secondary Bedrooms:** One of these is actually a loft/bedroom conversion, which makes it suitable for expansion space as your family grows.

Main Level Floor Plan

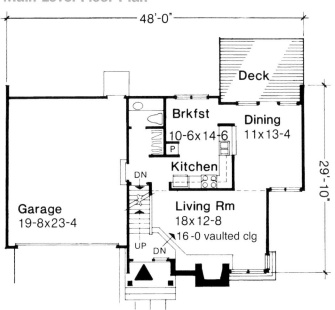

Upper Level Floor Plan

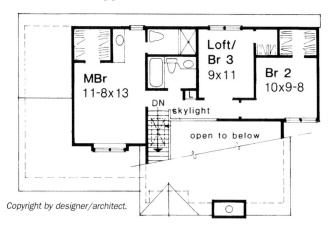

Plan #271025

Dimensions: 62' W x 57' D
Levels: 2
Square Footage: 2,223
Main Level Sq. Ft.: 1,689
Upper Level Sq. Ft.: 534
Bedrooms: 3
Bathrooms: 2½
Foundation: Basement
Materials List Available: Yes
Price Category: E

Images provided by designer/architect.

This traditional home's unique design combines a dynamic, exciting exterior with a fantastic floor plan.

Features:

- **Living Room:** To the left of the column-lined, barrel-vaulted entry, this inviting space features a curved wall and corner windows.
- **Dining Room:** A tray ceiling enhances this formal meal room.

- **Kitchen:** This island-equipped kitchen includes a corner pantry and a built-in desk. Nearby, the sunny breakfast room opens onto a backyard deck via sliding glass doors.
- **Family Room:** A corner bank of windows provides a glassy backdrop for this room's handsome fireplace. Munchies may be served on the snack bar from the breakfast nook.
- **Master Suite:** This main-floor retreat is simply stunning, and includes a vaulted ceiling, access to a private courtyard, and of course, a sumptuous bath with every creature comfort.

Main Level Floor Plan

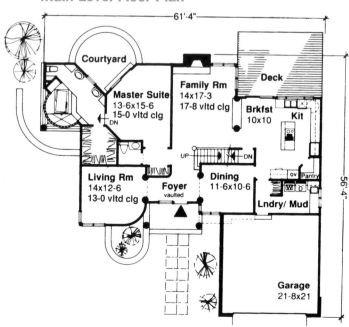

Upper Level Floor Plan

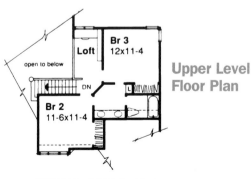

Copyright by designer/architect.

Plan #121001

Dimensions: 56' W x 58' D
Levels: 1
Square Footage: 1,911
Bedrooms: 3
Bathrooms: 2
Foundation: Basement
Materials List Available: Yes
Price Category: D

Images provided by designer/architect.

Detailed, soaring ceilings and top-notch amenities set this distinctive home apart.

Features:

- Ceiling Height: 8 ft. except as noted.

- Great Room: A soaring ceiling and six tall transom-topped windows make this a light and airy spot for entertaining.

- Formal Dining Room: The entry enjoys a pleasing view of this dining room's detailed 12-ft. ceiling and picture window.

- Great Room: At the back of the home, a see-through fireplace in this great room is joined by a built-in entertainment center.

- Hearth Room: This bayed room shares the see-through fireplace with the great room.

- Master Suite: Enjoy the stars and the sun in the private bath's whirlpool and separate shower. The bath features the same decorative ceiling as the dining room.

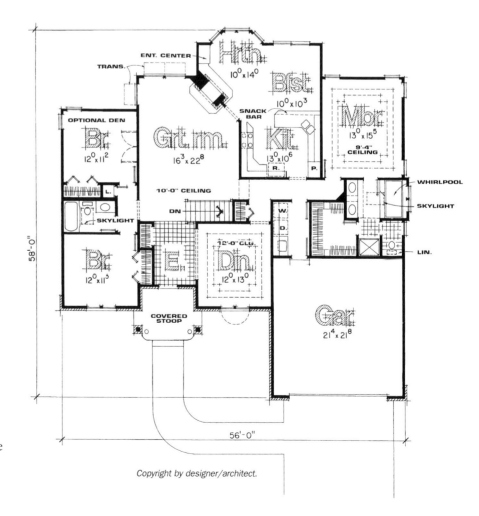

Copyright by designer/architect.

Plan #121070

Dimensions: 50' W x 58' D
Levels: 2
Square Footage: 2,139
Main Level Sq. Ft.: 1,506
Upper Level Sq. Ft.: 633
Bedrooms: 4
Bathrooms: 2½
Foundation: Basement
Materials List Available: Yes
Price Category: D

You'll love this design if you're looking for a bright, airy home where you can easily entertain.

Features:

• Entry: A volume ceiling sets the tone for this home when you first walk in.

• Great Room: With a volume ceiling extending from the entry, this great room has an open feeling. Transom-topped windows contribute natural light during the day.

• Dining Room: Because it is joined to the great room through a cased opening, this dining room can serve as an extension of the great room.

• Kitchen: An island with a snack bar, desk, and pantry make this kitchen a treat, and a door from the breakfast area leads to a private covered patio where dining will be a pleasure.

Main Level Floor Plan

Upper Level Floor Plan

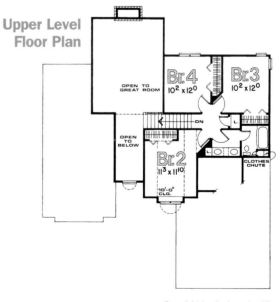

Plan #271027

Dimensions: 61' W x 44' D
Levels: 2
Square Footage: 2,463
Main Level Sq. Ft.: 1,380
Upper Level Sq. Ft.: 1,083
Bedrooms: 4
Bathrooms: 2½
Foundation: Basement
Materials List Available: Yes
Price Category: D

Images provided by designer/architect.

This post-modern design uses half-round transom windows and a barrel-vaulted porch to lend elegance to its facade.

Features:

- **Living Room:** A vaulted ceiling and a striking fireplace enhance this formal gathering space.

- **Dining Room:** Introduced from the living room by square columns, this formal dining room is just steps from the kitchen.

- **Kitchen:** Thoroughly modern in its design, this walk-through kitchen includes an island cooktop and a large pantry. Nearby, a sunny, bayed breakfast area offers sliding-glass-door access to an angled backyard deck.

- **Family Room:** Columns provide an elegant preface to this fun gathering spot, which sports a vaulted ceiling and easy access to the deck.

- **Master suite:** A vaulted ceiling crowns this luxurious space, which includes a private bath and bright windows.

Main Level Floor Plan

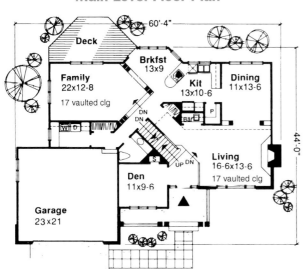

Upper Level Floor Plan

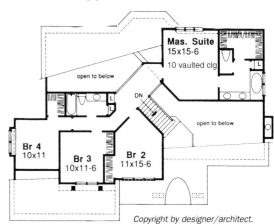

Copyright by designer/architect.

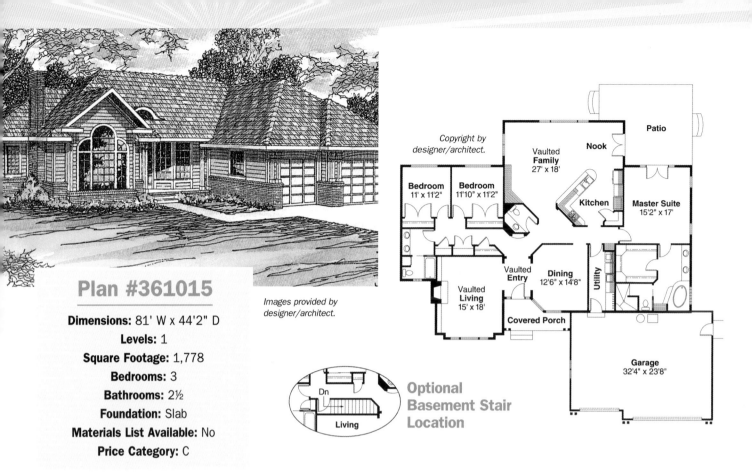

Plan #361015

Dimensions: 81' W x 44'2" D

Levels: 1

Square Footage: 1,778

Bedrooms: 3

Bathrooms: 2½

Foundation: Slab

Materials List Available: No

Price Category: C

Images provided by designer/architect.

Copyright by designer/architect.

Optional Basement Stair Location

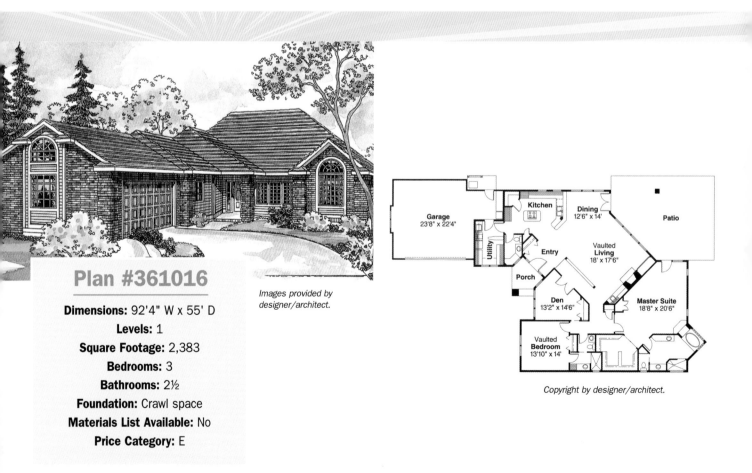

Plan #361016

Dimensions: 92'4" W x 55' D

Levels: 1

Square Footage: 2,383

Bedrooms: 3

Bathrooms: 2½

Foundation: Crawl space

Materials List Available: No

Price Category: E

Images provided by designer/architect.

Copyright by designer/architect.

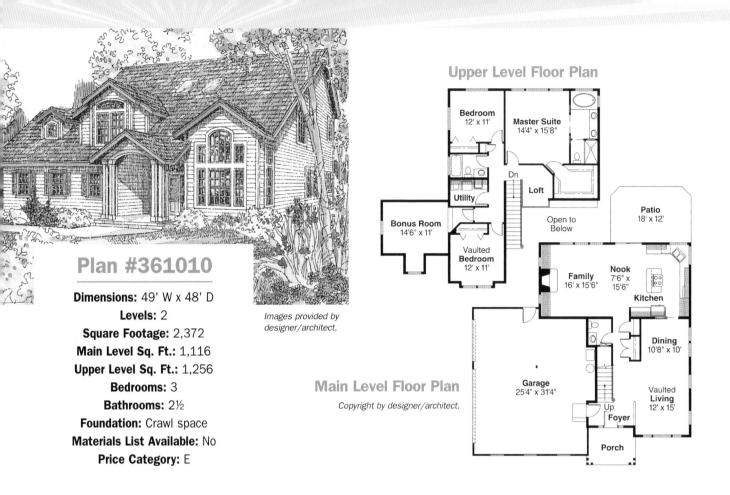

Upper Level Floor Plan

Bedroom
12' x 11'

Master Suite
14'4" x 15'8"

Dn

Utility

Loft

Bonus Room
14'6" x 11'

Open to
Below

Patio
18' x 12'

Vaulted
Bedroom
12' x 11'

Plan #361010

Dimensions: 49' W x 48' D

Levels: 2

Square Footage: 2,372

Main Level Sq. Ft.: 1,116

Upper Level Sq. Ft.: 1,256

Bedrooms: 3

Bathrooms: 2½

Foundation: Crawl space

Materials List Available: No

Price Category: E

Images provided by designer/architect.

Main Level Floor Plan

Copyright by designer/architect.

Family
16' x 15'6"

Nook
7'6" x
15'6"

Kitchen

Garage
25'4" x 31'4"

Dining
10'8" x 10'

Vaulted
Living
12' x 15'

Up

Foyer

Porch

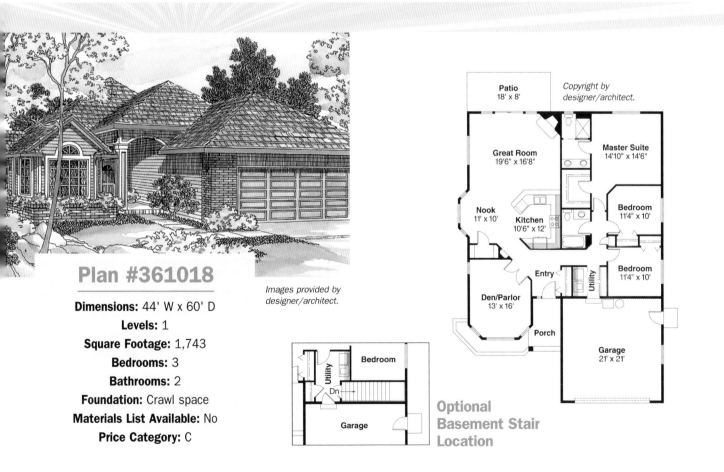

Patio
18' x 8'

Copyright by designer/architect.

Great Room
19'6" x 16'8"

Master Suite
14'10" x 14'6"

Nook
11' x 10'

Kitchen
10'6" x 12'

Bedroom
11'4" x 10'

Entry

Utility

Bedroom
11'4" x 10'

Den/Parlor
13' x 16'

Porch

Garage
21' x 21'

Plan #361018

Dimensions: 44' W x 60' D

Levels: 1

Square Footage: 1,743

Bedrooms: 3

Bathrooms: 2

Foundation: Crawl space

Materials List Available: No

Price Category: C

Images provided by designer/architect.

Bedroom

Utility

Dn

Garage

Optional Basement Stair Location

Plan #311005

Dimensions: 87' W x 57'3" D
Levels: 1
Square Footage: 2,497
Bedrooms: 3
Bathrooms: 3½
Foundation: Crawl space, slab
Materials List Available: Yes
Price Category: E

You'll love this home, which mixes practical features with a gracious appearance.

Features:

- **Great Room:** A handsome fireplace and flanking windows that give a view of the back patio are the highlights of this gracious room.

- **Kitchen:** A curved bar defines the perimeter of this well-planned kitchen.

- **Breakfast Room:** Open to both the great room and the kitchen, this sunny spot leads to the rear porch, which in turn, leads to the patio beyond.

- **Master Suite:** Vaulted ceilings, a huge walk-in closet, and deluxe bath create luxury here.

- **Bonus Room:** Finish this 966-sq.-ft. area as a huge game room, or divide it into a game room, study, and sewing or craft room.

- **Additional Bedrooms:** Each bedroom has a private bath and good closet space.

Images provided by designer/architect.

Main Level Floor Plan

Copyright by designer/architect.

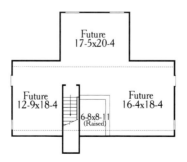

Bonus Area Floor Plan

Images provided by designer/architect.

Plan #121085

Dimensions: 42' W x 54' D
Levels: 2
Square Footage: 1,948
Main Level Sq. Ft.: 1,517
Upper Level Sq. Ft.: 431
Bedrooms: 4
Bathrooms: 3
Foundation: Basement
Materials List Available: Yes
Price Category: D

You'll love the spacious feeling in this home, with its generous rooms and excellent design.

Features:

- **Great Room:** This room is lofty and open, thanks in part to the transom-topped windows that flank the fireplace. However, you can furnish to create a cozy nook for reading or a private spot to watch TV or enjoy some quiet music.

- **Kitchen:** Wrapping counters add an unusual touch to this kitchen, and a pantry gives extra storage area. A snack bar links the kitchen with a separate breakfast area.

- **Master Suite:** A tiered ceiling adds elegance to this area, and a walk-in closet adds practicality. The private bath features a sunlit whirlpool tub, separate shower, and double vanity.

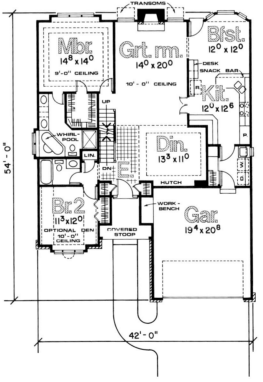

Main Level Floor Plan

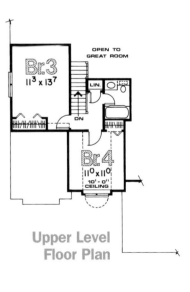

Upper Level Floor Plan

Copyright by designer/architect.

- **Upper-Level Bedrooms:** The upper-level placement is just right for these bedrooms, which share an amenity-filled full bathroom.

Images provided by designer/architect.

Plan #121086

Dimensions: 55'4" W x 37'8" D

Levels: 2

Square Footage: 1,998

Main Level Sq. Ft.: 1,093

Upper Level Sq. Ft.: 905

Bedrooms: 3

Bathrooms: 2½

Foundation: Basement

Materials List Available: Yes

Price Category: D

You'll love the open design of this comfortable home if sunny, bright rooms make you happy.

Features:

• Entry: Walk into this two-story entry, and you're sure to admire the open staircase and balcony from the upper level.

• Dining Room: To the left of the entry, you'll see this dining room, with its special ceiling detail and built-in display cabinet.

• Living Room: Located immediately to the right, this living room features a charming bay window.

• Family Room: French doors from the living room open into this sunny space, where a handsome fireplace takes center stage.

• Kitchen: Combined with the breakfast area, this kitchen features an island cooktop, a large pantry, and a built-in desk.

Main Level Floor Plan

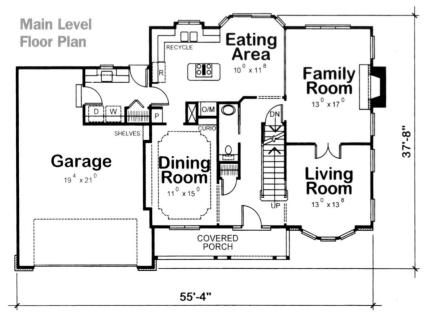

Upper Level Floor Plan

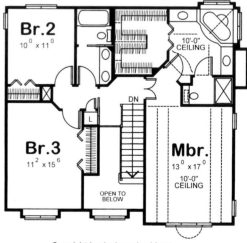

Copyright by designer/architect.

Plan #121090

Dimensions: 60' W x 58' D
Levels: 2
Square Footage: 2,645
Main Level Sq. Ft.: 1,972
Upper Level Sq. Ft.: 673
Bedrooms: 4
Bathrooms: 2½
Foundation: Basement
Materials List Available: Yes
Price Category: F

Images provided by designer/architect.

You'll be amazed at the amenities that have been designed into this lovely home.

Features:

- **Den:** French doors just off the entry lead to this lovely room, with its bowed window and spider-beamed ceiling.
- **Great Room:** A trio of graceful arched windows highlights the volume ceiling in this room. You might want to curl up to read next to the see-through fireplace into the hearth room.
- **Kitchen:** Enjoy the good design in this room.
- **Hearth Room:** The shared fireplace with the great room makes this a cozy spot in cool weather.
- **Master Suite:** French doors lead to this well-lit area, with its roomy walk-in closet, sunlit whirlpool tub, separate shower, and two vanities.

Main Level Floor Plan

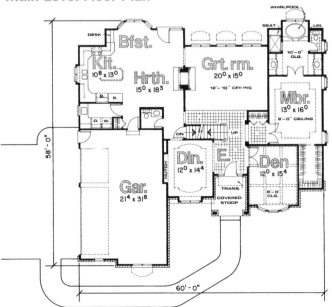

Upper Level Floor Plan

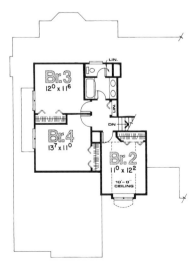

Copyright by designer/architect.

Plan #161027

Dimensions: 59'10" W x 37'4" D
Levels: 2
Square Footage: 2,388
Main Level Sq. Ft.: 1,207
Upper Level Sq. Ft.: 1,181
Bedrooms: 4
Bathrooms: 2½
Foundation: Basement
Materials List Available: No
Price Category: E

Double gables, wood trim, an arched window, and sidelights at the entry give elegance to this family-friendly home.

Features:

- Foyer: Friends and family will see the angled stairs, formal dining room, living room, and library from this foyer.

- Family Room: A fireplace makes this room cozy in the evenings on those chilly days, and multiple windows let natural light stream into it.

- Kitchen: You'll love the island and the ample counter space here as well as the butler's pantry. A breakfast nook makes a comfortable place to snack or just curl up and talk to the cook.

- Master Suite: Tucked away on the upper level, this master suite provides both privacy and luxury.

- Additional Bedrooms: These three additional bedrooms make this home ideal for any family.

Images provided by designer/architect.

Main Level Floor Plan

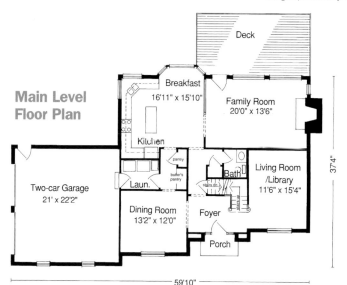

Upper Level Floor Plan

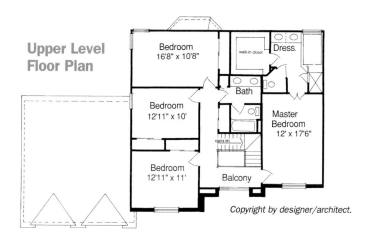

Copyright by designer/architect.

Plan #121068

Dimensions: 54' W x 49'10" D
Levels: 2
Square Footage: 2,391
Main Level Sq. Ft.: 1,697
Upper Level Sq. Ft.: 694
Bedrooms: 4
Bathrooms: 2½
Foundation: Basement
Materials List Available: Yes
Price Category: E

Images provided by designer/architect.

This home allows you a great deal of latitude in the way you choose to finish it, so you can truly make it "your own."

Features:

- **Living Room:** Located just off the entryway, this living room is easy to convert to a stylish den. Add French doors for privacy, and relish the style that the 12-ft. angled ceiling and picturesque arched window provide.

- **Great Room:** The highlight of this room is the two-sided fireplace that easily adds as much design interest as warmth to this area. The three transom-topped windows here fill the room with light.

- **Kitchen:** A center island, walk-in pantry, and built-in desk combine to create this wonderful kitchen, and the attached gazebo breakfast area adds the finishing touch.

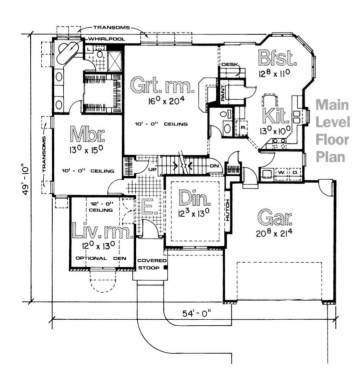

Copyright by designer/architect.

Plan #121029

Dimensions: 58'8" W x 54' D
Levels: 2
Square Footage: 2,576
Main Level Sq. Ft.: 1,735
Upper Level Sq. Ft.: 841
Bedrooms: 4
Bathrooms: 2½
Foundation: Basement
Materials List Available: Yes
Price Category: E

This gracious home is designed with the contemporary lifestyle in mind.

Features:

• Ceiling Height: 8 ft. unless otherwise noted.

• Great Room: This room features a fireplace and entertainment center. It's equally suited for family gatherings and formal entertaining.

• Breakfast Area: The fireplace is two-sided so it shares its warmth with this breakfast area—the perfect spot for informal family meals.

• Master Suite: Halfway up the staircase you'll find double-doors into this truly distinctive suite featuring a barrel-vault ceiling, built-in bookcases, and his and her walk-in closets. Unwind at the end of the day by stretching out in the oval whirlpool tub.

• Computer Loft: This loft overlooks the great room. It is designed as a home office with a built-in desk for your computer.

• Garage: Two bays provide plenty of storage in addition to parking space.

Main Level Floor Plan

Upper Level Floor Plan

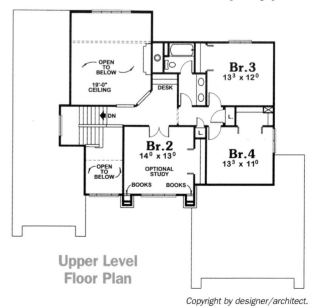

Plan #151034

Dimensions: 58'6" W x 64'6" D

Levels: 1

Square Footage: 2,133

Bedrooms: 3

Bathrooms: 2

Foundation: Crawl space, slab, or basement

Materials List Available: Yes

Price Category: D

You'll love the high ceilings, open floor plan, and contemporary design features in this home.

Features:

- Great Room: A pass-through tiled fireplace between this lovely large room and the adjacent hearth room allows you to notice the mirror effect created by the 10-ft. boxed ceilings in both rooms.

- Dining Room: An 11-ft. ceiling and 8-in. boxed column give formality to this lovely room, where you're certain to entertain.

- Kitchen: If you're a cook, this room may become your favorite spot in the house, thanks to its great design, which includes plenty of work and storage space, and a very practical layout.

- Master Suite: A 10-ft. boxed ceiling gives elegance to this room. A pocket door opens to the private bath, with its huge walk-in closet, glass-blocked whirlpool tub, separate glass shower, and private toilet room.

Plan #151117

Dimensions: 66' W x 55' D

Levels: 1

Square Footage: 1,957

Bedrooms: 3

Bathrooms: 3

Foundation: Crawl space, slab, or basement

Materials List Available: Yes

Price Category: D

You'll love this home if you have a family-centered lifestyle and enjoy an active social life.

Features:

- Foyer: A 10-ft. ceiling sets the tone for this home.

- Great Room: A 10-ft. boxed ceiling and fireplace are the highlights of this room, which also has a door leading to the rear covered porch.

- Dining Room: Columns mark the entry from the foyer to this lovely formal dining room.

- Study: Add the French doors from the foyer to transform bedroom 3, with its vaulted ceiling, into a quiet study.

- Kitchen: This large kitchen includes a pantry and shares an eating bar with the adjoining, bayed breakfast room.

- Master Suite: You'll love the access to the rear porch, as well as the bath with every amenity, in this suite.

Images provided by designer/architect.

Copyright by designer/architect.

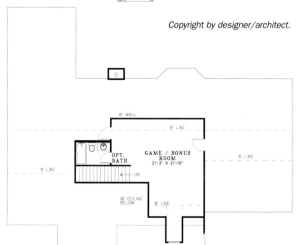

Bonus Area

Plan #361020

Dimensions: 38' W x 44' D
Levels: 2½
Square Footage: 1,434
Main Level Sq. Ft.: 1,318
Upper Level Sq. Ft.: 116
Bedrooms: 1
Bathrooms: 2
Foundation: Crawl space
Materials List Available: No
Price Category: B

Images provided by designer/architect.

Upper Level Floor Plan

Dn

Observatory 7' x 12'

Main Level Floor Plan

Deck

Kitchen

Sun Room 11'6" x 11'6"

Utility

Dining

Up

Great Room 15' x 21'

Entry

Vaulted Bedroom 12'8" x 17'2"

Entry Porch

Dn

Deck 16' x 6'

Up

Garage 15' x 28'6"

Up

Garage Level Floor Plan

Copyright by designer/architect.

Plan #361022

Dimensions: 34' W x 54' D
Levels: 2
Square Footage: 1,844
Main Level Sq. Ft.: 1,159
Upper Level Sq. Ft.: 685
Bedrooms: 3
Bathrooms: 2
Foundation: Crawl space
Materials List Available: No
Price Category: D

Images provided by designer/architect.

Main Level Floor Plan

Covered Porch

Bedroom 10'8" x 15'2"

Bedroom 11'4" x 11'8"

Utility

Kitchen

Entry

Up

Vaulted Great Room 24'8" x 25'4"

Deck

Upper Level Floor Plan
Copyright by designer/architect.

Master Suite 16'2" x 17'2"

Study 8'6" x 9'2"

Vaulted Loft 8' x 13'

Dn

Open to Great Room Below

Plan #381006

Dimensions: 59'10" W x 52' D

Levels: 2

Square Footage: 2,230

Main Level Sq. Ft.: 1,370

Upper Level Sq. Ft.: 860

Bedrooms: 3

Bathrooms: 2½

Foundation: Basement, crawl space

Materials List Available: Yes

Price Category: E

Images provided by designer/architect.

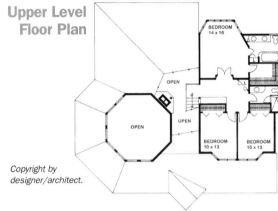

Upper Level Floor Plan

Copyright by designer/architect.

Plan #381009

Dimensions: 26' W x 46' D

Levels: 1

Square Footage: 950

Opt. Bonus Level Sq. Ft.: 210

Bedrooms: 2

Bathrooms: 1

Foundation: Crawl space

Materials List Available: Yes

Price Category: A

Images provided by designer/architect.

Copyright by designer/architect.

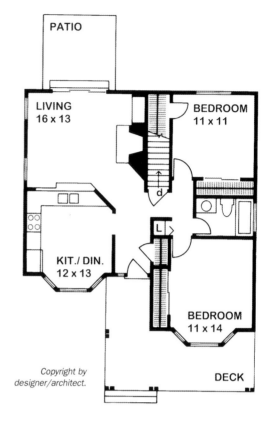

Plan #381016

Dimensions: 32' W x 39'8" D

Levels: 1

Square Footage: 910

Bedrooms: 2

Bathrooms: 1

Foundation: Basement

Materials List Available: Yes

Price Category: A

Images provided by designer/architect.

Copyright by designer/architect.

PATIO

LIVING
16 x 13

BEDROOM
11 x 11

KIT./ DIN.
12 x 13

BEDROOM
11 x 14

DECK

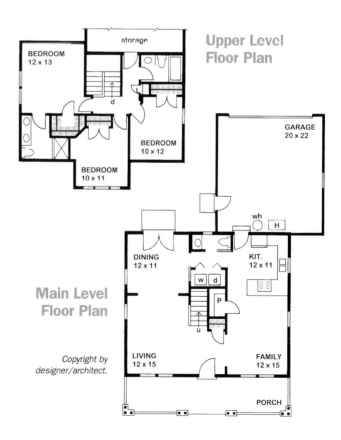

Plan #381018

Dimensions: 38'6" W x 56' D

Levels: 2

Square Footage: 1,540

Main Level Sq. Ft.: 865

Upper Level Sq. Ft.: 675

Bedrooms: 3

Bathrooms: 2½

Foundation: Crawl space

Materials List Available: Yes

Price Category: C

Images provided by designer/architect.

Upper Level Floor Plan

BEDROOM
12 x 13

storage

BEDROOM
10 x 12

BEDROOM
10 x 11

Main Level Floor Plan

Copyright by designer/architect.

GARAGE
20 x 22

DINING
12 x 11

KIT.
12 x 11

wh
H

w d
P

LIVING
12 x 15

FAMILY
12 x 15

PORCH

Plan #271053

Dimensions: 70' W x 34' D
Levels: 2
Square Footage: 2,458
Main Level Sq. Ft.: 1,067
Upper Level Sq. Ft.: 346
Bedrooms: 3
Bathrooms: 2½
Foundation: Daylight basement or crawl space
Materials List Available: No
Price Category: E

The octagonal shape and window-filled walls of this home create a powerful interior packed with panoramic views.

Features:

- **Great Room:** Straight back from the angled entry, this room is brightened by sunlight through windows and sliding glass doors. Beyond the doors, a huge wraparound deck offers plenty of space for tanning or relaxing. A spiral staircase adds visual interest.

- **Kitchen:** This efficient space includes a convenient pantry.

- **Master Suite:** On the upper level, this romantic master suite overlooks the great room below. Several windows provide scenic outdoor views. A walk-in closet and a private bath round out this secluded haven.

- **Basement:** The optional basement includes a recreation room, as well as an extra bedroom and bath.

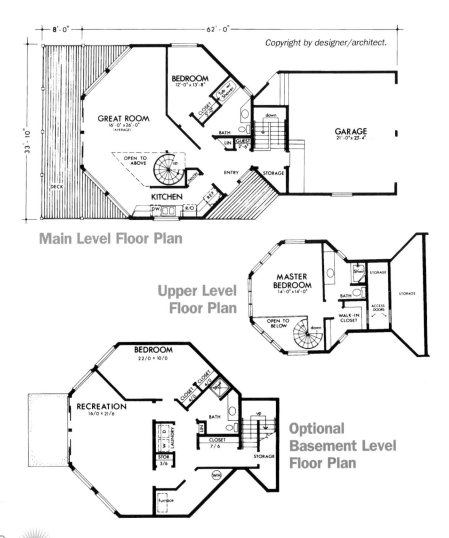

Main Level Floor Plan

Upper Level Floor Plan

Optional Basement Level Floor Plan

Plan #111047

Dimensions: 36' W x 54' D

Levels: 2

Square Footage: 1,863

Main Level Sq. Ft.: 1,056

Upper Level Sq. Ft.: 807

Bedrooms: 4

Bathrooms: 3

Foundation: Pier

Materials List Available: No

Price Category: D

Designed for a coastline, this home is equally appropriate as a year-round residence or a vacation retreat.

Features:

- Orientation: The rear-facing design gives you an ocean view and places the most attractive side of the house where beach-goers can see it.

- Entryway: On the waterside, a large deck with a covered portion leads to the main entrance.

- Carport: This house is raised on piers that let you park underneath it and that protect it from water damage during storms.

- Living Room: A fireplace, French doors, and large windows grace this room, which is open to both the kitchen and the dining area.

- Master Suite: Two sets of French doors open to a balcony on the ocean side, and the suite includes two walk-in closets and a fully equipped bath.

Main Level Floor Plan

Upper Level Floor Plan

Copyright by designer/architect.

Images provided by designer/architect.

Plan #361008

Dimensions: 42' W x 48' D
Levels: 2
Square Footage: 1,749
Main Level Sq. Ft.: 1,280
Upper Level Sq. Ft.: 469
Bedrooms: 3
Bathrooms: 3
Foundation: Crawl space, basement, or slab
Materials List Available: No
Price Category: C

This charming home is ideal for a small family whose members value spending time both together and apart.

Features:

- Great Room: This room opens to the deck for entertaining ease and has a vaulted ceiling and chimney for an airtight woodstove.

- Nook: You'll love the vaulted ceiling here and in the kitchen, and the many windows in this nook.

- Kitchen: The U-shaped counter area creates a step-saving design.

- Studio/Bedroom: The bath, walk-in closet, and door to the deck make this ideal as a master suite, at-home office, or studio space.

- Bedroom: Also with an adjoining bath, this room has a large closet and wide window area.

- Loft: This area can also be a master suite with a huge closet, great window area, and luxury bath.

Main Level Floor Plan

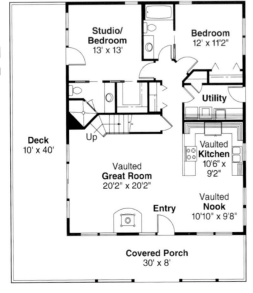

Upper Level Floor Plan

Copyright by designer/architect.

Plan #361007

Dimensions: 42' W x 40' D
Levels: 2
Square Footage: 1,306
Main Level Sq. Ft.: 1,047
Upper Level Sq. Ft.: 259
Bedrooms: 3
Bathrooms: 2
Foundation: Crawl space
Materials List Available: No
Price Category: B

This lovely, compact home is perfect for empty-nesters or a small family.

Features:

- Great Room: This spacious room has double doors to the deck, a vaulted ceiling, and a cozy area around the woodstove.

- Porch/Deck: The wraparound deck provides lots of space for sitting out to enjoy fine weather, but you'll want to sit under the roof when it's raining.

- Nook: Great windows and a vaulted ceiling make this room an ideal place for a dining area.

- Kitchen: The vaulted ceiling adds an unexpected touch to this step-saving kitchen design.

- Studio/Bedroom: Double doors from the deck provide a private entrance; you may want to use this room as a home office or studio space.

- Loft: The loft has an adjoining bath, spacious storage areas, and view to the rooms below.

Main Level Floor Plan

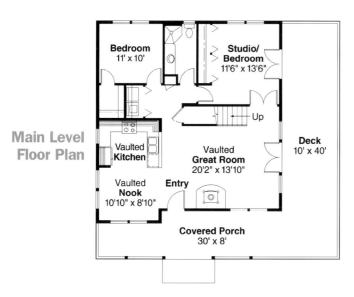

Upper Level Floor Plan

Let Us Help You
Plan Your
Dream Home

Whether you've always dreamed of building your own home or you can't find the right house from among the dozens you've toured, our collection of Southern-inspired home plans can help you achieve the home of your dreams. You could have an architect create a one-of-a-kind home for you, but the design services alone could end up costing up to 15 percent of the cost of construction—a hefty premium for any building project. Isn't it a better idea to select from among the hundreds of unique designs shown in our collection for a fraction of the cost?

What does Creative Homeowner Offer?

In this book, Creative Homeowner provides hundreds of home plans from the country's best architects and designers. Our designs are among the most popular available. Whether your taste runs from traditional to contemporary, Victorian to early American, you are sure to find the best house design for you and your family. Our plans packages include detailed drawings to help you or your builder construct your dream house. (See page 281.)

Can I Make Changes to the Plans?

Creative Homeowner offers three ways to help you achieve a truly unique home design. Our customizing service allows for extensive changes to our designs. (See page 282.) We also provide reverse images of our plans, or we can give you and your builder the tools for making minor changes on your own. (See page 283.)

Can You Help Me Stay on Budget?

Building a house is a large financial investment. To help you stay within your budget, Creative Homeowner can provide you with general construction costs based on your zip code. (See page 283.) Also, many of our plans come with the option of buying detailed materials lists to help you price out construction costs.

Is There Anything I Missed?

A typical construction crew consists of a number of skilled professionals. If you plan on doing all or part of the work yourself, or you want to keep tabs on your builder, we offer best-selling building and design books at attractive prices. (See our company Web site at www.creativehomeowner.com.) Our home-building books cover all phases of home construction. For more home plans, choose from our best-selling library of home plans books. (See page 288.)

Our Plans Packages Offer:

All of our home plans are the result of many hours of work by leading architects and professional designers. Most of our home plans include each of the following.

Frontal Sheet

This artist's rendering of the front of the house gives you an idea of how the house will look once it is completed and the property landscaped.

Detailed Floor Plans

These plans show the size and layout of the rooms. They also provide the locations of doors, windows, fireplaces, closets, stairs, and electrical outlets and switches.

Foundation Plan

A foundation plan gives the dimensions of basements, walk-out basements, crawl spaces, pier foundations, and slab construction. Each house design lists the type of foundation included. If the plan you choose does not have the foundation type you require, our customer service department can help you customize the plan to meet your needs.

Roof Plan

In addition to providing the pitch of the roof, these plans also show the locations of dormers, skylights, and other elements.

Exterior Elevations

These drawings show the front, rear, and sides of the house as if you were looking at it head on. Elevations also provide information about architectural features and finish materials.

Interior Elevations and Details

Interior elevations show specific details of such elements as fireplaces, kitchen and bathroom cabinets, built-ins, and other unique features of the design.

Cross Sections

These show the structure as if it were sliced to reveal construction requirements, such as insulation, flooring, and roofing details.

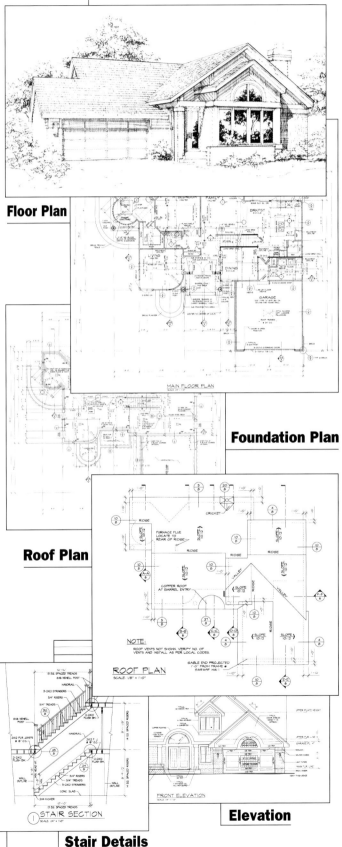

Frontal Sheet

Floor Plan

Foundation Plan

Roof Plan

Elevation

Cross Sections

Stair Details

Illustrations provided by designer/architect

Customize Your Plans in 4 Easy Steps

1 Select the home plan that most closely meets your needs. Purchase of a reproducible master is necessary in order to make changes to a plan.

2 Call 1-800-523-6789 to place your order. Tell our sales representative you are interested in customizing your plan. To receive your customization cost estimate, we will send you a checklist (via fax or email) for you to complete indicating the changes you would like to make to your plan. There is a $50 nonrefundable consultation fee for this service. If you decide to continue with the custom changes, the $50 fee is credited to the total amount charged.

3 Fax the completed checklist to 1-201-760-2431 or email it to us at customize@creativehomeowner.com. Within three business days of receipt of your checklist, a detailed cost estimate will be provided to you.

4 Once you approve the estimate, a 75% retainer fee is collected and customization work begins. Preliminary drawings typically take 10 to 15 business days. After approval, we will collect the balance of your customization order cost before shipping the completed plans. You will receive five sets of blueprints or a reproducible master, plus a customized materials list if desired.

Modification Pricing Guide

Categories	Average Cost For Modification
Add or remove living space	Quote required
Bathroom layout redesign	Starting at $120
Kitchen layout redesign	Starting at $120
Garage: add or remove	Starting at $400
Garage: front entry to side load or vice versa	Starting at $300
Foundation changes	Starting at $220
Exterior building materials change	Starting at $200
Exterior openings: add, move, or remove	$65 per opening
Roof line changes	Starting at $360
Ceiling height adjustments	Starting at $280
Fireplace: add or remove	Starting at $90
Screened porch: add	Starting at $280
Wall framing change from 2x4 to 2x6	Starting at $200
Bearing and/or exterior walls changes	Quote required
Non-bearing wall or room changes	$65 per room
Metric conversion of home plan	Starting at $400
Adjust plan for handicapped accessibility	Quote required
Adapt plans for local building code requirements	Quote required
Engineering stamping only	Quote required
Any other engineering services	Quote required
Interactive illustrations (choices of exterior materials)	Quote required

Note: *Any home plan can be customized to accommodate your desired changes. The average prices above are provided only as examples of the most commonly requested changes, and are subject to change without notice. Prices for changes will vary according to the number of modifications requested, plan size, style, and method of design used by the original designer. To obtain a detailed cost estimate, please contact us.*

Terms & Copyright
These home plans are protected under the terms of United States Copyright Law and may not be copied or reproduced in any way, by any means, unless you have purchased reproducible masters, which clearly indicate your right to copy or reproduce. We authorize the use of your chosen home plan as an aid in the construction of one single-family home only. You may not use this home plan to build a second or multiple dwellings without purchasing another blueprint or blueprints, or paying additional home plan fees.

Architectural Seals
Because of differences in building codes, some cities and states now require an architect or engineer licensed in that state to review and "seal" a blueprint, or officially approve it, prior to construction. Delaware, Nevada, New Jersey, and New York require that all plans for houses built in those states be redrawn by an architect licensed in the state in which the home will be built.

Before Customization

After

Decide What Type of Plan Package You Need

How Many Plans Should You Order?

Standard 8-Set Package. We've found that our 8-set package is the best value for someone who is ready to start building. Once the process begins, a number of people will require their own set of blueprints. The 8-set package provides plans for you, your builder, the subcontractors, mortgage lender, and the building department. **Minimum 4-Set Package.** If you are in the bidding process, you may want to order only four sets for the bidding round and reorder additional sets as needed. **1-Set Study Package.** The 1-set package allows you to review your home plan in detail. The plan will be marked as a study print, and it is illegal to build a house from a study print alone. It is a violation of copyright law to reproduce a blueprint without permission.

Buying Additional Sets

If you require additional copies of blueprints for your home construction, you can order additional sets within 60 days of the original order date at a reduced price. The cost is $45.00 for each additional set. For more information, contact customer service.

Reproducible Masters

If you plan to make minor changes to one of our home plans, you can purchase reproducible masters. Printed on vellum paper, an erasable paper that you can reproduce in a copying machine, reproducible masters allow an architect, designer, or builder to alter our plans to give you a customized home design. This package also allows you to print as many copies of the modified plans as you need for construction.

Mirror-Reverse Sets

Plans can be printed in mirror-reverse—we can "flip" plans to create a mirror image of the design. This is useful when the house would fit your site or personal preferences if all the rooms were on the opposite side than shown. As the image is reversed, the lettering and dimensions will also be reversed, meaning they will read backwards. Therefore, when ordering mirror-reverse drawings, you must order at least one set of right-reading plans. A $50.00 fee per order will be charged for mirror-reverse (regardless of the number of mirror-reverse sets ordered).

EZ Quote: Home Cost Estimator

EZ Quote is our response to one of the most frequently asked questions we hear from customers: "How much will the house cost me to build?" EZ Quote: Home Cost Estimator will enable you to obtain a calculated building cost to construct your new home, based on labor rates and building material costs within your zip code area. This summary is useful for those who want to know the total construction costs before purchasing sets of home plans. It will also provide a level of comfort when you begin soliciting bids from builders. The cost is $29.95 for the first EZ Quote and $14.95 for each additional one. Available only in the U.S. and Canada.

CompleteCost Estimator

CompleteCost Estimator is a valuable tool for use in planning and constructing your new home. It combines the detail of a materials list with line-by-line cost estimating. The result is a complete, detailed estimate—similar to a bid—that will act as a checklist for all the items you will need to select or coordinate during our building process. CompleteCost Estimator is only available for certain plans (please see Plan Index) and may only be ordered with the purchase of a set of home plans. The cost is $125 for CompleteCost Estimator.

Materials List

Available for most of our plans, the Materials List provides you an invaluable resource in planning and estimating the cost of your home. Each Materials List outlines the quantity, dimensions, and type of materials needed to build your home (with the exception of mechanical systems). You will get faster, more-accurate bids from your contractors and building suppliers—and avoid paying for unused materials. A Materials List may only be ordered with the purchase of a set of home plans.

Order Toll Free by Phone
1-800-523-6789
By Fax: 201-760-2431

Regular office hours are
8:30AM–7:00PM ET, Mon–Fri

Orders received 3PM ET, will be
processed and shipped within two
business days.

Order Online
www.ultimateplans.com

Mail Your Order
Creative Homeowner
Attn: Home Plans
24 Park Way
Upper Saddle River, NJ 07458

Canadian Customers
Order Toll Free 1-800-393-1883

Mail Your Order (Canada)
Creative Homeowner Canada
Attn: Home Plans
113-437 Martin St., Ste. 215
Penticton, BC V2A 5L1

Before You Order

Our Exchange Policy

Blueprints are nonrefundable. However, should you find that the plan you have purchased does not fit your needs, you may exchange that plan for another plan in our collection within 60 days from the date of your original order. The entire content of your original order must be returned before an exchange will be processed. You will be charged a processing fee of 20% of the amount of the original plan set, the cost difference between the new plan set and the original plan set (if applicable), and shipping costs for the new plans. Contact our customer service department for more information. Please note: reproducible masters may only be exchanged if the package is unopened.

Building Codes and Requirements

At the time of creation, our plans meet the building code requirements published by the Building Officials and Code Administrators International, the Southern Building Code Congress International, the International Conference of Building Officials, or the Council of American Building Officials. Because building codes vary from area to area, some drawing modifications and/or the assistance of a professional designer or architect may be necessary to comply with your local codes or to accommodate specific building site conditions. We strongly advise you to consult with your local building official for information regarding codes governing your area.

Blueprint Price Schedule

Price Code	1 Set	4 Sets	8 Sets	Reproducible Masters	Materials List
A	$290	$330	$380	$510	$60
B	$360	$410	$460	$580	$60
C	$420	$460	$510	$610	$60
D	$470	$510	$560	$660	$70
E	$520	$560	$610	$700	$70
F	$570	$610	$670	$750	$70
G	$620	$670	$720	$850	$70
H	$700	$740	$800	$900	$70
I	$810	$850	$900	$940	$80

Shipping & Handling

	1-4 Sets	5-7 Sets	8+ Sets or Reproducibles
US Regular (7–10 business days)	$15	$20	$25
US Priority (3–5 business days)	$25	$30	$35
US Express (1–2 business days)	$40	$45	$50
Canada Regular (8–12 business days)	$35	$40	$45
Canada Expedited (3–5 business days)	$50	$55	$65
Canada Express (1–2 business days)	$60	$70	$80
Worldwide Express (2–5 business days)	$80	$80	$80

Note: All delivery times are from date the blueprint package is shipped.

Order Form

Please send me the following:

Plan Number: _____

Price Code: _____ (see Plan Index)

Indicate Foundation Type: (see plan page for availability)
❏ Slab ❏ Crawl space ❏ Basement ❏ Walk-out basement

Basic Blueprint Package	**Cost**
❏ Reproducible Masters	$_____
❏ 8-Set Plan Package	$_____
❏ 4-Set Plan Package	$_____
❏ 1-Set Study Package	$_____
❏ Additional plan sets: __ sets at $45.00 per set	$_____
❏ Print in mirror-reverse: $50.00 per order __ sets printed in mirror-reverse	$_____

Important Extras

❏ Materials List	$_____
❏ EZ Quote for Plan #_____ at $29.95	$_____
❏ Additional EZ Quotes for Plan #s_____ at $14.95 each	$_____

Shipping (see chart above)	$_____
SUBTOTAL	$_____
Sales Tax (NJ residents only, add 6%)	$_____
TOTAL	$_____

Order Toll Free: 1-800-523-6789   By Fax: 201-760-2431
Creative Homeowner
24 Park Way
Upper Saddle River, NJ 07458

Name _____
(Please print or type)

Street _____
(Please do not use a P.O. Box)

City _____ State _____

Country _____ Zip _____

Daytime telephone ( ) _____

Fax ( ) _____
(Required for reproducible orders)

E-Mail _____

Payment ❏ Check/money order *Make checks payable to Creative Homeowner*

❏ VISA ❏ MasterCard ❏ American Express ❏ DISCOVER

Credit card number _____

Expiration date (mm/yy) _____

Signature _____

Please check the appropriate box:
❏ Licensed builder/contractor ❏ Homeowner ❏ Renter

SOURCE CODE | CA800

Copyright Notice

All home plans sold through this publication are protected by copyright. Reproduction of these home plans, either in whole or in part, including any form and/or preparation of derivative works thereof, for any reason without prior written permission is strictly prohibited. The purchase of a set of home plans in no way transfers any copyright or other ownership interest in it to the buyer except for a limited license to use that set of home plans for the construction of one, and only one, dwelling unit. The purchase of additional sets of the home plans at a reduced price from the original set or as a part of a multiple-set package does not convey to the buyer a license to construct more than one dwelling.

Similarly, the purchase of reproducible home plans (sepias, mylars) carries the same copyright protection as mentioned above. It is gener-ally allowed to make up to a maximum of 10 copies for the construction of a single dwelling only. To use any plans more than once, and to avoid any copyright license infringement, it is necessary to contact the plan designer to receive a release and license for any extended use. Whereas a purchaser of reproducible plans is granted a license to make copies, it should be noted that because blueprints are copyrighted, making photocopies from them is illegal.

Copyright and licensing of home plans for construction exist to protect all parties. Copyright respects and supports the intellectual property of the original architect or designer. Copyright law has been reinforced over the past few years. Willful infringement could cause settlements for statutory damages to $150,000.00 plus attorney fees, damages, and loss of profits.

Index

Index

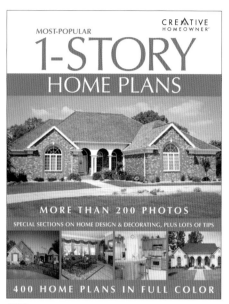
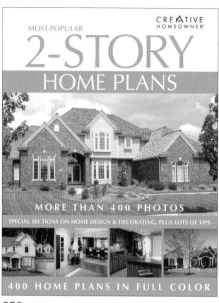
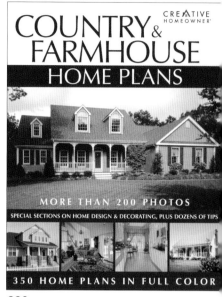

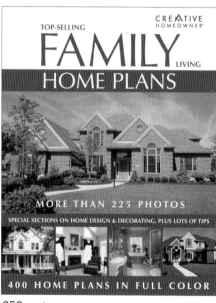